Vanished

Book 4
Crocodile Dreaming Series

Novel by

Graham Wilson

Copyright

Vanished

Graham Wilson

ISBN 9780645588736

Contents

Acknowledgements

Thank you to the readers of the previous version of this book. Your comments, mostly positive have encouraged me to keep going with this book and series. Reviews, including negative ones, give great insight into how to improve the telling of a story and, along with professional editing advice, are invaluable in seeing places where the story and how it is told need to be improved.

Particular thanks to Candra Hodge who did a structural and editorial review of this book. It provided many ideas for improvement which I have incorporated.

Thank you to my family and close friends, particularly my wife, Mary, who supported me on my writing journey.

Thank you to the many backpackers and other foreign travellers I met while living in the Northern Territory. Some of you shared my travels, many shared your wider experiences of the world you came from and personal experiences travelling in this land. From you came a major part of the idea for this story.

Most significantly thankyou to a large unseen crocodile, probably still living in a remote Arnhem Land billabong, who almost had me for dinner. The teeth marks are still visible on my leg today, giving me my own close encounter to recount in outback bars.

The silent power of this predator stays with me still and, along with aboriginal mythology and other stories, has fed my fascination for these huge ancient creatures, barely changed since the time of the dinosaurs. Some of the largest I have seen, living in very remote places, rival those in my imagined stories.

Background to Story

This is the fourth book in a series of five books called the Crocodile Dreaming Series, named for the central role which a large and ferocious predator, the saltwater crocodile, plays in these stories. This series is principally set in the Northern Territory, a huge, largely undeveloped part of the north of Australia. Crocodiles dominate its coastline. Their danger is an ever present part of living here, and is told in the stories of its aboriginal inhabitants.

In the first book an English backpacker, Susan, comes on holiday to Australia, and goes travelling in the outback with a local man, Mark. Too late she realises this man has terrible secrets hidden, involving the disappearance of other travellers. She only just escapes with her life, but Mark dies. She hides this fact in the hope that no one will ever know.

In the second book Susan tries to get on with a new life back in England. But Mark's body has been discovered and the police link her to his death and charge her with murder. She has this man's diary and needs to understand what he did and why, which she hopes the diary will reveal.

In the third book Susan is in jail in Darwin, Australia, on trial for murder. She has decided to plead guilty but refuses to say what has happened. She actively seeks to conceal Mark's role in the disappearance of other girls. She becomes suicidal in her desperation to escape from what appears a hopeless situation. The one person, a helicopter pilot, who could help her, has vanished too. Finally, the police discover the other missing girls and she may have acted in self-defence. She is released on bail while they investigate what this means.

This book picks up the story following Susan's release from jail. It tells the story of four vanished girls, at first only known from passport photos, and the search for them which goes on in Australia and across the world, with a remote hope that one or more could still be alive.

Prologue 1 – Vanished

I had a daughter once, but she went travelling. The last time I talked to her was on the phone from Melbourne. She had just left her job on a ship to go travelling in the Australian outback. She sent me a postcard from Adelaide, a day later. Then she vanished from the face of the earth.

It is four years now and I have heard nothing. Before that her communications were irregular, a postcard from here, a letter from there, at times a telephone call. Weeks and months could pass between each one. But always there was something, no matter how infrequent. Four years is too long for nothing. My fear grows, fear for her, fear for how it may have ended.

She was always a wild one who went on her own way, travelling to the furthest parts of the globe, to Antarctica, Africa, Alaska, Australia and South America. She was a true adventurer, one who desired to follow in the footsteps of her early Viking ancestors. I can imagine her crossing a distant sea. But I cannot bear the not knowing, thinking she may be no more and that I will never know!

Part 1 - Emily

Prologue 2 - The Small Hours

It was a small hour of the morning, its number around three or four. Her mind was sharply awake but, for a second, she did not know where her body was, except it was in an unfamiliar bed.

There was the sound of another person drawing breath, in and out, a regular rhythm, but not loud. She moved her arms around to explore the bed space. A body was lying nearby which was the source of breath sounds. It was hard and angular shaped; a body of elbows and bony protuberances. It was a man who was sharing her bed, now in this most alone hour.

As she felt his shape her memory returned. If he'd delayed his return just a little longer neither she nor he would be here. She would be a cold object in a box; her spirit, if such existed, gone. Great tenderness for this man washed over her. It was as if he had reprieved her from death row a minute before execution, even if her demise would have been self-done.

She ran her fingers through his straggly hair and over a bony shoulder. She pushed her body tightly up against him, wrapped her arms around and hugged herself to him. He was all bones and angles, so wasted from walking, but she loved his shape and comfort. Her body was so distended with her swollen child-full belly; his, in contrast, was so empty from three months of eating lizards and frogs. Yet, he was here and he was hers. She loved his body, she loved every bit of him.

He stirred in his sleep. Coming half-awake he rolled towards her, speaking in a thick, sleep filled voice.

"I can't believe I am lying here with you. I have no words to say how wonderful it feels. It is something I half-dreamed of, as I walked forever, but never dared to imagine."

Now she could feel his body rousing against her, his maleness was his one full part. She wanted it to fill her again. She rolled onto her back bringing his hand to that place. They made love, he trying to be careful of her enlarged belly. She laughed, telling him. "They are well protected in there. You are as light as a feather; you will do no harm."

Their bodies released in one of life's tender moments.

He muttered, "Susan, my beautiful Susan."

She felt happy; so, really, really, really, happy. She felt new surprise at her ability to love, to know complete gladness after what had been. She must never lose this moment of surprise by joy.

Vic drifted back to sleep. Soon she could hear his regular breathing again. Her mind stayed in a place of dreamy wakefulness, remembering what had been, only bare hours before.

Other memories crowded in of the day just past.

They had left the courtroom together, along with a crowd of friends and family, all of them desiring a celebration and catch up while walking the short distance to the hotel. Vic hobbled along beside her for his promised plate of steak and chips washed down with a cold beer.

The food was good but the night was an anti-climax. Vic had eaten so little for weeks that he could only manage a third of his dinner. She had a numb mind from anxiety and exhaustion of spirit. Vic had barely slept for the past three nights as he had driven himself to keep walking. Now, with his mission accomplished and alcohol washing through his bloodstream, he could barely keep his eyes open. Others wanted to take Vic to the hospital, in order to recover and fix his leg while they took her to a hotel bed in a room next to her parents or Anne in order to protect her from herself.

But Susan declined, saying "Vic has walked for three months to get here today and save me. It is my turn to mind him. I am staying with him tonight."

No one could argue with that.

Ever reliable, Alan suggested a solution. "My flat is empty now that I am sharing with Sandy. Why don't you both stay there tonight?"

They both nodded in gratitude, but decided this hotel where they were eating, was easier for this first night and they would go to Alan's place tomorrow. Soon they were in the hotel room, alone. In a minute Vic was asleep, stretched out on the bed. Susan showered and found one of Sandy's light dressing robes, wrapping it around her body. She sat on the bed beside Vic, one hand on his shoulder, the other fondling his hair, simply taking pleasure from touching and looking at him.

After half an hour he stirred and looked up with an incredulous grin. "I dreamed of you. Here you are, way more beautiful than in my dream."

She took off her robe, placing her naked body along his. His body was unwashed, dirty, skinny and smelled. She did not care. She wanted to join her body fully to his. Soon they were in a place of joined togetherness. Then they slept, bodies entwined, in a deep and dreamless sleep.

Susan lay there contemplating this past which her mind had just lived. It slowly came to her, it was all a dream, an exquisitely beautiful dream, one that had yet to happen, a part of her future not her past.

She was alone in this bed. Buck had taken Vic to his own separate room, next to theirs and she had gone with Anne to a room in her hotel, her own separate room. Here she too had fallen into an exhausted sleep.

There was a flash of disappointment in this unrealised part but then she understood it was simply a prelude of what was to come in their next night which she would ensure was spent together.

Chapter 1 - The Morning After

Susan woke with bright light streaming into bedroom.

She knew, with that certainty that comes with great clarity after crisis, that, from today on, she would become a new person, one named Emily. She would leave behind her alter-ego, Susan, the person in whose skin she had lived this last year. She saw it in the same way a snake sheds it skin and there is a new full formed skin underneath, but still an integral part of the whole.

She planned to remake herself, both anew and by return to the life of her own happy childhood. Once this was done her Susan persona would fade from collective memory. It had happened that way for Mark's identity when she had told the world his real name. Mark Bennet had slid away, along with all the other Mark Bs. Instead, the world now only remembered Vincent Bassingham. In the same way, she too she would shed her "Susan" name, a name redolent of horror. Those she cared about would now only call her by her name from childhood and school.

It was an idea that had formed in her mind over dinner last night- an alternative way of escaping her own past self now that Vic had come back. It seemed like a good plan, a way in which she could build a new life with her almost-formed children.

She stretched in bed. This bed was unbelievably soft and luxurious after where she had slept over the last few months. Her brain was struggling to take in the changes that a day had made. Yesterday, she could see no future ahead of her and had convinced herself this was what she had wanted: an escape on any terms even including her own ending.

Today, those last months had a surreal feel. She was glad to be alive! She was glad that somehow, whether through a fluke, divine providence or perhaps the efforts of her friends, she had stepped through two doors. She could now look from outside into her two cages of yesterday, the cage inside her mind which refused to see other options and the cage of a jail cell which had sealed away her body for months.

She climbed out of bed and stretched, revelling in a sense of freedom. It was a freedom she had previously taken for granted. All of a sudden, she could come and go as she pleased, again. She could catch the hotel lift and walk outside without anybody to say she couldn't. Beyond her window she could see it was a bright sunny day. Her room was high up, a short walk from a cliff top. Beyond the cliff lay miles of water looking to a distant shore. This must be Darwin Harbour; it seemed big and empty with barely a handful of boats dotting the horizon.

She found a bathrobe and went into the shower. She stripped off in front of a full-length mirror. Her body was much changed since the last time she had a full view of herself. Her arms, legs and face looked very thin, almost gaunt. They contrasted with her large, bloated belly. She felt the weight of her babies pushing down; it was a bare six weeks to go until the due date.

As she came out of the shower, a discrete tap on the door signalled a visitor. She put the safety latch on and opened cautiously, not wanting to find a TV crew and camera in waiting. It was a breakfast tray someone must have ordered for her last night. She felt inordinately pleased with this simple service and brought it inside.

A minute later her phone rang. It was Anne, checking to see if she was awake and inquiring whether to come over to her room or, alternatively, inviting her to come out and join them for breakfast. She told Anne to come in five minutes and share her breakfast tray, but only for her to come.

Emily felt full of thanks to Anne, the friend who had stuck to her through thick and thin. She must talk alone with Anne before she faced the wider world. Yesterday was a reprieve. Today a mass of unresolved issues were bubbling below the surface that she needed time and more mental clearness to deal with. Last night, she had pushed them away out of sheer relief. Today, however, she needed a clear head to think rationally about them.

Emily felt she would feel too confronted if she had to deal with a whole lot of people, no longer kept away by a prison, wanting to know plans for her future. In contrast, Anne and her could talk sensibly, on a one on one basis, on how Emily could start taking baby steps back into the scary outside world.

Her thoughts turned to Vic. She felt another welling up of affection. She had spent the first part of the night with him, sitting next to him, minding him and holding him close, giving comfort to his broken body, in a similar way to how he had begun to heal her broken mind, but exhaustion had intervened.

He had come with her from the court to the nearby hotel bar where his cherished beer, steak and chips had been ordered. He had finished the beer quickly, perhaps too quickly. He had eaten some chips and a few mouthfuls of steak, but at that point the exhaustion overwhelmed him.

So Buck and his wife, Julie, took Vic to a hotel room next to theirs where they could give him the attention he needed. Really, he should have gone to hospital, but he would not agree to that. So Buck, as a friend, took the responsibility to ensure his care. Emily felt pulled to go with Vic, to lay her body alongside his and hold him as he slept, but she knew she must find some time to talk with and thank the others, Anne and David, her Mum and Dad, Alan and Sandy. It was not deep conversation, but the togetherness and simple relief felt good to them all. She sat with them all, smiling and chatting, until her own fatigue flooded her, then Anne brought her to her own room.

During the night she had dreamed of Vic, of loving him and joining her body to him. Tonight she must do it, make the dream become real. One thing she knew after her months locked away was that she would take the chances for happiness that came to her; she would not waste them or die wondering about what might have been. She was confident that Vic had real affection, maybe love, for her. She had spent too long on her own, now she wanted to be with him, and she thought he wanted to be with her. She would do all she could to make it happen without delay.

There was a knock on the door, it was Anne. She came inside and they hugged and giggled with girlish delight. Together they ate every morsel of food on the tray, then they found biscuits, chips and chocolate in the mini-bar and devoured them all too. They sat facing each other, knowing the time had come for honesty, not knowing quite where to start, each waiting for the other. Each started to talk and then stopped, not finding the words, walking around the edges of the elephant that sat between them.

Emily took a deep breath. The time to speak of this was now, now they must talk. Then Emily must face the world. But first she must see Vic again, to tell him she wanted to be with him and make plans for tonight. Her dream of last night would be tonight's reality.

At last Anne spoke. "Can you tell me the truth now?"

Emily replied, "Yes, I think so, but I will only be brave enough to tell it once. It will cost too much of me if I ever have to go there again. My mind almost came apart yesterday, with me deciding to end it all. That person and place still sits looking over my shoulder, lurking in the shadows. I fear, if I let that person back into my mind for a second time, I will never be able to leave there again.

"So can you listen and maybe write it down. I will tell it like it happened, from my mind as I lived it. And, after that, I will speak of it no more. After I have told you I must then put it from my life and start to live again in another place where it cannot reach or touch me. I think that is the only way where its power of evil can be gone."

Anne said. "In that case I must get a tape recorder. Then, as you speak, it is there for me later. That way I need not remember it all at once. When you are finished the telling I will write it out in full as I do with my barristers' tapes. After that you need speak of it no further."

Emily nodded. "This will be the story of Susan, the other half of me. When it is told Susan will live only in words and paper. I will live again as

Emily. No one else will know that Emily is my real name. To the readers of those words, I will be Susan and Emily will disappear.

Anne nodded seriously. “OK Susan, no Em, if that is what you want then I will tell it that way.”

They agreed to meet after lunch and start the telling, to tell it in parts each afternoon until the telling was done.

Now, this morning, she would go and see Vic, David, her parents and all the others who had helped, not least Alan and Sandy. Until the story was done her nights would belong to Vic, her mornings with her friends and family and her afternoons would be with Anne for the telling.

She knew there were a few parts she would slide past unmentioned, the note she had discovered on the aeroplane which told her Mark’s true feelings, after she had killed him. That was private, just for her. With it went his will; she was not prepared to let others read it without her first knowing its full contents. Also she would tell no one the true location of the diary; they had the copy; that was enough. And she would not tell about the bag of jewels, they were Mark’s private present just to her and she was not ready to give them away. She only wanted the pendant and ring he’d given her, but it was linked to all the other things. She could not reveal one without the other being discovered too. Perhaps, in time, she could retrieve just those things.

Chapter 2 - The Telling

Anne and Emily enjoyed a morning of laughter with their other friends, first coffee and cakes in the hotel lobby, where Vic, David, Buck and Julie joined them, followed by her parents, cousins and Alan and Sandy, forming an ever increasing circle.

At first they just chatted and exchanged news and banter. Then she asked them all, if the media tried to get to her through them, to say she needed to rest and be left alone for now. They all agreed.

Next she told them all of her changed identity to Emily, saying it was her middle name and had been her childhood name. Her Mum and Dad were used to the dual identity, a part of how they saw their daughter.

At first Vic and the others were a bit perplexed, it seemed too simple and easy, but as it was explained by Anne who was now well used to her friend's two faces it started to make more sense. They agreed that if it was what she wanted they would all play their part.

Vic had the most reservations; he said he knew her as Susan and he wanted to keep this person alive. She quelled that by taking his hand and asking him to come and walk with her, just him by himself. She said she wanted him to show her the town which she had never seen.

So they walked the town, she keeping hold of his hand. Once they were well alone she turned to face him, saying that now she was free she wanted to spend as much time as she could with him, both the days and nights together. It seemed a bit forward, inviting him to be her lover, but he had a huge grin as she said it. From then it seemed easy and natural, a promise of things to come.

She stepped up close and kissed him mouth to mouth, telling him she wanted him the way that a woman does a man. She said she hoped he did not mind her full and bloated body, but that, if he would have her, she did not intend to let that stop them sharing their bodies as lovers.

She knew that Alan and Sandy had offered their empty flat and put it to him to arrange for them to stay there together from tonight, just the two of them. Vic said Alan had already offered it for his use, said he could stay there while he recovered. Vic was sure it could accommodate two not one.

Then she asked him to walk with her down to the beach, below the cliff. She stood there with her feet in the wavelets and asked him to put his arms around her from behind, to hold her tight to give her courage.

She could feel his maleness against her. She took his hands and placed them on her breasts, telling him this was how she wanted him to hold her, now and tonight when they were back together again.

After standing with him holding her like that for a long time she said. "Now it is time for me to become Susan, each afternoon to tell Anne her story until it is finished. Tonight, when I leave Anne, I want you to hold me again, encased in your arms like this. I will become your Emily again as you hold me. I need you to help me become her, new and whole again."

She returned again to the lobby where her parents still sat, though her other friends were gone. She told them that from tonight she would be staying with Vic; he was special to her and she wanted to be with him.

Then she found Anne and began her story. On this first day, the Thursday, she told of the first meeting Mark until the leaving when she went to Sydney and then of the re-meeting in Alice Springs up until the big waterhole on the Frew River. This was the time when no clouds could be seen in her sky.

On the second day, the Friday, she told of her discoveries of the many identities and passports of the other girls and her sending the text Anne, then of the second last night on the crocodile river with the running tides, a deeper, but shadowed perfection.

On the third day, the Saturday, she told of the knowing from the text reply and the ending, the ending of his life, the ending of her innocence, and then of her first plan to escape through the hiding of it.

On the fourth day she told of her life in a cage, consumed by the crocodile spirit dreaming, until her whole life was but a part of by this madness. She told of how desire to go to the place of crocodile spirit had possessed her until it was the only way she saw to escape, that was until when the gods of fate opened a window and Vic was returned to her.

Then she looked up at Anne and said. "It is done; I have spoken all I know. It is not within my power to tell it again, or even to correct it or to change it in any way. You must take and tell this story of Mark and Susan to those who need to know. I want to know nothing of this or anything which comes from it. I will be only Emily and Emily will vanish from this story. I will no longer know Susan or share her memories. Perhaps that is enough to let me be free again."

After she finished the telling each day she went out into the evening calmness and walked on the beach until the spirit of Susan and that of the crocodile faded from her into the harbour dusk. Then she found Vic and put her arms around him. He and she held each other through the night and through their joining she rebuilt her strength for another day.

In the mornings she would share coffee, breakfast and laughter with her friends, and walk with them and see the sights of the town. In the afternoons she would close her mind to Emily and be only Susan for the telling. In the nights she would try to become only Emily again, to give her love to Vic, who had need of her as she did of him. But in this giving and loving of the night a part of her always became Susan again. In the small hours it returned to a crocodile spirit dreaming. Here another man found a space in her dreams. Yet each morning when she awoke again it was Vic whose arms held her and she was glad it was him.

Anne found herself consumed by the story. She sat, both appalled and enthralled as it unfolded, occasionally forcing herself to ask questions to clarify odd bits of the monologue. The two faces of Emily-Susan were but a part of the larger tale.

Emily had been her friend from school, though her real name was Susan Emily McDonald. However, as a small girl she had adored her own Aunt Em; her father's younger sister, who had died tragically when young. So, at that time, she had decided she wanted her Aunt's name to be the name people called her and she took the name Emily to use. It was first year high school, the same year they first met, when their friendship had started. Anne had first known her as Susan. Then, only a couple months later, after her Aunt's death, the name change occurred. It seemed weird at the time, but everyone soon got used to it. By the end of school her first name was forgotten, now all knew her only as Emily, even though she had never officially changed her name.

So her passport had Susan as her first name and when they had gone on holidays to the beaches of the Mediterranean she was Susan again. It began as a game; she remembered them sitting on the plane together as they left England for their first holiday together.

Emily had announced, part mocking, "Seeing as my passport calls me Susan, I will call myself that while I am away, you know, tell that name to any boys we meet. It will become a second me, my alter ego."

Then, during her University years, she'd used Susan more and more. She still responded to Emily, it was what family and close friends mostly called her, but the lecturers used Susan, and she made Edward call her Susan. She said it was too kitch for a couple to be Edward and Emily, shortened to Ed and Em.

It was strange, but as the years had gone by it was as if two people had started to live within the one, Susan the outgoing extrovert, party animal and traveller, and Emily, a quieter and more studious twin, careful and competent at everything she did. More and more Anne had called her friend Susan, but her family still mostly called her Em, and Anne lived in both worlds.

Once Anne had asked her what was the name she used for herself inside her head. She had replied, "Emily, but I like the idea of a braver and wilder me. That is who my friend Susan is."

So, weird as it sounded, it made a strange sort of sense, this girl who was two people, choosing to split herself and pass the bad memories and experiences to the one part which she would shed, while she returned to her earlier self again, the person too cautious for this to ever have happened to.

Anne found that swapping between the two personas of her friend was almost effortless, it was like using someone's name and nickname interchangeably. She slid into this narrative form without effort. As her friend spoke, she saw the person sitting there as Emily, but she heard the words which came from Susan's mouth.

So Anne sat and listened as the tape recorded. It was a story which began like a bright shaft of sunlight. But, even before the first day was done, she could see roiling dark clouds begin to form in the far distance, climbing up the horizon and rolling relentlessly forward. As later days unfolded this darkness became all encompassing.

At times she tried to test what happened using her own moral code and sense of courage. Would she have gone to the police earlier? Would she have acted to save herself by killing a man she loved in the way her friend had or would she have stayed, frozen in terror, become passive as a victim? Could she have accepted the punishment meted out to her for what she perceived as the greater good, to save a man's reputation and to protect her children?

Some parts she found incomprehensible, at other times she found herself marvelling at the bravery of personal choices, never did she form the view she could have acted better or feel entitled to sit in judgement. Her friend was a harsher judge of her own actions than another could be. A part of Anne felt privileged she had been entrusted with this story. Mostly she just listened.

It was so good to have her friend back, to see the real Emily standing behind Susan. But she knew this Emily was in a very fragile place, that she must be protected and kept away from shocks which would damage her slowly rebuilding self-esteem.

By the end of the fourth day, when the telling was done, Anne began to feel easier. It seemed as if a huge weight had been lifted off Emily as

Susan separated from her. Now Emily walked with lighter and brighter feet, the skip returned to her step.

As the story unfolded, as well as compiling the tapes, Anne wrote notes of urgent follow up actions to undertake, based on the knowledge imparted. Highest on the list was to retrieve a small metal box which held passports of four lost girls. While she had never been to the site she had a clear description of the location, the place where the little hill was. She knew where the box was buried in relation to the hill. So, once the telling was finished, as Emily went off to find Vic on the Sunday night, to spend a last night with him before he was taken to hospital to have his broken leg set straight, she picked up the phone and called Alan on his mobile.

She told him she had the full story on a set of tapes that she would transcribe over the next week or two. But, in the meantime, the one most significant thing he needed to know was about was the box which Emily had buried. She described the hill as told by her friend.

Alan remembered Susan's little slip, her unintended revelation of something hidden made in the pre-trial meeting. He knew immediately that this was it, recounting his own futile search of a few days before.

Anne described the square flat stone where the hill ended at its furthest edge, alongside which the box was buried.

Alan even remembered this place, saying "I stood on it, looking out across the surrounding country wondering where else to search. It is hard to believe it was at my feet the whole time."

Then Alan asked her if she and David would like to come with him when he went to this place to retrieve the box. He would get on the phone to his boss now and organise it for the morning. It was the highest priority so he was sure it would happen.

Anne and David had planned a picnic together for tomorrow, their last day before David returned to Sydney. Anne would then stay on to provide company and support for her friend until the babies were born.

While Alan had given Vic and Emily the use of his flat for as long as needed, Anne was hoping that Emily could be persuaded to soon come to

Sydney and stay there with them until the babies were born. Emily's cousins lived there too. Together they would provide a stronger support network than what was here in Darwin. It would be good to put distance between Emily and this place of horrors.

Anne's initial inclination was to decline this trip, begging a prior picnic engagement. But another part of her had a strong curiosity to see the site of the events which had consumed so much of her life. She said she needed to check with David.

Alan said he would be leaving at eight o'clock tomorrow morning, with a couple vehicles, accompanied by Sandy and two other men. If they wished to come they should be at Sandy's place before then.

Anne felt comfortable in leaving Emily alone tomorrow. As well as Emily's own parents being there she would be spending the day with Vic who was booked into surgery after lunch. Emily would stay with him in recovery until the evening before returning to a quiet night on her own, by which time they should be back in town.

She made her pitch to David, "How about we take our picnic out on a site visit to that buried box place with Alan and Sandy tomorrow. Alan is organising to excavate the box I told you about last night. I would really like to see the place with my own eyes, not just as exhibit photos."

She could feel David's interest was as piqued as her own. He readily agreed. Instead, they decided to have a night out on their own tonight, time for a celebration for just them two, a first step towards planning their future life together. They could at last think of this with enjoyment now that Susan-Emily was no longer the centre of both their lives.

Chapter 3 - The Crocodiles and the Box

Despite spending more than a month in Darwin, neither David nor Anne had ever travelled beyond its rural outskirts. They had a real sense of adventure as they drove out of town with Alan and Sandy, sitting in the back of a large Toyota Landcruiser Station wagon. They went down the Stuart Highway, the same way they went to Berry Springs last Christmas. They came to a big sign left, proclaiming 'Arnhem Highway', pointing to Kakadu. They took this road. From here it was all new to them.

First they passed through a town called Humpty Doo, just a few shops and a string of houses and larger blocks. The name gave it a picture book feel, akin to a Humpty Dumpty place in a children's story. After it was left behind there was only featureless scrubby land until they rounded a small hill and came out onto a wide expanse of swampy plains.

A minute later they crossed a wide expanse of brown water signed 'Adelaide River', with advertising tours to see the jumping crocodiles. This gave Anne goose bumps as it brought home to her the reality of this place, this wide placid river with a sense of hidden danger.

Soon the open plains were left behind and scrub land resumed. They rounded more low hills and, before she realised where they were, they were crossing another river. The sign 'Mary River' flashed past. Anne saw a broad tree lined river pass below.

She called out to Alan in the front. "Could you stop for a minute, Susan told me something about this place. I need to remember it."

It came to her. Susan described discarding tools and heavy items from Marks truck, stopping in the middle of this bridge and throwing them into the water. She suspected most things did not really matter but they might want to try and search for the number plates and the guns left here.

She recounted her memory of Susan's words while Alan and Sandy listened attentively, "Susan said she stopped at the far end of the bridge, behind us. Then, after listening and looking for sign of anyone else nearby, she realised it was a good place to dispose of all these last heavy things of Mark's that she could not burn and had not thrown in the waterhole. She reversed back onto the bridge, far enough to be fully out over the water, and then she threw them all over the side, into the water below."

Alan was nodding. "Yes, well worth checking out. Maybe it's a needle in a haystack, but who knows. I doubt we will find any number plates, but the guns are worth looking for. Even some of the boxes and tools may tell us where they came from and help us track other places where Mark has been."

They reversed back, got out and peered over the side.

Anne tried to imagine her friend standing here on that dark night, exhausted, terrified, fleeing for her life, but almost to safety. It felt surreal as she gazed over the water below, with only reflected trees, sunlight, and an occasional bird and insect to break the calm. She could not reconcile these two competing images in her mind.

They drove on. In half an hour they were at the billabong. It looked like nothing much at all; an open car parking space, a few blackened stone piles, some dense shady trees with a papery bark and, on the other side of the clearing, a pool of dark blue-green water, about a hundred yards wide, extending out of view in both directions.

Alan walked them around the site. He pointed out the hill that sat low on the horizon. It matched Susan's description. He showed them the locations from the main features of their investigation.

As he talked on Anne was overcome by a huge sense of unreality. How could she align this beautiful, peaceful place with all the horror seen through Susan's eyes and told to her in the last few days?

She said, "Where are the crocodiles? I feel I should be able to see them. The way Susan talked this place is full of them. Yet, instead, I hear birds singing, the water is still and there's nothing in sight."

Alan replied, "You are right, it takes a long time before those of us who live her get a real sense the hidden danger we cannot see. After we search at the hill we will come back here for lunch, Sandy has packed a picnic. Then, if you sit quietly and watch, you will begin to understand. It is hard for visitors to grasp what lies below the surface of these places."

They walked over to the hill, along with a police photographer and a man carrying a pick and shovel. Alan carried a thin metal rod to probe the soil for soft areas. At the far side of the hill Alan pointed to a flat rock in the place where the ground became level. It was singular and distinctive. He asked Anne, "Do you think this is the place she described?"

Anne looked carefully and shrugged, "Maybe." As she came close, she saw a smaller flat rock, about a half a metre across, resting of the earth surface, right next to the large flat rock. She pointed to it. "That is the place, I am sure."

Alan walked over and stood alongside, "Isn't it amazing, only three weeks ago I stood right here, on the bigger rock and looked all around, wondering where to search, how to try and find whatever it was that Susan had hidden. The one place I did not look was at my feet. If I had done that, I might have guessed this was her hiding place.

The photographer clicked his camera several times as he recorded it all. Then Alan bent over, lifted the smaller flat rock and placed it aside. With the steel rod he probed the ground underneath. At the edges it was hard but in the centre it went straight in. About a foot down it hit something hard which sounded metallic.

Anne's heart pounded. Everyone else had the same tense look on their faces that she was feeling.

The man with the shovel carefully dug the soft centre soil away, an inch at a time. When the hole was knee deep Anne heard the shovel make a scraping sound. It was definitely metallic.

A shiny metal corner was exposed. More photographs. Alan bent down. He pushed away the remaining dirt. A rectangular metal box object, around ten by fifteen centimetres, was revealed.

He turned to Sandy, "Yours from here, I think."

Sandy put on disposable gloves. Then, grasping the very edges with the fingers of opposite hands, she lifted the box out and placed it on the dirt beside the hole. She took a plastic specimen bag and carefully slid it inside.

They all stood around, looking, knowing that inside this object was a story of vanished lives. It seemed too easy, almost unreal.

It was a remarkably ordinary box, shiny metal with traces of rust in a few places. And, as Anne had described, recounting Susan's words, they saw transparent tape around the edges to seal the lid to the bottom part. Sandy would take it back to the laboratory to open. That was really it, the end of the search, a mere ten minutes' work. A few more photographs, but the evidence gathering was done.

They returned to the billabong for their picnic, all sombre now. They sat in a patch of deep shade ten metres back from the edge of the water, under a large paperbark tree leaning back over the land. There was a muted sound of fruit bats squabbling in some nearby trees alongside the billabong and a few bird noises were heard occasionally in the distance.

Nobody said a word. They sat, gazing out over still water. There was barely a breath of breeze. The day was hot but not sweltering in the shade.

Anne was lost in her own thoughts and the others appeared the same. Finally she spoke, perhaps reflecting other thoughts. "It is strange being here now that Susan has told me what happened and how it all unfolded. So far I am the only one with that full story inside my head. I have told David some parts. In a few days I will have it transcribed. Then you will all be able to read her own words, hear her own voice and relive her actual experience.

"Even though I know it happened inside my head, I can't make it feel real. I can't see her reality, feel her panic, feel her complete terror. I should be able to see it through her eyes, now, as she told me. My eyes see only a picture of shady trees and an empty billabong, pretty but with nothing else.

As she spoke Anne saw a movement in her furthest vision, far across towards the distant shore, in a place where tree leaves hung low on the water and formed the deepest shade. The movement slid slowly from deep shade to bright sunlight. As the sunlight reflected she saw eyes glisten. They watched her with implacable patience.

Now it was real, her mind had connected with this being, the hairs on her arms stood up and goose bumps ran down her spine. She took David's hand and pointed. The creature, still far out, was sliding and gliding in an empty water-space with no apparent motion. It was a shape shifting shape that moved inexorably towards them.

Now they all watched, mesmerised, gripped by strange inability to move. It came to half way and still kept on coming; now it was closing in on the bank where they were. They stayed paralysed, barely able to breathe, still fully unable to move, while it slid without visible motion towards them. It seemed to have a power to make the invisible water flow in their direction and it sat within this invisible flow. As it shape shifted forwards, first its scales separated and became discrete things, then the knobs on its head and eyes took shapes of their own.

At last Anne realised that the invisible motion had stopped. Before them, resting in the water a bare ten metres away, was an object of ancient saurian stock, her mind labelled it as a creature pulled out of ancient aboriginal dreamtime legend. Its length equalled the distance which separated them. Its girth surpassed the biggest river trees. It rested, unmoving, save for an occasional eye flick. It made no other move, it was at rest, now parallel to the bank, watching with a single eye.

None of the other watchers spoke or moved, all seemed trapped in this mesmeric miasma. After an long, uncounted time, it sunk beneath the waters, inch by inch, and was no more.

Anne shook her head. She said to David, "Was that real? Or was it something only I saw, an imaginary creature inside my mind."

"No, it was real. Hard to believe any creature could be so big, so still and so silent. And, although it is undoubtedly dangerous, I felt no sense of danger as it looked at us. Do you think that is the crocodile Susan tells of, the one that came and took Mark's body away from the others?"

Anne nodded, "Yes, it must be, I cannot imagine there are any other crocodiles here that big. What do you think Alan?"

He replied, "Yes, that must be the one, it is far and away the biggest I have ever seen. Sandy and I have seen it once before. I have never heard others tell of it. It did something similar the day they found and removed the other part of Mark's body, the forearm. That day only Sandy and I saw it. We did not tell others of it then, of how it came close by and watched us, as if trying to communicate, that story sounded mad.

"That day it stopped close by the edge, motionless, like now, and it looked at us the same way before it went away. I could have sworn that day it was trying to tell us something, perhaps seeking the return of the body parts we had taken, signalling its loss.

"Today it does not seem to be trying to send a message, only telling us it is still here and it is waiting, waiting for us to return what we have taken away."

They looked out over the water again. Of this huge crocodile there was no more sign. But now two other large sets of eyes and noses had taken its place, slowly cruising up and down in the middle of the billabong, separate and yet linked through some commonality of presence.

Anne wondered if these were the other two crocodiles Susan had spoken of, the participants in the human feast on that fateful day. Their size matched Susan's description and their joint purposeful patrol seemed to connect them. However, she felt these were only crocodiles; large and dangerous, but without the mind-numbing life presence of the other.

Now they all started talking as they ate their sandwiches. The ordinariness of the day returned. They talked of other things, each unwilling to try and put words around what they had seen.

But this place would never feel the same for Anne; she knew there was something here, like a spirit of this place. It was seeking and calling for a kindred spirit. She thought of Susan and of her crocodile spirit dreams. A chill washed over her. She did not think she was superstitious, but here there was something no ordinary words could fit around.

Anne now felt a strange, unfathomable anxiety for Susan-Emily. It was as if this creature was telling her, mind to mind, there was unfinished business, and it would never release the hold over what it owned.

Anne's mind told her that Emily had created a separate life from the Susan of that day. But her emotions told her that this link was not so easily broken. The spirit of this creature would keep calling to Susan, like a restless soul it would not let her find peace. She shivered and tried to dispel her morbid imagination, the idea this crocodile being could summon its own.

Chapter 4 - Secrets of a Box

Alan and Sandy delivered the box to Police Forensic Section before they returned to work in the mid afternoon. They were told that Forensics would first check the external surfaces for fingerprints and other residue and would open it about 4 pm. They were invited to witness the opening and see what the box's contents were. They shared a cup of coffee as they waited and chatted about their day, deciding they would have time for an hour in bed together before they joined Anne and David for an agreed two couple dinner.

They returned at the due time and watched as a forensic technician carefully examined a thin layer of clear sticky tape which sealed the lid to the base of the box. At first he tried to lift it off as a single piece, the way Susan had described to Anne, but this proved impossible, the months in the ground had caused it to deteriorate. So he sliced through the join with a very fine scalpel, separating the lid from the base and lifting it off. Inside the only contents were two envelopes, each about an inch thick.

He lifted out the first envelope, lifted the flap and disgorged four packages, each a series of identity documents fronted by a driver's license, two from the Northern Territory, one from Queensland and one from Western Australia. With each license was a range of other documents, the sort required for an identity check, an electricity bill, a rates notice, a credit card and a couple other variable items.

Each group was held together by a rubber band and each was an MB name in the way that Susan had described through Anne. Mark Butler came first, with a Katherine address and seemed to be the most used. Mark Bennet came next and seemed to also be well used, then, little used, appeared to be the identities of Mark Brown and Mark Brooks.

There was nothing remarkable about any of this, although it would give many days of work for the various state police forces running to ground all these aliases, checking bank accounts, license and address details and any connections which flowed from them. Alan had an officer reporting to him who was responsible for this part. This person now clicked a digital image of each document bundle and then of each document as it was separated.

Then they came to the second envelope. Alan had a sinking feeling in the pit of his stomach, mixed with anticipation. He knew that once he had the identities of these girls, assuming it was as told by Susan, he would need to contact the police forces of their home countries, seek their assistance and soon after this he would be having agonising conversations with their next of kin. At one level he would be giving them new information which may resolve long uncertainty. At the same time he would be dealing a hammer blow to whatever fragile threads of hope they still held for each person's survival.

As expected this envelope held four passports. He watched as they fell onto the table. First came one from Sweden, followed by a French one, both with the EU insignia, then came one from the USA and finally one bearing the distinctive United Kingdom insignia. As each hit the table it felt like a blow, the unknown identity of a person, once vibrant and alive, now likely dead and buried in some distant corner of this country.

He watched with morbid fascination as the technician opened each passport and held it carefully by its edges as the photographer clicked away, page by page. The first, the Swedish woman named Elin Tordquist, looking to be in her mid twenties, strikingly beautiful with golden Nordic hair in dense tresses and a face with a striking intensity; words like elfin, and Viking Queen would have been the first words that tripped of his tongue if he was asked to describe her. The assurance in her eyes was no childlike girl but a woman used to being decisive, organising, taking risks but keeping control. He wondered about her story, where was gone.

Then came a girl with long black hair, Mediterranean but softer, she too looked self-contained; more understated beauty than the classic form. There was a soft femininity to her face but also an edge of mischief and a sharp appraising intelligence. Her name was Isabelle followed by what looked like a typical French surname that he would have to ask Sandy how to pronounce, she had studied French at school.

Then came the American girl, she must be the Amanda of the text message that Susan had sent to Anne, she was pretty in a more conventional way, the typical post high school girl image of one of those innumerable American TV soaps.

Last came the UK girl, with a Scottish place of birth in Inverness. She had similar long black hair and looks to the French girl though a bit more groomed and poised looking, as if had she spent time getting her hair done and her face made up before her photo.

There was something tugging at the edge of Alan consciousness, a resemblance that he could not quite place, it was part the face, but most strongly a look, she really reminded him of someone else, he compared her photo again to the French girl. Despite some differences the similarity was striking. He wondered if it was this, the strong resemblance between the faces and the look of these two girls which ran a bell in his brain. No, he knew it was more than that.

It came to him like an outside image projected into his eyes, he realised what it was. If one superimposed the images of the two girls and blended a few of the differences what one was left with was an almost exact replica of the face of Susan Emily MacDonald. But even more it was the look, as if Susan was looking directly at him from a merging of these two photos. It was so clear it gave him goosebumps.

He looked at Sandy, she had seen it too. She said, "They look so like Susan it is scary, there is something strikingly similar and compelling in the faces of those girls, these could almost be the same person's picture, taken in different times and places with different hair styling and makeup. But, most of all, they have the same look; it is the way they look out at the world; with a dreamy but searchingly intent look out to a distant horizon, it must have caught Mark's attention, like a re-meeting sequence.

"And I have not told you of the photos I was sent of Mark's mother, Rosita, from her brother Antonio. In early photos as a teenager and young mother, she had that look too. It was gone in later photos, when she had the look of a battered housewife, but it was there as a young mother.

I showed it to Susan last time I visited her in jail, but she did not seem to see it, she was fixated on the pictures of Mark as a boy. She mostly just looked at the one photo of him with his Uncle, smiling proudly as he held up a fish he had caught. She connected more with photos of Rosita near the end, when she was defeated by life, had lost hope and walked a path of no return. I think she saw herself in them, what she was becoming.

So I think it is right, that a thread runs from Mark's early childhood mother to his girlfriends, a look and faded memory he carried that he was always trying to recapture. Even the Swedish girl, Elin, despite many other differences, shares something of the searching intensity of that captured look, although I cannot see it in the American.

Chapter 5 - Five Day Interlude

After a first night of loving Emily and Vic settled into a comfortable and almost entirely private existence. They both went out with their groups of friends and family, sometimes alone, sometimes together, but the rest of the time, apart from storytelling with Anne, it was just them and they desired no one else.

Vic's mother and sister had come up from Alice Springs to welcome his return. He introduced Emily, they had all had a meal together and she liked them both. Now, at times, when she went off with her family and friends, Vic too would go off with his too.

But these hours of separateness were minor interludes in a private world that contained only them. Each evening, as dusk fell, they would walk on the beach and partake of a brief meal with others, but it never lasted long. They both most desired to be in a place of solitude with just the other. So they would return together to Alan's apartment and begin by linking their bodies and holding the other close. Then they would talk, tell of memories and stories as the night hours went by. Sometimes they shared a drink together, a beer or a pot of tea, sometimes they snacked on food with which Vic stocked the fridge during the afternoons when Emily was with Anne; occasionally they watched something on TV together. But mostly they shared of themselves with each other.

The flat was ideal, private and secluded on an upper floor, with a view of sky and distant sea to the north, and with no sense of neighbours. They would talk until sleep overcame them and they would sleep with their arms around each other. Sometimes they would wake and make love again, but mostly it was the companionship they most treasured.

Emily told Vic of her days and nights in the empty cell, with only the crocodile spirit as her company, and how she had ached for a man's arms to hold her. Then she had thought that any man would do; now she knew this man was the one she really wanted.

Vic told her of the solitary place in his mind when he walked, mile after mile, day after day, counting his steps to measure progress. As he walked what he most wanted was to see her face and bathe in her smile. Now he had all that and more and he was utterly content. Then they moved on to telling each other stories from their lives before.

Vic told of his childhood in an Alice Springs town camp, his love of football and of the determination of his mother and sister that he become something more than a town camp bum or even a champion footballer; something that would give him real success that would carry through his full years, even something he could pass on to his family.

So he had built a dream, an aerial work business, both the flying and the machine maintenance, with helicopters at its centre but maybe expanding into fixed wing aircraft as time went by. His first helicopter had been a start; he had almost paid off the loan and was starting to earn his own money now. But first he had to recover from the setback of losing that machine. He hoped the insurance would give him money for something newer without too much debt.

Emily told of her life in England, her riding and studies, her desire to learn about animal behaviour and early human history, to visit the famous archaeological sites of Africa and Australia, and to learn of other cultures from around the world. She told him about her former loves and boyfriends including Edward and David, but largely skirted around Mark. Four days passed together, wrapped in their own private world.

One day, as they were talking, she could see that Vic had a story to tell her which was on the tip of his tongue, but he was stalling over it. She asked him what it was about. He said that there was a story about Mark he was going to tell her, but then he had hesitated, wondering if it was a no go area.

Emily took a deep breath, trying to think what she should say. Mark's name had only been mentioned between them on the first day, something about him helping Vic escape through a crocodile, a half told tale which came out as part of the tangle of facts when they first met again. It had not been returned too.

She herself, no longer Susan but Emily, tried to keep separate from the Mark memories. But Mark had been a part of her life too; Vic would not be here without him. She needed to find a way to allow Vic to keep alive the good memories of his friend and for her to also find a way to think about him without it threatening her fragile peace of mind.

She said. "I am not ready for you tell me stories about Mark yet. I know he was your friend and he was much more than that for Susan.

But I must keep myself in another place from that time, a place with only you, and not him. There is a danger for me in even thinking about him so I think it is better if I do not think or talk about him, perhaps one day I will be able to do so with affection and nothing more."

Vic nodded; it was true, this story told of danger in his friend, a spirit which neither he nor others could control. He wished he had not spoken lest this man had the power to harm his Emily-Susan still.

On the first day together, the day after the trial, Emily made Vic show her his leg. She had examined it, doctor like, feeling the lump in the bone where healing was happening. She looked closely at the bend in the place where the bones had re-joined.

She said, in her best no nonsense manner, "Vic, tomorrow you must go to the hospital and make arrangements for that to be set straight. Talk to Sandy, she knows people there and will ensure you get someone good to fix it."

She could see Vic wanting to procrastinate. "I will, I just don't want to stop being with you any time soon. Surely it can wait for a couple weeks."

Emily shook her head, "No, the healing of the bone is well advanced. Each day it gets stronger and it will do more damage to reset. It needs to happen next week, sooner is better. You are too important to me to be left with a crippled leg. Please do it for me if you won't do it for yourself."

So, the next day, the Friday, Vic went to the hospital and met with the best orthopaedic surgeon. There was a gap in his surgery list for Monday, so he was booked in. He would need to stay in hospital for two or three days after the surgery until they were happy that the incision site was not getting infected and would heal well. Then he would have to spend about a month on crutches until the reset bones, which would be joined with a metal plate, began to knit. But, if he followed directions fully, the surgeon said he was confident that, within three months, Vic's leg would be as good as new.

Vic had never had an operation and felt nervous, but both Emily and Sandy, who had come along too, assured him it would seem like next to nothing for a man who had walked on a broken leg for hundreds of miles. In the end he held up his hands in surrender and it was all agreed.

Now they had their four nights and the days in between them. It was too precious to waste. A couple times it was on the tip of Vic's tongue to propose marriage; he loved this girl so totally.

But he decided he'd get his leg fixed first. Then, once he could run and jump, he would bring her next to the ocean, pick her up and carry her across the sand and into the milky sea. Then he would ask her the question.

Emily delighted in and returned his love. In her own mind their future together was sealed, she felt she'd made this pact with God for his safe return, it had been her unspoken prayer for a month in her cell until the debris of his helicopter was found floating in the sea. Now, as he'd been brought back to her, so must she give of herself and there was no trace of regret in the giving.

She had a vague awareness of something else, a Mark with a crocodile face, swirling through her darkest hour dreams. But the dreams would fade each new day and she was filled with delight at the sight of this man sharing her bed each morning when she awoke.

Chapter 6 - Hospital

All too soon Monday came around. They were told to go together to the hospital between eight and nine o'clock in the morning. Vic was ravenous when he woke, he had been eating double over the weekend and she could feel the hollowness of him refilling. However the doctor's orders were clear, "nil by mouth" on this day.

So she played the policeman, enforcing the rule while he grimaced, pleading, "So Hungry."

She returned her sweetest smile, "Tough, can't the man who lived on lizards and frogs for months survive a few hours without breakfast of bacon and eggs. Don't worry; I'll have a double burger waiting when you wake."

"So long as it is you holding it, I guess I can last that long," he said.

All too soon the taxi was waiting downstairs. They packed light, a change of clothes in an overnight bag they found in the cupboard along with toothpaste and shampoo, and a couple novels from the bookshelf.

The hospital was familiar from her pregnancy visits and several of the nurses knew her by sight, now a minor celebrity. They waved and smiled. She was due for her own check up on Wednesday and hoped that would be the day that Vic was discharged. After filling in lots of forms they were taken to a private room and Vic was shown his bed. They settled in, both sitting on the bed, side by side.

The morning passed in a steady stream of visitors, Buck and Julie popped in to give best wishes, half an hour later it was Vic's mother and sister, followed by her own parents and cousin, Ruth, who had stayed over the weekend and was flying back to Sydney tonight. Anne sent apologies; she, David, Sandy and Alan were tied up. For half an hour she had a nice chat with her Mum, Dad and Ruth. She liked the way they had accepted Vic into her life, sensing this man's importance to her. Then it was just them again. She could tell Vic was anxious, she thought it must be about the operation. She asked, "What's the matter? Are you scared about what they are going to do today?"

He shook his head, "No, not really, I just have this bad and anxious feeling in the back of my mind, as if everything since I came back and since they let you out of prison is too good to be true. I wish I did not have to leave you, even for a few hours."

She hugged herself to him, "Well I am here right now and all is fine. So let us just keep enjoying what we have, one day at a time. I will stay here today until you wake up after the operation and I will come back each day until they let you out."

A knock on the door came. It was a nurse with a sedative, saying it was now half an hour until he was taken to be prepped for surgery. Then they were left alone for the last half hour. Vic became dreamy and started to doze in bed. Susan sat next to him, resting a hand on his shoulder, willing it all to go well. It seemed only a few minutes until the orderlies arrived with a trolley to take him to the theatre.

Susan walked alongside, holding his hand until the surgical theatre doors where she had to leave him. She gave him a last wave and watched until the trolley turned the corner out of sight. She knew she needed more clothes, almost nothing she had fit her anymore. Last Friday her father had given her an envelope holding $1000 cash with this in mind. So, for the next couple hours, while the surgery proceeded, she decided she would go to Casuarina Shopping Centre and buy a couple loose fitting dresses, that gave space for her babies, and some other bits and pieces, nothing too much, as in about a month her shape would change back and ordinary clothes would fit her again.

Outside a taxi was waiting and it brought her to the shops. She bought a cheap overnight bag and a selection of loose fitting things, two shapeless dresses with a floral pattern and a couple of tracksuits and T shirts for comfort, along with a pair of runners and some undies and socks. Then she indulged in a large ice cream. In sympathy for Vic she had skipped her own breakfast too. Now, with the babies taking a huge share, her blood sugar had fallen away and she was really hungry.

It was time to get back to the hospital; another taxi had her there in no time. Vic was still in the theatre and they indicated it would be at least another hour before he was out and awake, but all was proceeding fine.

Emily went to the café and bought a plate of hot food and ate it, while she distracted herself with flicking through magazines to pass the time. They were all old editions. She was pleased, not wanting to take the chance of stumbling across herself in the pages.

She returned to the waiting room outside the theatre. Vic had just come into the recovery ward, the operation completed. It would be another half hour before he was recovered enough to come back to the ward and she could see him. The time passed with excruciating slowness but at last his trolley came out and she walked alongside his barely awake form. He would open his eyes and try and look around then drift back to sleep. She took his hand and held it and, when he looked her way, she gave him a reassuring smile.

In the room the nurse fussed around, checking his observations and then saying, "As he comes to his leg is going to painful. I have a shot of fentanyl to give him for pain relief, but it will keep him groggy for a few hours.

Vic opened his eyes. "You're right, it does hurt big time, but at least this time I have a pretty girl to hold my hand and another to give me a jab to make it all float away. Last time it was just me and a huge crocodile for company, so this is definitely an improvement."

They all laughed.

Then the nurse asked. "Ready for your jab now?"

Vic nodded, "You bet, anything to kill the pain. Christ my leg hurts."

Soon it was done and the nurse left. At last it was just them. She took his hand, held it and stroked it. "I am so glad it is done and now I have you all to myself," she said.

"Me too," he said, fixing her with a boyish grin.

They sat for a while. Vic's eyes kept closing, as he drifted off, but each time he would pull himself back, and look at her. Finally he said, "I need to keep looking at you, over and over, to convince myself you are real. Did I tell you I love you?"

She smiled back at him, "I think it's the first time but I guessed it, and I love you too."

Then he said, "I think I would really like to be married to you."

"Me too," she said, "but I want you to ask me when you are properly awake, and not full of drugs, before I say yes."

He nodded. Now it was as if he had set his mind to rest. He drifted off into a deep sleep.

Chapter 7 - No Escape from Evil

Emily sat there watching Vic sleep for a long time, her mind in a dreamy state of happiness. He was OK, he had asked her to marry him and even though he was in a befuddled state, she knew it was real. And she had as good as said yes, loving the idea of linking her life to this man, who made her smile inside every time he turned his warm brown eyes her way.

She roused herself from the reverie. The outside light was fading. Vic would sleep for hours yet. She must go home, fix dinner and sleep herself.

It was her first night on her own, when not in prison, for longer than she could remember. She was happy it was so; she could go and have a meal with her parents, or Anne and David, or even Alan, Sandy, Buck or Julie. All were her friends; all had invited her and any would be delighted to hear she was available. But, nice as that thought was, this was a night for her and her alone, the first tiny step towards getting on with her own life outside. She needed to face that world again, not as Susan but as Emily. She must face it with her head held high in her new-old identity.

She walked through the foyer, passing alongside the café. She saw newspapers for sale. She could not remember how long it was since she had sat and read a newspaper or watched the TV news – months and months. On impulse she picked one up, not even looking at the cover. She passed the money over to the man at the counter before putting the newspaper into her overnight bag.

She felt tired as she sat into the taxi, feeling in her shoulders the tension which she must have held inside herself on Vic's account. The babies were getting heavy and pressing down and she could feel her ankles were puffy.

Soon she was inside the flat on her own. She put on the kettle and made some toast, feeling suddenly flat, tired and very alone. Part of her wished she had gone out somewhere for dinner, having someone else to fill the empty space with conversation would have been nice, along with a hot ready cooked meal. She knew she could still ring and do it; someone would soon call round to collect her. But her back was aching, there was a headache at the edge of her consciousness and, overall, she was really tired from an unaccustomed day of walking around.

No, she would just have her tea and toast, stretch out on the couch, read the paper and maybe watch a bit of TV as she fell asleep. Tomorrow was a new day. She could get herself organised then.

She pulled out the paper to read, placed a cushion at one end of the couch for her head, lay down and stretched out. She picked the paper up, but she could not keep eyes open. She fell into a deep, dreamless sleep.

She woke up thirsty. The clock on the mantel said the time was after eleven at night. She had slept for four hours. The room felt oppressive. She had not turned the air conditioner on. It was hot and stuffy. But it was more than that, there was some portent of doom pushing into her mind, like the crocodile spirit was seeking to return.

She went to the sink and filled a glass of tepid water, sipping it with distaste. She was filled with anxiety, source unknown. She picked up the paper, thinking reading may distract her. The front page was some boring story of a prime minister's announcement, pure poly speak.

She turned to page three. Her face jumped out at her. She looked at the caption. It read "Two Faces of Susan Emily McDonald."

Below were two photos, one of a bookish looking school girl in uniform, captioned "Emily". It must have been a final year high school photo when she was studying hard to get good grades. The second, "Susan" was a typical party girl photo, her in a skimpy bikini, on a holiday, drink in hand, flaunting her body and exuding sex appeal, one of those half drunken snaps on a friend's camera, taken up close and showing the world way too much body with almost nothing to cover it.

Off to the side of those photos was one taken on the day she walked from court, was it only last week, her face sedate but dazed looking – she remembered that numb relief feeling.

The story continued. "Who is the real Susan Emily McDonald? Is she studious and serious Emily, the model pupil with the butter wouldn't melt in her mouth manners? Or is she the wild and raunchy party girl, Susan, known to give it out to many, many men in wild parties?

"We don't know all their names as she cut swathes through the social circles of London and Sydney. But there was Edward, budding business entrepreneur, son of a powerful stockbroker, dumped when she got bored. Then there was Mark, aka Vincent Mark Bassingham, the NT man from nowhere, who she fed to the crocodiles when he tried it on. Then there was David, son of the squattocracy, old Sydney town money with an impressive stable of sports cars. And last, but not least, is Vic, helicopter pilot from Alice Springs. Rumour has it she is currently holed up with him in a sleazy Darwin apartment. She won't talk to us, but she has plenty of words and more to share with her succession of boyfriends. Will Vic share the same fate as the others when the wheel turns?

"We ask again, who is this real person? Who is Susan Emily McDonald? Rumour has it that she is trying to say she is the victim of a crazy psychopath. Could it be that she is really the dangerous one who, like the spider, weaves her web and, when she has captured her prey and sucked out all its juices, she discards what is left like an empty husk. Rumour also has it she is possessed by a crocodile spirit and uses a psychic power to lure, stalk, ambush and consume her victims like the fabled saltwater crocodiles. We think this is one dangerous schizophrenic person; the two faces of Susan and Emily are but two faces of evil no matter which is their name."

She put down the paper, her hands were shaking. She was so shocked she could think of nothing to say in her own defence. Perhaps it was true. Perhaps she had been infected by evil, the evil had consumed her soul and she could never escape it. Pretending to be Emily was pointless. Emily was every bit as contaminated as Susan was!

Emily found herself walking around the flat in endless and pointless pacing. Her mind was in turmoil. She found herself reverting to the Susan persona, the actor, the person of endless self-control, the one who had survived all alone for months in jail.

Perhaps it was just one nasty journalist who was running this line. She remembered the wave of support she had felt from the crowd in the court that afternoon. Was that only five days ago?

A new lifetime seemed to have begun now, she was with Vic, and the past world had a surreal and unreal feel. As she calmed she saw that running away in any form was pointless. She just had to know the truth and face up to it.

Nothing could be that bad if you were secure inside yourself. She had Vic who knew her and what she had done and yet still loved her, he had asked her to marry him, after all. He would help give her strength to deal with this. And there were a mass of family and friends in her corner who knew the truth, or at least part of it and they had not condemned her: Anne, David, Alan, Sandy, Buck, and of course her Mum and Dad and Sydney cousins.

But another part of her hated drawing them all back into this, this place of endless rumour mongering and dredging up muck. Her friends had stuck to her through everything, but this was totally unfair to them, what she had done was wrecking all their lives.

She could feel her mind flip flopping backwards and forwards between exultation and despair.

She saw a computer sitting on a desk in the corner of the room. She had never noticed it before, although it had obviously always been there.

The thought flashed into her mind to get a wider perspective, see what others were saying. Surely this vicious story was just an isolated outlier of something much more balanced as people began to understand the facts. But then, of course, the judge had suppressed all the facts. What was out there for others to know was only gossip and speculation.

Still, she was better off to know what was being said. She walked over to the desk and pressed a key on the keyboard. The screen came to life. It showed a log in screen, two user accounts: Alan and Sandy, then a third guest account. She clicked onto the guest account, no login was required. It opened Internet Explorer and Google. She typed in her name and started to look down the page list.

Innumerable articles were there, the page count ran to thousands. Some were main media sites like the Guardian and Times in her hometown, and the Australian and Sydney Morning Herald here. But far and away the most common, including those with the highest ratings, were blogs and chat rooms. She knew she should not look at them but found herself powerless to stop.

It was like a vortex was sucking her down and it was appalling. What these people wrote made the newspaper she had read tonight sound tame. "Kill the bitch, cut her babies out, feed them to the crocodiles before they breed," was but one pretty typical variant.

But those that upset her most were the ones about Vic, speculating the whole thing was a hatched up plot between him and her. They had now got the last obstacle out of the way, she was released from jail and away free to cash in with him. His helicopter crash was a fabrication. In fact he had hidden away until the time was right, so as not to arouse suspicion. Now he and his witch girlfriend would collect Mark's riches. It was speculated that Vincent Bassingham had multiple flats and other property bought with cash. Gossip from the outback also told about him having a big stash of cash and jewels. So Witch Susan and this evil man, Vic Helicopter, who was her partner in crime were now about to cash in the bonanza.

But God help Vic, he was probably just another pawn captured in her evil web. In a year of two he would get his comeuppance too, with no reward from her for his help in doing the foul deed.

She put her hands to her eyes in horror. It was all so unbelievably vicious, how could anyone say these things about this dear kind man who she loved and who had saved her life. But perhaps they were half right, she really was evil and the evil within her would fall on him and harm him too. That was an idea too awful to contemplate. She wished she could tear her soul out and give it to the crocodiles if that would stop the madness. Better that than to harm him further.

She got up and started her restless pacing again; now opening and shutting cupboards in some sort of pointless ritual, looking for something, she knew not what.

In a high cupboard she saw a square bottle of brown liquid with the words “Bundaberg Rum” on the label. She remembered the happiness shared with Mark as they drank together from a bottle like this in the desert when she first came to Alice Springs. She lifted the bottle down, uncapped the lid and smelt the contents. The remembered smell burst into her brain. She wished she could go back to that time when life was simple and she was happy.

She found a glass and splashed some into it, then added a dash of water the way she had been shown. She swallowed a mouthful; she could feel it burning her insides. She knew it was bad for her babies but she was unable to care. She thought if she drank the bottle maybe it would all be over, like she had planned in the hospital. Her babies would feel nothing, they would go to sleep forever along with her and hopefully wake in the better place that their father was calling them all to go to.

She poured a second glass and forced herself to drink it. She felt dizzy, feeling the alcohol flooding her brain. She went and sat down on the lounge, carrying the bottle to continue with her drinking. She would just lay her head back for a minute before she poured another glass.

Chapter 8 - In a Pool full of Crocodiles

Susan opened her eyes. She was floating in a pool of water, looking up at high trees and clear blue sky in their middle. The sun was warm and she felt happy. She was lying in the centre of the pool, it had a circular form.

She felt something brush her arm. She turned her head to the side. There was Mark. He had come back for her. He reached for her hand and brought her to him. She looked down at her body. She was wearing her blue bikini, the one the men in her life had loved. Her belly was flat and smooth. She wondered where her babies had gone. She turned again to Mark. She saw that her babies were swimming with him, one holding each hand. They were smiling up at her.

She sensed movement at the periphery of her vision and looked to one side, then looked to the other side, feeling growing amazement at the sight.

Circling around them, maybe five metres out, was a school of crocodiles, all big, following each other, nose to tail, cruising in an effortless flow. Now, coming past her, was the mother of all crocodiles, looking just like the one she had seen that day on the Mary River. It passed her by and went behind her. Then drifting into her view came an even longer one, she recognised it as the one that she and Mark has seen that day on the Victoria River, perhaps it was also the one which Mark had sent to help Vic on the Fitzmaurice River.

Of course, it all made sense now. They were family, her new family. They were welcoming her and Mark and her children. They were saying, "At last you have come to be with us, to swim amongst us. Welcome, welcome from us your totem brothers and sisters."

Huge big crocodiles came nuzzling up to Mark, like friendly puppies. He lifted his children and placed them on the back of the biggest one. Then he reached for and lifted Susan, placing her alongside. Lastly he pulled himself up from the water and sat behind her on the creature's broad back. She could feel his arms around her, holding her and her babies in safety. She felt so happy. They cruised off and joined the circle in its endless procession.

Her dream faded but, as it left her, she had an overwhelming desire to return to Mark; her and her babies together. They would be minded and safe there with their crocodile family.

She found herself waking in the flat, roused like a dream walker to a new and altered state of consciousness. She could see what she should do. She should pack up her few things and make her way back to Mark, to the place where she had left him. She would find him there again.

Chapter 9 - Forever Running

Emily found herself awake and lying on the lounge. The light was still on and the three quarters full bottle of rum sat on the coffee table beside her. She felt disgusted at what she had done; indulging in this self pitying binge, trying to wash away reality with the contents of a bottle. The dream was startling and clear. But she knew it now for what it was, just a dream, a lovely dream which she ached to re-enter, but still just a dream.

She must pull herself together. She loved Vic; he needed her and she needed him. She could not let this crazy stuff in her mind take her away from that. But lurking in her subconscious was this incredibly strong pull, the desire to run away from it all and re-join the crocodile world, just to know the joy of seeing Mark one more time.

She stood up and rinsed her face under the tap in the kitchen, trying to clear her head from the sleep and alcohol daze. She should take herself off to bed now. Maybe, if she lay in the place where she and Vic had shared these last nights, there would be enough of his smell and presence to keep the other demons at bay.

She got up and picked up her overnight bag, carrying it with her to the bedroom. She saw the strappy sandals which Anne had lent her, pale pink with silver buckles, lying on the floor. They were cooler and more comfortable for Darwin weather than her own shoes, giving space for her swollen feet. She picked them up and brought them with her, turning off the light as she left the living room.

In the dark of the flat she could make out the faint outline of the bed in the bedroom, the sheets rumpled from this morning, she had forgotten to make it with their early departure. She crawled onto the bed, hugging Vic's pillow to her face, drawing comfort from his smell. She pulled a sheet over her shoulders and lay on her side, slowly inhaling and exhaling the odour of the man. She felt herself calm. Despite the awful vindictiveness of all that was out there Vic would help her through. She felt herself sliding down into sleep again, not quite happy but safer for now.

As she slid deeper into oblivion she felt the crocodiles reforming in the pool around her. Now they were clawing at her, pulling at her, nudging her back towards them. She screwed her eyes tightly closed, wishing for peace and to be left alone. Was there no end to this?

As the Emily part of her mind asked the question, the Susan part of her mind replied. *Why do you keep trying to push me out? We are two parts of the same person. I will not be sent away by you. Mark wants me back and I am going to him. You can do what you like; go with your new man, Vic, if you want. But I belong to Mark, my children are his children. I will return to him. Stop me if you can, but I am in charge now.*

Emily watched in horror as Susan climbed out of bed. There was something glowing softly on the mantel piece, its light reflected softly in the mirror above. Emily watched as Susan walked over to it and took it in her hand. The light coming from it grew brighter as if it responded to her touch. Susan held it up, cupping it in the palm of her hand, brought it to her face. As it came close Emily realised it was Mark's crocodile totem, the one he had shown her on their helicopter trip in the Gulf, that day so long ago. Emily was puzzled at how it came to be here.

But Susan had no uncertainty. She brought it right to her face and touched it to her lips. As she did the totem connected. Now she was only Susan again; Emily was pushed away to furthest recesses.

Emily watched from an outside place, trapped behind a mind wall. Her Susan-self picked up the sandals and strapped them to her feet. Then Susan picked up the overnight bag of clothes, her travel pack. Lastly she put the crocodile totem into an empty plastic shopping bag, the one lying on the floor from her visit to Casuarina.

With her overnight bag in one hand and the shopping bag with the crocodile in the other, Susan walked out the door, down the steps and out onto the street. Emily was powerless, she must walk where Susan went. She saw that everything was deserted, not a person or a car was in sight.

She realised that her Susan-self was going somewhere. In her Susan mind she knew she was returning to Mark and the crocodile pool, to bring her babies to the safety of her crocodile family. She did not know how Susan would get there but Susan knew the way; down the highway for twenty miles, turn left, follow signs for Kakadu until just after the Mary River when she would head north, following the road to the billabong.

She supposed Susan could walk there even if it was a long way, but perhaps someone would come by and give her a lift. But, for now, at least until a car that was going the right way came by, Susan would walk. Every step would bring her closer.

So Susan walked. An hour later she was still walking and an hour later she walked still. Her feet were hurting now and she wanted to take the sandals off. She put them in the shopping bag with the crocodile totem.

Now Susan could see some traffic lights in the far distance. She felt like she had walked for half the night, but at least that was a destination to aim for. At last she reached the traffic lights where a big sign read "Stuart Highway". As Susan turned onto the start of the highway, just past traffic lights, she saw there was an occasional car passing. She saw a white one coming her way. It looked life Mark's Toyota. Perhaps he would drive her there, or at least arrange a lift for her with one of his friends.

Susan stuck out her hand to wave the car down. It pulled to a stop. The guy was around Mark' age, maybe a little older, but then she had not seen him for almost a year. Susan asked him where he was going.

He replied, "I'm going fishing on the Mary River, an hour and a half's drive from here. I always leave early as the fishing is best at dawn; that is when the barra feed the best, though one always has to keep one's eyes out for a big crocodile of which there are plenty in the place I go."

Susan said, “That’s good. I want to go to a billabong on the Mary River too. I am glad you can take me there, it beats walking.”

The man gave her a curious grin, but then nodded, as if to say, “The world is full of unusual people and what is one more.”

Susan smiled brightly in response. She knew this man had been sent by Mark to help her to return.

From a great distance Emily watched Susan, unable to stop her.

Chapter 10 - Gone Girl

Vic woke up in the hospital on Tuesday morning. His leg was hurting a lot but he had slept well in his drug-infused trance. Now, he was ravenously hungry. He remembered Emily/Susan's promise to bring him a double burger in the hospital when he woke up.

He found her double name thing kind of strange, though he got her "Emily" desire to be separated from the "Susan" identity with all the muck that was going around. He had begun to call her Emily over the last few days at her request. But he had not really got this new name fully into his mind. The "Susan" part of her still burnt so bright. He loved the picture in his mind that went with it: she was the girl he had met and fallen in love with. This was the main reason it was hard to change her identity in his mind.

But, hell, it was the same adorable person. If it helped her get her life back together that was fine, though it seemed silly for her to think she could just vanish using her middle name. The media was unlikely to be conned for long by that when they were looking for a story. But, if it made Susan feel better, then she would become Emily to him.

He remembered how he had told her he loved her and had proposed to her in a half-asleep state last night. And she had, more or less, said, "I do." He only had to say it a second time (when he was not spaced out) for her to say a proper "Yes". It made him feel so pumped up and happy to think of spending the rest of his life with her.

Right now, though, he really wanted to see her. He picked up the new mobile phone he had bought last week- since his other one had went in the river with the chopper. He dialled her temporary mobile phone number. It was Ruth's spare phone according to Emily.

It rang without being answered. Perhaps she was in the shower and making herself beautiful to come visit him. As if she needed that! She was ravishing the way she was, particularly when she woke in the morning with her eyes mussy from sleep. It was impossible to improve on perfection. But, then, she did scrub up well, too. He even found her big round belly sexy- hard to believe a belly-full of another man's child could be such a turn-on. He pulled back from his lustful thoughts, though. He did not want to give the nurse tidying up around him in the room the wrong idea.

The nurse said, "Good morning, Mr Campbell, can I get you anything?"

Vic replied, "Well, my girlfriend promised me she would be in early with a double burger. But, failing her arriving right now, something else for breakfast would be just great! I am so hungry I could eat a whole cow in one sitting."

She replied, "Breakfast should be here in about half an hour. In the meantime, I can get you a cup of tea and a couple biscuits if you like."

Vic nodded, "And, while you are at it, is there a paper around? Yesterday or the weekend's one would be fine as I've not done much reading of late."

Five minutes later, she was back with a tray carrying a cup of tea and plate of biscuits, just plain family-type, good to dunk. A minute later, she was back with a pile of newspapers: Sunday, yesterday and today's.

He started with today's paper. There was only political rubbish on Page 1. He turned to Page 3. Emily's photo jumped out at him. He read the reporter's name, James Wilkinson, then the headline: ***"Two Faces of Susan Emily McDonald continued."*** The rest of the shocking article followed:

"Following yesterday's sensational story about the dual identity of a convicted murderess, strangely released on bai, further details suppressed by the judge, we can report that yesterday she accompanied her new boyfriend to hospital for a supposed operation to repair his broken leg. Meanwhile the person in question went off in a taxi alone to an unknown destination. It is a strange state of affairs: a convicted felon who has served none of her sentence to be free to come and go on her own."

More sick rubbish followed this- mostly nasty speculation into Susan's private life and her former lovers. Vic could feel anger welling up inside him. He wanted to get hold of this James Wilkinson guy and rearrange his pretty face. How dare he treat Susan like that?!

Vic hoped Emily had not seen or read this- it was vile! He decided he should read yesterday's story, too. It was better to know what was being said, even if it was a pack of lies.

He soon found the story in yesterday's paper. He read, with his hands shaking and mind reeling. He did not care what the reporter said about him, Mark, or even Susan's former pretty-boy boyfriends: David and Edward. But, to treat her like a slut or a common criminal and say these things about her, when she was the most honourable person he knew, it made his blood boil!

He must talk to her quickly in order to tell her not to read it! He must say to come and see him straight away! He could protect her and keep her away from all this stuff. He dialled the number again and again. The phone kept ringing with no answer.

He had an awful premonition. She should be out of the shower by now and would have seen his missed call. Even if she did not pick up in this instance, she would ring back in another minute.

Vic remembered back to yesterday now. While he was waiting to go into surgery, he had this terrible feeling that it was all about to go awfully wrong. Emily's reassurance had pushed the feeling away.

Then, last night, this feeling had been at the edge of his consciousness until he had got out the "love" word and she had returned it. After that, he had felt so happy and the foreboding had been forgotten again.

But, now, it hit him with both barrels: an awful sense of loss. Something bad had really happened to her! *Calm down, calm down*, he told himself. He called her again and again- still no answer.

Vic decided to call Alan's number. Sandy picked up after a few rings. He asked Sandy if she had read yesterday or today's paper about Susan.

She said, "no." She then explained how they had gone out to dinner with David and Anne last night, as David was on his way back to Sydney today, so they had slept in late this morning. Now, Alan was in the shower and getting ready for work. Sandy asked him, "What's this all about?"

Vic told her about what all he'd read in the paper and added how he had tried to call Emily this morning but could not get an answer from her. Now, he was really worried about her. "What if she, too, had read the paper and did something really stupid!!"

Sandy was all practical common sense, as usual. She reassured Vic, "I am sure she has just gone out for an early morning walk, walking along the beach or something like that. She must have left the phone behind by accident. Why don't you give her another half-hour and try to call her then? Once Alan is dressed, I will ask him to go over there and check on her- just to be safe."

Vic thanked her and hung up.

Now, his breakfast had come but his appetite was gone. Vic forced himself to slowly eat all the food that was on the plates, in order to pass the time, before he tried to call Emily again.

A half-hour had finally passed since he had last called Emily. He called two more times, five minutes apart. Each time, he left the same message: "Emily- ring me, please, as soon as you can."

Just as Vic hung up the second time, his own phone rang in his hand. He looked at it with a flash of hope, hoping to see her number come up. Instead, it was Alan's number.

He picked up, saying, "Vic here."

Alan's voice came down the line. "This is strange. I am here at the flat. There is no sign of Emily, but nothing is gone, either. However, the paper is open at the page of yesterday's story- so she must have read it. Yet, her clothes are all here and the bed looks like it has been slept in. There is nothing else I can see to get excited about. Perhaps she has gone out for breakfast or something like that. I will ask around downstairs and see if anyone has seen her around or leaving this morning."

Vic said, "Thanks," and hung up without saying goodbye.

He thought, *This is crazy, me sitting here in hospital while she has gone missing. I must get out and go and look for her.* He rang the nurses call bell.

In a minute, the nurse came into his room. Vic told her he was checking out as soon as could be arranged. He just needed her help to get him a set of crutches so he could walk without putting weight on his leg.

She protested these statements and called the doctor- who answered immediately. In a minute, the doctor and senior nurse were both in his room telling him to "calm down, Sir." They informed him that he risked damaging his leg and undoing all the benefit of the operation **IF** he did not stay in bed for **at least** two more days.

Vic would hear none of it. Finally, he got them to bring him a set of crutches and he signed his discharge papers.

Then, he was in a taxi heading back to Alan's flat.

When Vic arrived, Alan and Sandy were both there now. They were looking around, perplexed, as he hobbled in on his crutches.

"What are you doing here?! We've barely begun to look for her! we don't even know she's missing! You should still be in hospital!" exclaimed Sandy.

Vic could feel panic coursing through him. It was his sixth sense- not something tangible. He agreed there were lots of explanations. Deep down, though, he knew it was not that simple. It was something to do with the level of commitment Emily and he had towards each other. It told him, without a doubt, she would not just go off somewhere without letting him know.

Alan, as always, was a master of practicality. He held up the phone which Emily had been using which showed the missed calls from Vic. It had been next to the bed. "OK. First, we need to contact her parents and

Anne- just in case she has gone visiting either of them early in the morning. Sandy can do that.

"Then, we need to contact all the other people she knows: Buck, her lawyer, the doctors in the hospital she regularly sees. That is in case the babies have come early. I will do that.

"What I need you to do, Vic, is walk carefully around the flat, see if you can spot anything of hers which should be here and is missing. Or anything out of place since you were last here. While you are at it, have a close look at the bed, too. See if you can tell whether she has slept in it since you were last here together. The same for the bathroom and kitchen- see if there are signs of her having being here, since you were here yesterday morning together.

"At this stage, we don't really know if she even came home last night- except for the paper, but that's assuming that was not from yesterday morning. The phone could have been left here since yesterday. Do you know if she brought it to the hospital?"

Vic was sure there had been no newspaper in the morning. She could have hardly opened it without seeing the story! IF she had seen it, he would have surely known. In fact, at that point, he would have cancelled the surgery until he knew how it affected her. As for the phone, he could not remember seeing it at the hospital. He thought she'd brought it, but was not quite sure. He checked the call log. There were no outgoing or received calls since the day before yesterday- just Vic's missed calls this morning. So that did not help any.

Vic looked at the bed, felt the pillows and looked at the shapes of the body outlines left in the bedclothes. He could almost swear that Susan had slept here last night: the pillow he normally used had traces of lipstick and her smell on it, as if she had cuddled it to herself. It was not conclusive but, when he added that to the open newspaper, he felt almost sure that she had come back here last night after leaving him in the hospital.

Then, he saw a bottle of Bundy Rum and a glass next to it in the lounge. The bottle had not been there when he had left yesterday. He did not much like Bundy and he and Susan had not drunk from it together. He saw finger marks on the glass. It had a small amount of what smelt and looked like rum in the bottom. He called out to Alan, "When you're finished, can you come and look at this?"

Alan and Sandy were both busy on the phone. Vic decided to look around some more and saw the computer in the corner. He went over to it and pressed the keyboard. The screen came to life, instantly.

He saw Internet Explorer was running with a series of web pages open in the browser. He started reading: it was an awful story about Susan by an internet troll, totally vile! "Cut the babies out of the bitch and watch the crocodiles jump to feast on them" it proclaimed.

Vic felt mortified that someone could write this about his beautiful Susan. He looked at the web page history. The most recent page about her had been opened at 11:45 PM last night. Now, he knew for sure she had been here at that time and had been reading this poison! He knew it would have completely destroyed the fragile self-esteem she had just begun to rebuild.

He brought Alan and Sandy inside to show them what all he had discovered. Now, they all knew this was really something to be frightened about. It seemed, after reading this, she must have run off into the night to God knows where. Her friends and the hospital confirmed that nothing had been seen or heard of her since she was at the hospital with Vic.

Alan decided it was time for a full-scale missing person's search with the police raising the alarm through the media to seek any sightings. He called his boss and was told that, in five minutes, a squad car would come to bring them all to the police station. At the same time, a second car would come and secure the site for subsequent investigation.

Emily's family and close friends had also been contacted and asked to come to the police station to give statements about any contact they had with her in the last 24 hours. It was an inconvenient request as her parents and David were each scheduled to leave on midday flights for England and Sydney, respectively. However, all other plans were off until Emily was found.

Vic's leg was hurting and he felt woozy from yesterday's operation. Despite these facts, he resisted all entreaties to depart the scene and go off and have a rest. He said he had returned to Emily once before, against the odds, and was fully determined to find her once again.

A news conference was called for just after lunch. Thus far, a series of searches of the beaches and local parks had found nothing. At the news conference, Vic, Anne and her parents all spoke of their concern about her absence. Vic told of discovering that she had read the awful articles in the paper and on the internet, that her mental state was very fragile and that he was very fearful for her safety. He asked for anyone who had seen anything, particularly between midnight and daylight this morning, to come forward with this information.

This conference went on air and was run on all the local TV and radio channels. Now, all they could do was hope and wait.

In the late afternoon, the others returned to their hotel rooms after a fruitless day of searching. Alan and Vic, however, stayed on at police HQ. Alan was coordinating the search while Vic sat and watched on helplessly. He knew there was nothing further he could do, but he refused to give up and go to bed until all the efforts of the day were finished.

About eight thirty that night, a call finally came in. It was an early morning delivery driver. He told of returning to Darwin from Palmerston, driving a flat-back truck, after delivering goods to the Coles Supermarket about 5 AM. He said the Berrimah lights had changed red just as he was coming up to them. As he slowed down at the lights, he thought he had seen a girl who matched Susan's description flag down a white Toyota tray-back going in the opposite direction. While he was still stopped at the lights, he had seen this person climb into the passenger side of the vehicle which had then driven away-heading south on the Stuart

Highway. As best he could guess, the time was about quarter past five in the morning.

At the time, he had thought it was very early for a backpacker to be looking for a lift. He also thought the girl looked fat or perhaps pregnant, though his side-view of the girl was not very clear once the Toyota had stopped, he could only see her head then. He had called only now because he had just seen Susan's photo on the late-night news. It was the first he had heard about the search today.

In five minutes, Alan and Vic were in a squad car and going to meet the witness. He was a pleasant young bloke and was trying very hard to be helpful. He had no description of the car driver. All he could say about the vehicle that stopped was, "It was a white Toyota tray-back which looked like it had a few boxes on the back, nothing distinctive." However, he was fairly sure that the girl he'd seen was Susan- although, he'd only glimpsed her in half-light from across the road. He was also fairly sure, when he had seen her, she was carrying a small bag, "at least nothing bigger than a backpack", in one hand.

So that was it. The next day, the search was widened across the NT- particularly focused on the top-half. However, nothing was found or reported which helped locate her. Within a week, lots of vague reports of people who looked like Susan were coming in from all parts of Australia. But, again, none came to anything.

Police opinion became that she had run away to an unknown place. Based on the sighting of her going with the man in the Toyota, serious fears were held for her safety when she was not found after an extensive media fuelled search. It was all too general. Too many white Toyotas were registered in the NT and nobody came forward to admit to having given this girl a lift.

A week passed. Then, it was two weeks. Then, it was a month. Still nothing was found. The police now raised a warrant for the arrest of Susan Emily McDonald for absconding on bail- should she ever be found. The judge who had originally released her on bail reluctantly confirmed the warrant and asked Alan to press on with his investigation of the other missing girls.

The papers had taken to calling Susan, “Gone Girl”- based on the book and movie of the same name. Slowly, “Gone Girl,” slid away from peoples’ memories as other stories came and went. Only her closest friends continued the search, refusing to give up.

Vic and Anne were both plagued by guilt: Vic for allowing the operation to happen despite his fears, Anne for leaving her friend unattended this critical day. But nothing made a difference; nothing could bring “Gone Girl” back.

Chapter 11- A Clue

It was now almost six weeks since Emily had vanished. Time had drifted by, out of March, through April and into May. The weather was getting cold at night. Charlie had decided to go and camp on a waterhole on the Mary River for a night. He had a plan to fish in the morning, once there was some warmth in the sun. Now, it was "Yegge"- the season after the knock-down late wet season storms had gone, and when coolness came with a dry south-easterly wind during the day. By night, when the wind dropped, there was still wetness in the air as the land gave up its moisture.

Since Charlie had found the man's head, he had avoided his favourite billabong on the Mary River, because the big croc had spooked him. He missed his fishing. This Mary country was like a link to his father who was gone now. On top of that, Rosie wanted a big catfish for another curry and this river was still the best place to get one. He decided to go to a different place on the same billabong, maybe a mile further along. It connected to where he had gone last time, but he felt it held a different crocodile spirit and would be safe. It was also another place his father had shown him. It was outside the locked gate, so more people came here. Despite this, it should be quiet on a Thursday morning since the weekend warriors would not be here before tomorrow afternoon. He should have the place to himself.

It was an hour after dark when he arrived. Already the night was chill. He parked on the opposite side of the cleared area from the water and took out a big torch to have a look around.

As he walked across the open camping area towards the water, he saw a plastic bag lying on the ground. It annoyed him when people came to these places and did not take their rubbish away. There was obviously something in the bag or it would have blown away on its own.

Oh, well, he supposed he'd do the right thing, pick it up before it ended up in a dugong or turtle's guts. He had seen on TV how turtles confused plastic bags with jelly fish. Their guts got all blocked up from eating the bags and they died. It was bad not to care for the land and sea by leaving trash lying around.

He lifted it up. It was surprisingly heavy. He looked inside. It had a pair of shoes: woman sandals. There was something else at the bottom, sort of dark and stripey. He put in his hand and the thing jolted him- like an electric shock! He pulled back his hand quickly. It felt like he had been bitten!

God, I hope it's not a snake sheltering in there which fanged me.

His heart skipped a beat and he felt panicked. *Stupid fucker* he was for putting his hand into something like that without looking better at it first. It was one of the first lessons of being a blackfella *–always look real good before you poke around in holes in the ground or in other hidey places that you can't see into properly.*

Charlie looked at his hand- no sign of punctures. *Calm down old fella,* he said to himself, *your imagination is getting the better of you.*

He set the bag back on the ground and picked up a forked stick. One by one he lifted the sandals out of the way with the stick, setting them on the ground alongside the bag. He looked into the bag again with the torch.

As he did, he exclaimed, "Oh Fuck!" He'd seen this object before; Alan had shown it to him when he'd first found it. It was that bloody crocodile totem, the Baru one from those Yolgnu tribes. The one Alan said belonged to the man of the head. He'd felt freaked out by it when he was last shown it- knowing as he did that it had crocodile spirit magic inside it. It was not his totem and, as an initiated man of another tribe, it was dangerous for him to touch it. No wonder it had bitten him. It was its way of saying, 'hands off'.

He looked again at the sandals. They looked kind of familiar. Sort of thing a young white woman would wear: one who looked like Sandy or red-haired, Anne.

The thought struck him. These had not arrived here by accident. Someone had brought them and left them here. It screamed out to him of the missing girl, Susan. The one Alan was searching for. The one some people said had run away and others said had returned to Crocodile Man. He had not paid all the garbage in the papers much mind, himself, but he knew it was really tearing up Alan and Sandy- the way she had just vanished suddenly. They were blaming themselves, as were the other friends of the girl.

There was that sighting of her getting into the white Toyota. Maybe she had come out here with a fisherman who had offered her a lift. It was all maybe, maybe, maybe: too many maybes.

Well, Charlie did not know much about police stuff, but last time he had taken something away- he did not really get into trouble, but he knew it could have been a problem if Alan was not his friend.

Today, Charlie would do the right thing. He would leave this stuff right here, where he'd found it. He would drive back to Darwin. He knew where Alan lived and he had his private telephone number. He would try to call him from the Bark Hut since it would only be about ten pm when he got there. If he could not get an answer from him, he would drive right up to his house and bang on the door until he woke Alan up.

On second thought, he would skip the Bark Hut, he might as well go home and sleep in his own warm bed since nothing would happen until the morning. He would at least let Alan know tonight, though. Then, in the morning, he could come back and show them what he had found. He was sure it was important- even though he had no idea what it meant.

To make sure no pig, dog or big bird came rooting around and disturbed it, Charlie put the sandals back into the bag next to the croc totem and covered it with his upended metal bucket. In addition, he put a heavy stone on top of this to keep it in place.

Chapter 12 - The New Billabong Search

Alan was sound asleep when he felt Sandy shaking him awake. He did not know what time it was, but it seemed like the middle of the night.

Sandy said, "Someone has been ringing our doorbell and banging on the front door off the street. I don't know who or what it is, but they are very determined. You'd better come down with me to see who it is."

Alan pulled on a pair of shorts and T-shirt while Sandy wrapped a dressing gown around her body. They were both half asleep as they stumbled down the stairs to the building lobby. Through the glass panel they could see a dark-skinned man standing outside in the light and trying to peer inside.

Suddenly, Alan realised who it was: "It's Charlie!" he exclaimed as he went to open the door.

"Charlie, what is it?" Alan asked, perplexed.

Charlie surveyed them both with searching eyes, noting their sleep befuddled look. "More-better I come inside to tell you it. I have found another thing at the Crocodile Man Billabong."

They ushered him up the stairs without hesitation. Sandy put the kettle on while Alan sat Charlie down at the table.

"How about you start at the beginning," Alan said. "But, first, let's all have a cup of tea to wake us up."

Charlie nodded, "More-better that way."

Soon, they all held a steaming mug of tea and were eating Tim Tam biscuits. Charlie began his story: "That waterhole, that one where I found that head. I not go back there because of bad crocodile spirit, not since before I found it. But now, Rosie wants another catfish, big like last time. I know another place, maybe one mile, maybe two miles, further long same billabong. My father showed me this place, long time ago, when I was boy, same as other place, big catfish live there, too. I think, *Different crocodile's home, no bad crocodile spirit live there.*

"Tonight, after Rosie and I have early dinner, she to go play cards with friends. Me, I drive there to camp, new place longa same billabong. Think safe place. Want to catch another big catfish in the morning. Once I get there, I take big torch and walk around to look- make sure no bad spirit hiding.

"In middle of car park place, back from water, I see plastic shopping bag on ground. I think, *Is rubbish which lazy person left*. Plastic rubbish- it real bad, it poison turtle and dugong.

"I pick it up- heavy bag: something inside. I shine torch in. I see ladies' sandals, and underneath something else, dark and stripes. I put in my hand to take out and it feel like bite me- bad pain in hand. Think, *Maybe bad snake is inside bag, it bite me.* But, no mark is on my hand.

"I get long stick and take out sandals, then look inside bag again. Now I see that crocodile totem, that Baru. Same one you show me, one you find along-side of billabong where I find man head and you find footprint. That place right there, same one, same Baru you show me before.

"I know, when you show me last time, it bad one. That time I tell you, 'Baru spirit not my totem, it dangerous to me.' Today, when I try touch it in bag, it bite me on hand. I already know not to touch. Now, it bite me to say the second time, 'I bad spirit, you not touch.'

"You tell me one time already, you think Baru missing when that Susan- lady go missing. Now, I find it back near billabong. Me, I think it say, *Maybe she come back to billabong.*

"I reckon I need to come and tell you straight-way. This time, I not bring anything away. Just leave Baru and shoes in bag on ground there, in that place where I find it, until you come and look."

Alan and Sandy questioned Charlie back and forth until it was clear they had the story straight – that he had found the same carved crocodile that Alan had shown him before and a pair of pink woman's sandals together in the bag.

Then, Alan rang police HQ to organise a team to come out in first thing in the morning to search the new billabong area. He debated about calling their other friends to tell them the news but, in the end, decided he needed to do an initial investigation before he told them anything. Then, Alan and Sandy could go from there. Alan was unsure if it would lead to anything- he was not even sure it would be the same crocodile totem. After all, similar things were for sale in tourist shops across the Top End. But, still, Charlie was convinced it was the same one- said he could feel the same spirit inside it, the exact same one as the other time.

Alan thought he had to trust Charlie on that for now. He remembered the day he had shown it to Charlie. It was a Friday, just after the trial and before the sentencing. It had also been the day he had gone back to the billabong, to search the site a second time, looking for whatever Susan had hidden. The thing he would eventually find out was the box with the passports that they had just recently found.

As Alan came back to town that day, he had stopped by Charlie's place with a six pack- wanting to get his wisdom on anywhere else to look. He had shown Charlie this new discovery of the totem and Charlie had refused to touch it. Charlie had said it was a crocodile totem called a Baru from the Gove country. He had told Alan that, as an initiated elder of another totem, he must never touch it! It would bite or hurt him or his family if he ever did.

That day, after they had finished a beer each, Alan had taken it home. As best Alan could remember, he'd just dropped it on the computer desk he had at home and had never officially logged it as evidence. Although, he did remember he had noted its discovery in his field notebook. It had then been forgotten by him when he had travelled out to Gove the next day- and again on his return. That had been because of his rush to get to Katherine, in order to try and trace the phone calls. These same phone calls led to the discovery of the subsequent texts- the very thing which had finally cracked the case!

By then, the totem had seemed unimportant and had slid out of his memory. When Susan disappeared from the flat, he'd vaguely wondered what had happened to it and remembered mentioning to Charlie how the totem was gone. He was fairly sure he knew where he'd left it and it was not there. In addition, he'd asked Sandy if she knew where it had gone to, but she had no knowledge of it at all. After that, it had been forgotten again by Alan. He hadn't deliberately forgotten it, but it had seemed so unimportant at the time.

Suddenly, this very crocodile totem had come back into the centre of attention. If Charlie was right, someone had taken it back to the billabong. The only someone who could have done that was Susan. Therefore, if it was confirmed as the same exact object, it must mean that she'd gone back to the billabong. That was good news for nobody. Hence, it was best to be sure she had done all this before Alan let this particular cat out of the bag.

Now, Charlie was saying he would go home to bed. He added, however, if Alan called for him in the morning, he would come out with him to show him the way to the place where the bag was found. Alan arranged to pick him up at six am. It would mean Alan would have to be up at five o'clock- but it was too important to let it wait any longer than that. Sandy would not be able to come with them to examine it on site as she was due in court tomorrow morning. Alan planned to get a second car organised to follow him out to the billabong, if it proved to be new evidence in the Susan/Emily missing case, bringing two more of his team. They could secure the site while he came back to town to make arrangements for whatever needed to happen from there on out.

The sun was still low in the eastern sky and a steamy mist was rising from the water surface into the cool air as they pulled up alongside the billabong. Alan made sure to keep well-back from where the upended metal bucket lay visible on the ground. They walked across to it- Alan making sure Charlie followed directly in his footsteps and stayed well behind him.

While they slowly approached the bucket, Alan tried to remember when it had last rained. It came to him suddenly- two days of rainy weather in the middle of April, about three weeks ago, was the last rain they had around here. He could see Charlie's tire and footprints from last night. It did not look like anyone else had been to this place since before it had last rained. It looked like it must have been a heavy shower when it had rained as Alan could see the outlines of some dried puddles- their smooth dried-mud surface still evident along with only a few leaves fallen on top of them.

Alan and Charlie finally came over to where the metal bucket sat. Alan lifted it and set in down a couple of feet to the side of where it had been, upon a piece of unmarked ground. Under it was now revealed to be a Target shopping bag, with the logo still clearly visible on the side facing up. Charlie pointed out the outline of where it had sat before he had found picked it up- about half a meter to one side. Clearly, it had been there since before the last rain as its outline in the dried dirt was still clear.

Using gloves, Alan opened the bag and looked inside. As described, he saw the pink sandals sitting on top of a dark object. As Alan looked at the sandals, he thought they definitely looked familiar to him. He had a feeling he had seen Anne wearing them before. Maybe they were, indeed, hers. He had vaguely remembered the fact that: when they compiled an inventory of everything anyone could remember that Susan had brought with her into the flat, Anne had listed them among her belongings and they were not found during their subsequent search. It had been presumed Susan was wearing them when she disappeared as none of her other shoes seemed to be missing.

Alan carefully picked the sandals up and placed them in one specimen bag. Then, he picked up the shopping bag and peeked inside, again, to glimpse the Baru totem. It certainly looked the same to him. He placed the bag with the totem still inside it in a separate specimen bag. He would bring these into town to check. There was a good chance they would find fingerprints or even some DNA on these- assuming they had sat inside this closed bag since they were originally left here.

He organised for his other two men to do a careful search of the rest of the site with minimal disturbance. This was to see if it warranted a full-scale search or not. He was not too hopeful- the rain seemed to have washed away any sign of visitors from before today. Once they had checked more carefully, though, he would see what they came up with and decide then. In the meantime, Alan and Charlie were headed on their way back to town.

Chapter 13 - Searching for Five Lost Girls

It had been an excruciating two months since Charlie's newest find at the Crocodile Man Billabong. The police had confirmed the sandals and the Baru had been with Susan at some point- her fingerprints were on both and her DNA was on the sandals. They also now had Mark's diary, proof of his multiple identities, Susan's testimony spoken on tape and as a transcript, four passports of vanished girls- along with a new vanished girl to add which added up to five sets of distraught families. Yet, at the same time, they had almost nothing! Nothing had given them real clues as to where any of these people could be found now- not even a clear location of anyone's last resting place.

Alan felt like screaming in frustration. He had wanted this case- first to make his reputation, then to seek Susan's salvation. Yet she was gone, and he could not find her. In addition, he could not find any of the others either.

The only redeeming feature of this whole mess were the friendships which now sustained him. Strangely, most important was his friendship with Charlie- that wise dark-skinned elder who could look past this place of blockage and sense something beyond it. This gave Charlie equanimity and, in turn, this gave Alan a shred of continuing hope.

The other friendships were the gang, so to speak, of: Anne and David, Buck and Julie, Vic, and, of course, his own dearest Sandy. Whenever the others came to Darwin, they would always have a gathering of some sort. Sometimes it would be held at Alan and Sandy's flat, sometimes at a restaurant or hotel, but mostly these gatherings were held at Charlie's place so they could all eat a ritual meal fish curry and catfish. This meal was best but, when it was not at hand, there were plenty of other delicious substitutes at Charlie's place and each one would be washed down with ice cold beers.

At one of these gatherings, David had an idea: "We have tried this on our own now for more than two months and it has not got us very far. Why don't we turn it on its head and try to enlist public support?

"There is no longer anything much to hide- all the private secrets of these girls are being ferreted out and fed to the tabloids, but that is just scuttlebutt to feed the sensation seekers. However, while these rumours circulate, our search is getting drowned out by them There must be somebody out there who remembers something! I don't mean regular police publicity calling for assistance, but something much bigger.

"We need two things: a sympathetic story of each girl, which the public will remember and be moved by, and we need public attention which will bring in money. This money will be used for rewards, investigations, but, most of all, to buy publicity that will reach into people's distant memories.

"I have connections in the commercial media of Sydney- why don't I ask them for assistance? Perhaps just one company or perhaps they all could come on board to turn it into some sort of public appeal- both to raise awareness and to seek funds for this cause.

"Perhaps, we could call it the Lost Girls Fund. Not just for them, but for the many others who have disappeared without a trace across Australia: money to fund ongoing investigations run on behalf of distant parents or families. Most importantly, it's money to find these girls! Money to bring them home if possible or, if not, to place a memorial to remember them where they last were."

Everyone agreed it was a good idea. Alan said he would need to clear it with his bosses but thought it made sense. David said he would pursue his part on his return to Sydney- once Alan gave the go ahead, that is.

Chapter 14 - Lost Appeal

The friends left it to David to use his contacts and see what he could arrange. He started with a journalist who worked in a major TV current affairs program who he had known over several years. David had dealt with him when the accusations against Susan first surfaced. This man had been surprisingly sympathetic to this story- perhaps because he already knew David at a personal level. Despite the desire for sensationalism, the man had done an initial balanced report- leaving aside the many suspicions swirling around about Susan's role in Mark's death at that time. Since then, he had steadfastly resisted the urge to sensationalise in all events that followed.

David and this journalist knew each other well enough to go for a quiet beer and an "off the record" chat. At the end of the chat, it was all agreed. This man, Mathew, was strongly enthusiastic about the cause. He, himself, had a cousin who had vanished over a decade ago and knew the anguish this part of his family was still going through. He said he had good friends in the two other major commercial TV channels and thought it might even be possible for these channels to get together and cooperate on this event.

With this friendly chat, a deal was struck. The stories on each channel would share some common threads but, in addition, each would pursue a part of the story using their own contacts and networks. Each station would have their own night set aside for them to run a feature story so they were not be competing head-to-head during the television event.

All the stations would also be provided with access to both Anne and David in order to allow them to tell of their knowledge of what had happened in this event. Then, each channel would focus on their own stories relating to either these four girls or to other missing people who had vanished somewhere in Australia without a trace.

Each TV station would make a public announcement asking people to get in contact with them about missing people they were trying to trace. They had deliberately widened the scope beyond the missing girls, to focus on missing people more general, and so the name had become the *"Lost Appeal."* Together with Anne, David and Vic, the stations would then work with the local police and missing people organisations to profile a wide range of missing people. They would tell these tragic stories in a way that would capture the sympathy of others, in hope that some of those missing would be found.

Of course, many parts of the current police investigation could not be detailed. But the fact that four passports identifying these four girls as missing had been in the possession of one, Vincent Bassingham, was now public knowledge- in addition to the trial and subsequent disappearance of Susan.

There was plenty of meat left on the story and plenty of leads for each channel to chase. The dates were set, three consecutive nights, one for each channel to run their profile story. After each night's story, the channel would launch part of the appeal, all using the same hotline number for information.

It was a hectic time pulling it all together in time and establishing a charitable foundation to handle the donations expected. Finally, though, all the bits were in place and the programs went to air.

All of the nights got huge ratings. All the channels claimed it had ended up benefitting them. Their journalists were fired up with their own personal motivations to discover the stories of many missing girls and, also, of a few missing men. It was not targeted at the big end of town but at ordinary families who had known such people and shared the pain.

At the end of the week, well over a million dollars had been raised to pursue the investigation. The following week, the trustees met and agreed to fund further publicity and build memorials to remember those who had gone missing somewhere in Australia and had vanished without a trace. Also at this meeting, Anne had an idea which she put up to the trustees. She had Susan's story on tape and wanted to write it. It was the best memorial she could think of to remember her beautiful friend by.

Anne had now talked to the other four sets of parents. They, too, wanted their daughters' stories to be told. Therefore, if the trust would agree to assist her in this pursuit, she would find time to travel directly to the families and get all their stories, too. Then, she would sit down and write them up into a book. She believed, once a book was done, it would raise further funds to go into the trust. It may even lead to further programs which would both contribute financially and with publicity to keep the search alive.

Anne said she would not concede defeat. She did not believe that Susan was no more. And, even if she was, at least telling her story would leave her footprints in the world so others would know and remember her, too.

After two hours of heated discussion and debate, it was finally agreed. An allocation of $100,000 was set aside for Anne to travel and gather whatever information she could on these lost girls. It could also be used to pay her living expenses for as much of the next year as was required while she wrote. Anne promised she would have a draft of the full story by the next Christmas. In addition, as she compiled it, she would make available any useful information that came out to help others in the search to find the lost girls.

Chapter 15 - Anne's Story

Anne now had a war chest of a hundred thousand dollars. She had set herself the task of finding out the stories of all the lost girls and recording them in one book- along with Susan's story. The money would fund her to go to the countries of origin of all the girls, to gather information about their lives and to help with any investigations that flowed from these stories. It would also help pay for her multiple trips to Darwin to work with the NT police in searching for additional clues on Emily's whereabouts.

Anne was determined to take only minimal expenses for her own living costs. David had offered to fully support her over the year, but she did not want that either. Time enough for that when they were married- a plan that sat somewhere over the rainbow of when she finished this.

Alan and Sandy cleaned out the spare bedroom at their Darwin flat for whenever Anne was in town. She found this was very helpful for it saved hotel costs and gave her company along with some perspective. They were both the source of innumerable good ideas for her journey of discovery. Plus, Sandy had her own different and unique insight into Susan's mind, something that even Anne had not shared in talking to her friend.

Anne knew the book could end up being a best seller. It was one of those stories that, even if told badly, would be riveting. She intended to tell it the best she could! She already had several publishers beating a path to her door for publishing rights a year from now. She ignored these offers. In her mind, any money the book raised would be first used to repay what the Trust had given her and, after that, would go into funding the Trust's ongoing activities. IF she signed on with any publisher, they would obviously feel the need to take some of the proceeds received from sales of the book. There were even talks of film or documentary rights, perhaps even a TV mini-series. While Anne was willing to cooperate with this for the additional publicity it would bring to the cause, it was too soon to think of this idea before she had even got the stories from the families. If a film happened, again, it would be done through the Trust so the money could go there.

Anne wanted no private benefit for herself from this unfolding set of tragedies. Her only motivation was to make a small step of reparation for her failure to protect her friend. She had already met all the parents in association with the police inquiry and the appeal. All had welcomed her offer to write the story and use it as a way to try and find their daughters and to raise funds to help others like them.

Each family had promised her free access to any material they held from their girls. They agreed she could do with it as she chose, with them having no right to censor what was found- unless it raised information about crimes which should be referred to the police or it was very harmful to their girl's own reputation. In this case, they would all try to work out an acceptable way to tell these parts of the stories that was sympathetic but still truthful.

In giving this undertaking, Anne sensed they all trusted her motives and understood her pain, based on their own. She felt charged with responsibility to be faithful to these girls' lives and stories- both the good and the bad. She knew she still had to be kind in the telling of even the bad parts.

In addition to this, having seen Mark through Susan's eyes as she'd told her story, Anne knew she must be faithful to her friend. She must not to take the easy way out and present Mark as a monster. Instead, she must try to see him from the inside: the good with the bad. She must take the insights from his diary and try to understand them. Then, she must truthfully reflect the character they showed. She suspected, even from the small amounts she had read thus far, that gaining an understanding this man and his motives was actually a very complex thing.

To this day, Anne had deliberately refrained from the serious study of his diary. After all, it was police evidence. Despite this, at the request of the lawyer David retained to assist them in her journey to find more information about the Lost Girls, she'd been provided with a copy for her own private reading, which was not to be further copied by anyone. The diary was to allow her to use the information contained within, in combination with Susan's story, to better understand the full story of what had happened.

In addition, Anne had agreed to cooperate fully with the police in their own investigation. The judge had made a confidential order to this effect, but in reality, no order was needed. She and Alan, who was leading the police inquiry, were driven by the same motivations: to discover the truth, to find her friend again and to find out the fate of the others. They talked of minor details almost every day.

Both Alan and Anne had copies of the 'Susan' tapes and transcripts. They had spent two days locked in a room together, listening to every detail and cross checking the transcript for accuracy.

Now, even though Anne had fully intended to start on reading and understanding the diary almost a month ago, she had done little more than skip here and there as she dipped into odd bits. She now must spend a couple solid weeks on the reading until she had fully absorbed all the contents. Then, she would arrange to spend two weeks in Darwin talking in detail to the police officer, who was reporting to Alan. Alan was leading this component of the investigation. Together, they would work on the task of trying to sort out the people described in the diary, particularly these girls, and the dates and places where they had been. Then, while Anne went overseas to try and gather their other stories, to better understand the history of the four girls whose passports were found, the police would try to track Mark's contacts and that way to corroborate dates and places he'd visited through other sources.

In her initial look at the diary, it rapidly became apparent that it was not a chronology: things were out of order. There were stray reflections, creative pieces and factual descriptions interspersed throughout- their beginnings and endings often blurred together. In many places, the language he used was so cryptic that separating fact from reflection was very challenging- particularly for many of the early entries, where there was little ability to corroborate from other sources.

Names, of course, were another challenge. Some names obviously referred to these four girls but did not really fit the passports' names. First, there was an "Elfin" whose story was told a bit later in time than when the Swedish girl disappeared, as if written after the event. Her real name was Elin, but otherwise she seemed to match her description.

There was also a "BB" who may be Isabelle since once he had called her "my beautiful B with the beautiful mind." Also, a few times there was a "Belle" or "Bella" who may well be the same person.

There was also a "M" and sometimes an "A," whose stories seemed to run together. She could be Mandy and Amanda. Some of what Mark said about her was far from nice: "scheming conniving bitch" seemed to refer to her in one place. But, at other times, he was quite tender about her: describing her as another piece of damaged goods that he felt soft about. Anne thought this was the girl Susan described who had come at Mark with a knife and, at that point, he'd killed her. However, this was far from clear.

Then, there was a "J" and once a "Josie" who matched none of the names and dates in the passports. Josephine was Amanda's middle name, but the dates and places seemed wrong. In the end, it sounded like he had hunted and shot this girl from behind like a wild animal. It was a very disturbing sequence but, also, filled with parts of remorse and tenderness.

It seemed like, over time, the diary morphed from an initial thing with parts of light and fun told in earlier places, to a story with overwhelming darkness at its core near the end. Several times, he talked of the "crocodile within which is driving me effin crazy", but he also seemed to take a dark and perverse joy in communing with crocodiles by feeding them and seeming to draw sustenance from his interactions with them.

The only girl whose identity seemed clear throughout the diary was "Kate," often called "Cathy." She seemed to fit with Cathy Rodgers, the Fiona of the passport. She initially emerged as someone with a light shining from within after some very dark parts of the diary- where Mark seemed to become quite crazy. But, even here, it was cryptic. He described meeting her in Adelaide, saying that when she smiled at him it was like someone turned on a light in her face and that turned on a light in his brain which made him feel good. He also said she was one of those rare kind, generous souls who tried to do good, but this goodness was her undoing. He told in detail and reflected on what seemed like some very dark and disturbing secrets that Kate had told him as they travelled together- being raped as child by an uncle. He said that, because of this, Kate was broken and damaged inside. He said she was fucked up in the head like himself. In one place, after describing a truly harrowing bit where she told how the same was done to her sister, too (who had then committed suicide), he had written in heavy underline, "Bastard must be made to pay – I will hunt him down!!"

The Diary was an endless jigsaw of puzzles within puzzles.

What Anne really needed to do was read it fully two or three times from start to finish. Through this, she hoped to try and place herself inside Mark's mind, absorb his idioms and see the world as he saw it. Then, she hoped, it would start to make more sense overall. That was a job for another day.

Meanwhile, Anne tried to keep herself busy and think of nothing but the work in progress: next steps and more next steps. Her legal secretarial training proved useful in giving her a task focus, an organising mind and good systems.

But, lurking behind it all was a fear of what she might find at the end. Or worse, what she might not find- an inchoate fear of nothingness as the ending to a year of her life. A year of toil, labour and searching, where the only output was a book of stories in which life was still absent.

One life would be enough- even if it was not Susan's life. She was not very religious, but she would still pray every night, before she drifted off to sleep, that at least one girl could still be found alive.

A fortnight later, Anne found herself in Darwin sitting with the detective who was trying to unscramble the diary. In the meantime, she had fully read it once, and then gone through a second time to make notes in the margins about the things that seemed significant to her.

Now, Anne and Detective John Arthur were working together off its large photocopied pages, along with a whiteboard to one side, trying to make a chronology of events. She was beginning to see an overall pattern of Mark as damaged goods and understand he was drawn to others similarly damaged. None of the girls had what one would describe as full and happy childhoods- except Susan and, maybe, Belle. Even for Susan, there was a way in which the loss of her Aunt Emily had caused her great distress and split her personality. Belle was less clear-cut but, even for her, there was a sense that she was searching for something or someone. Amanda, Cathy and Elin had all had very difficult times in childhood as had the phantom "J."

All were vulnerable and searching for new identities. The dangerous sense of wildness and brokenness in Mark's character seemed to connect deeply with each them because of this desire.

With this understanding, Anne now felt she was ready to begin.

The first significant event in the diary, which seemed to predate the first diary entries by at least a few months, was the story of Elin, Mark's Elfin Queen.

Part 2 - Elfin

Chapter 16 - The Waiting

Elin remembered winters best as a little girl. She'd lived in a town in the far north of Sweden. It was a place where, for the summer, the sun barely set. In the winter, on the other hand, the sun barely rose at all. It would make a low circle around the white-covered hills and, for a full month, never rise at all. Then, it would suddenly be just a glow appearing on the southern horizon around the time they ate their family lunch for, at most, an hour or two. In this chilly winter half-light, her father would take her out to walk across the snow on the days when the cold was not too extreme and a winter blizzard did not blow in.

There was something magical in this half-light: a place of imagined beings which lived in the half-shadows, glimpsed but never quite seen. At these times, her father would tell her stories of their Nordic ancestry: of gods and warriors. Indomitable spirits who could survive in this land and, when the winter ice was gone from the fiords, these brave souls would sail out in their ships to raid and gather resources for their families. Sometimes, they would discover new and unknown places, even whole new worlds. These legends lived on in Elin's mind far beyond her childhood. They gave her a soul filled with wanderlust and, as she grew from a child to a woman, a restless spirit which ate at her.

In the rest of Elin's life, other things changed too as she grew- though these memories had blurred edges. Around when she was ten, her mother got really sick. They tried treating her and all her hair fell out. She got better for a while- but then she got sick again. That time, however, she never got better again.

Elin remembered that awful, cold day. It was coming into winter and they stood around the hole in icy ground, throwing in gifts and bouquets of flowers into it for her mother. Her mother's body, itself, was wrapped in linens and placed in a small boat. This boat was the very same one her mother and father had sailed in together around the lakes and fiords of Sweden and Norway when they had first met as two children in the local village school. Then, the boat and her mother were covered in the icy dirt. Her father spoke of how her mother could continue to sail the boat over wide oceans as a new warrior queen.

Her mother, Elle, was the love of her father's life. Their family had always been herself, a brother, a little sister and her parents. They had all been very happy together until her mother got sick.

Both her father and mother loved the early Norse customs. So, on that sad day, they followed the way of their warrior ancestors from time immemorial and had done their own boat burial. Her father had dug a huge hole to fit the boat. It had taken him several days before the burial.

Then, he had placed his Elle and their much-loved boat together into the ground. Elin's father did this so the boat could carry Elle into an afterlife where he still had a dream of meeting Elle again when he made his own journey there. It was what Elin's father had promised Elle as she lay dying and, as he always did for her, he had faithfully fulfilled his promise.

The years that followed Elle's death had been hard and lonely years for them all. Their mother's bright smiles and golden hair had lit up all their lives and, in her absence, they felt a great hole.

But, life had continued on despite this. A year later, they had moved to Stockholm. Her father had got work in a factory there. Elin had moved from the village school to a big school in the city and still got good grades. But, her friends, family and teachers all said that Elin had a restless soul. They said it was a sort of wanderlust- endlessly dreaming of the Viking legends and how she could, at least in some way, recreate them in her life to come. She had taken her mother's looks, not in totality, but the golden hair and the blue eyes were her legacy. Her sister had the rest of her mother's face- the chin and nose. Elin's facial features were stronger, like her father's. Regardless, Elin was striking in her own way- if not a full classical beauty. She could sense the power this gave her to make her way in the world.

Elin had her first man when she was fourteen- a teacher in her school. She had stayed behind after lessons and was working away at her desk. She could feel something inside her drawing her to him. He was married, but young and handsome nonetheless. She wanted to know what this boy-girl thing was all about. He had come up behind her as she sat at her desk and, after initially putting his hands on her shoulders, he had fondled her breasts. She was a willing participant to this all and had even encouraged his advances. They had ended on the carpet in the classroom- with the blinds drawn and the doors locked to keep any curious passers-by out, of course. It happened a few more times with him before she moved on to other pursuits. She learned that moving on from people was easy to do. Even though she had shared her body with them, none of them had gotten deep into her soul, to the place of her dreams.

After that, Elin experimented with other men, and even a couple of women, learning how to fully pleasure her body and theirs. One of her girlfriends helped her get a prescription for the Pill, which she had then taken religiously. She did not want any babies spoiling her adventures!

All these events were only brief encounters, though. There were merely something to meet her physical needs. Mostly, she lived in her mind and dreamed of Viking gods and goddesses: travelling with them to places where nobody she knew had ever been before. She did not know how she would satisfy this wanderlust of hers. It was just always there and she would not let it go and settle for an ordinary life!

At University, Elin enrolled in History and Archaeology with a focus on Norse Studies. She also had a minor in Natural History, specifically the plants and animals of the Arctic Kingdom. While at University, she began to read about the great whaling adventures of the Nordic and Icelandic seamen in which they went on expeditions covering all the world's oceans in order to bring their bounty home. It was not that she wanted to kill whales, but the sense of adventure and sailing into danger brought passion to her soul.

Instead, Elin soon became captured by a modern variant of this- the need to protect the masters of the ocean, those magnificent creatures of the deep from the new commercial marauders. She realised that there was nothing courageous in these new, steel sided ships with explosive harpoons- which killed with no risk to the sailors at all. So very different from the way of her distant ancestors using the longboats. That was when the contest was something of bravery and equality; where only the few most-skilled hunters succeeded and returned with their bounty. The seas were a fitting graveyard for those who failed with brave hearts.

One day, when her lectures were out, Elin was wandering aimlessly around the harbour. She saw a Greenpeace ship was docked there, in Stockholm, taking on provisions. She struck up a conversation with a crewman on the gangplank. He told her this boat was seeking to disrupt the commercial whalers of the modern day and to protect the world's oceans from their depredations. On impulse, she enlisted. She was already a competent sailor of small boats. It was an ongoing pleasure she had shared with her father in his later years. Her only regret would be the actual leaving of her father, for whom she kept alive her mother's image. But Elin knew that, in her absence, her mother would still live on in his memory as a Viking queen of old.

Now Elin was a deckhand, unpaid but fed, off in a quest for fame and glory as they ran their campaigns to harass and disrupt the whalers of the world. It began in the Arctic and soon moved on to the north Pacific, focusing on the Japanese Scientific Kill. Then, it moved to the Antarctic. This was a place she fell in love with from her first glimpse of the ice-covered Antarctic Peninsula, teeming with its penguins, seals and countless flocks of other birds, all with its backdrop of ice in all its myriad-colour tones.

Most of these boats took on provisions or were based out of Australia or New Zealand. Soon, Elin came to regard these places as her second homes. It was on one of these stopovers, when she had three weeks in Port Melbourne with nothing in particular to do, that she decided to go and see the inside of what she had been told was a vast, empty continent. The night train was leaving soon for Adelaide. She bought a ticket on impulse- the way she had made most decisions in her life

Her plan was to go the whole way across to Perth, then explore around there. She had heard that Albany, to the south, was a famous whaling town. Elin wrote a post card to her father, telling of her plans, while waiting for the train to depart at Southern Cross Station.

In Adelaide, she spent a day walking around the town. While it was a nice quaint city with spacious parklands and attractive old buildings, it did not really excite her. She wanted to see the outback- the real place far-out past wherever civilization ended. She found out there were tours running to the heart of the inland: places with names like Marree, Coober Pedy and Lake Eyre, largest salt-lake in the world. This seemed a much more interesting plan. She decided she was happy to make her own way without all the tour things added on. A coach was leaving for Coober Pedy at half past seven tonight, due in just after six the next morning. That was good for her since she could sleep on the bus at no cost for her funds were limited.

Next morning, in the early dawn, she collected her backpack from the bus and walked uptown in Coober Pedy. She was ravenous and decided to treat herself to a big plate of cooked breakfast before she checked out the town. Walking along the main street, she found an early opening cafe.

It had only one other guest in it who was starting a big plate of bacon, eggs and sausages, with a couple tomatoes and mushrooms on the side. The food smelt and looked delicious.

Elin sat down at the table next to his. When the waiter came, she pointed to this man's plate and said, in her best and politest Swedish-English, "I would like one meal just like that plate, if you please. I am not sure what you call it."

The man eating looked up and fixed her with a weather-beaten smile. "Oh, you just call it 'The Works'. Bacon, Egg and Sausage with the works, but most locals just call it 'The Works'. I promise it's as good as it looks."

He talked to her with a distant smile, his eyes crinkled up around the edges. He was looking both at her and way past her, but with a burning intensity for both her and the other place. She felt something grab in the pit of her stomach that she had never felt before.

It was not primarily sexual- through there was that mixed in. It was a basic primal attraction, an almost mindless 'fatal attraction', as she had once seen in that movie of the same name. It spoke of danger.

Elin had lost count of the number of men she had shared her body with over the years. If she felt in the mood, and they felt in the mood, it was something she did when the moment was there. She liked the feeling of a man thrusting with abandon, body out of control, as she clawed at his back, and sometimes bit him, while she thrust back. No doubt- she would do it with this man. She knew already this part would happen between them. It would be good and wild- the way she liked it.

But, it was more than that- something much sharper. It was the element of buried danger that excited her. Taking up with this man would be going past life's "safe places." She gone past life's safe places in her travels and in the physical ordeals she had put herself through. But- she had never done it with a man.

It was almost predatory. Both of them were looking at the other like two hungry carnivores eying off the other to feast on- the female spider and her mate. Except, in this case, the mate was her equal or more of a threat. Her sixth sense told her this man was dangerous, seriously dangerous, though not in a callous way. But, at the same time, he disregarded the danger to himself and to others along with the consequences which may follow his actions. Elin had heard of bored sailors playing Russian roulette with a loaded pistol. It was somehow akin to that. They would take the shot; some would survive and some not. She now grasped that in doing this death dance with others lay the supreme thrill; a place she had eternally searched for in a tame world. All of this passed through Elin's mind in a fraction of a second as she appraised her co-diner.

Breaking from his intense gaze, she held out her hand and said coolly and politely, "I am Elin. How are you?"

He responded by gripping her hand with a firm and callused one. "Name is Mark, Mark B. for short. I am what folks round here call a 'local to the Outback'- that is anywhere out the back of Australia."

"I am from Sweden, though I think of myself as more of a Norse Viking warrior from an earlier time, as my father was always telling me stories of our Viking ancestor heroes," she said.

Mark gestured, "Why don't you join me and be my Viking Goddess?"

Elin moved her chair to his table. They ate with a muted conversation. It was what came after that mattered for both of them. He shared his food with her as she waited for hers. In return, she shared her food with him. Their hands and knees brushed in passing. She felt a thrill and she knew he felt it, too.

When they had both finished, he said, "My truck is out back. I have worked here in a mine digging for opal for a month, but this morning I am up early to travel. Tonight, I will be 900 kilometres north of here, up in western Queensland at a place called Birdsville. To get there, I must go around Lake Eyre, a huge salt lake, and then I must cross a big desert full of stones.

"Will you come with me?

"I sense you, like me, are an adventurer who takes life as it comes."

She said, "I have been waiting to make this journey for a long time. I think I have been waiting for you to find me.

"Yes, I will come."

Chapter 17 – The Journey

Elin and Mark set off driving into the early sun. It was February so, even though the early morning was still cool, there was intense heat in the sun. It was mid-morning when they came to William Creek. There was not much there, just a roadhouse hotel and some old railway relics. By now, the heat was baking- the thermometer on the hotel verandah read 38 degrees Celsius. Mark told Elin it would get a lot hotter yet, probably reaching around 47 degrees Celsius by three o'clock.

Rather than pushing hard to cover the miles he had originally planned, he said to Elin, "Now I have a companion, I am happy to only go part-way today. There are a few places I would like to show you along the way."

Elin nodded, "I am your willing guest- take me where and when you will, Mr. Outback Man."

They both had a beer and then a second one before Mark indicated it was time to head on. He said they were heading for Coward Springs, an oasis in the desert, where the old cameleers used to stop on their trips following the mound springs. Here they would have a swim in the oasis springs to refresh themselves before going on to Marree.

It was much hotter by the time they came their oasis, the cabin thermometer read 43 degrees Celsius as they pulled up at the campground which was only a few old buildings scattered under pepper trees. Date palms, their images wavering in scorching heat rising across open ground, marked the watering place.

Mark paid the fee to swim and bought them both an ice cream which melted almost faster than they could eat them. They walked across to the pool and the surrounding shade. They were the only people outside in the ferocious heat. By the time they had walked the hundred yards to the water, every pore in Elin's body was dried out and blasted with the warm air.

She went to jump in, but Mark put his arm on hers to hold her back. "First, I want you to experience something that very few people have enough patience to try," he said.

Mark sat on the edge and she sat down next to him. He said, "Feel the heat as it blasts into your body, that fifty degree hot wind that feels like being inside a fan forced oven."

Elin put her mind into that place where it was only her body absorbing the heat. She pulled her hair free and tipped her head back, pushing her body out like a sunbather revelling in the sun.

Mark nodded his approval. "That's it, drink it in, feel it heat and dry you to your core. Now, do as I do" He slowly lowered his feet into the water, an inch at a time. She, in turn, mirrored his action. The feeling was indescribably delicious. The water was cool and refreshing, but it was the contrast that struck her most. As her feet went deeper, she felt wonderfully refreshed and cool. They both sat there, side by side for several minutes, revelling in the pleasure: the cool water, so delicious as it chilled them from below, all the while counter-posed against the blasting hot air above.

Elin looked at Mark, he was watching her finish her ice cream, his own long gone. He had a lascivious look on his face. "By God it is hot! Looking at you makes me even hotter," he exclaimed. Standing, he walked over, scooped her up with his arms and stepped into the pool.

She laughed in delight as the cool water doused all of her. The water was chest deep and the cool water made her nipples erect under her thin shirt, showing them in perfect outline in a watery silhouette.

Elin slowly unbuttoned her top, exposing her breasts. "I think you have been trying to look at these so I thought I would give you a full view."

Now, Mark's mouth was on one breast and his hands were pulling her pants down. She wrapped her legs around him and he pushed deep into her. *God! It felt good.*

He carried her to the bank and laid her on the baking hot ground. She felt prickles and sharp stones prick the skin on her back and butt, along with the baking heat of the ground, burning into her skin. It aroused her even more, like multiple love bites, exquisite in its pain.

Elin flicked her body and rolled Mark over. Now, it was his back in the dirt and prickles. She pinned him to the ground as she worked herself back onto him, laughing as he squirmed with discomfort. She could feel herself coming with the wildness of it. As she began to lose control, he rolled again and pushed her underneath, laughing at his ascendancy. Now, they both came in a great rush as he pounded his body within hers.

As she felt herself come down off the mountain of pleasure, she stroked his head and hugged him to herself. "Thank you. I have had some wild bonks over my life, but I think this one under the baking desert sun with prickles in my back and bottom takes the cake."

He gently kissed her on the lips and said, "Me too."

After a few minutes more of swimming and playing, he asked her if she was ready to head on. She nodded. She would have been happy to spend a lazy afternoon with him here, but was game for whatever came next.

As they drove on, the air shimmered with heat haze. They came around a corner in the road. A huge expanse of white glittered before them, running away endlessly into the horizon. "That is the start of Lake Eyre," he said. "Right now, its surface is hot enough to cook an egg. It would kill us in half an hour if we tried to walk over it. Now, we will drive past and look at it. Tonight, when the moon is full, if you are made of brave enough stuff, we will walk on it."

As they drove through the full midday heat their world took a surreal feel. Even though the air conditioning was working well in their four-wheel drive, nothing could remove the heat blasting through the glass windows and shimmering off the salt lake and sand hills. Elin felt she had entered a trance as the relentless heat mirage blasted into her. Mark had his eyes squinted with the strain of the sun-glare.

Finally, they sighted buildings in the distance and came into a small town. No one was in sight, so they pulled up outside a sign which read Marree Hotel. The cabin thermometer in their Toyota read 49 degrees Celsius. They walked through the swing doors into a dark interior which felt so restful after the sun's glare. There were more than a dozen people at the bar and a blast of cool air washed over them as they came close. The bartender said, "Howdy MB, bit of a bloody hot day for driving across this God forsaken country. Do you want to introduce me to your lovely passenger?"

Elin said, "Hello, my name is Eli. Does this man usually bring his other visitors to such desolate places?"

The bartender replied, "Well, you are a rare one. Not many have the stamina to travel on a day like this. Hottest day so far this year. Over fifty degrees out there in the sun and, even in the shade of the verandah, it is 48 degrees. No wonder you look like you need a drink."

They stayed for two hours, slowly sipping drinks as they felt the fluid ooze back into their pores. At first, they drank lemon lime and bitters. Then, as their hydration returned, they shifted to beers.

When the clock passed five in the afternoon, Mark stood up and said, "Well, that will do me for the day. Got a mile to make!"

It was still baking outside but, with the sun sitting low in the sky, the ferocious glare was gone. They drove on, following the signs for Birdsville, heading out of town. Now, the sun was behind them, lighting up the desert scrub in a range of colour tones: golds, russet, oranges, olives and browns. As they drove, they slowly veered from a heading of east to north. An hour further on, they approached a turnoff to the left.

Mark looked at Elin and asked, "Are you game for a full moon walk out on the lake? While it looks solid on top of the salt crust, underneath parts are like jelly. It can be really scary if you fall through, like quicksand only worse. But it is beautiful for those with the courage to dare."

Elin looked at him and laughed. "If you are brave, I am too. Plus, I am with a true outback bushman. I trust him to know what to do."

Mark grinned in a self-deprecating way, "Out here, there are no certainties, even for bushies like me. It is a game of Russian roulette. Mostly, fortune favours the brave. Sometimes, even the brave lose."

"That sounds like my Viking ancestors throughout their long and chequered history, whether discovering new worlds or hunting whales. Whoever got it wrong died, such was their warrior way."

The sun was a hand's breadth above the horizon as they came to where the track ended at the edge of the lake. From their elevated position in the sand hills the surface still shimmered in heat haze. But a thing of magic was happening- it was becoming a rainbow surface, as all the light's many colours refracted off the surface crystals, taken in, splitting and rebuilding from the hues of the late afternoon light.

Elin looked out and said, "Wow! It is like Antarctica when the light hits the ice sheets, so barren and yet full of an eerie and remote beauty that it takes your breath away."

Mark unpacked a box from the back of his truck. It was an ordinary looking tin box and inside were things to make a meal: a frying pan, a billy can, along with some metal plates and cups and some tins of food.

The heat was still beyond hot on the sand but there was something restful in the view. Mark pulled out a square glass bottle of brown liquid. He poured an inch into two tin mugs then added water from a canvas bag tied to the back of the cabin. He passed one to Elin and said, "To your best health and a good trip to nowhere."

Elin raised and clinked her mug to his, "Nowhere beats any other anywhere right now."

She did not know why but she felt more content than she could ever remember, sitting here in a desert place with this man she had only met this morning. It was as if his soul met with hers in a place of dangerous emptiness. In the centre of this dangerous emptiness lay a powerful bond of empathy between them. Moved by affection, she slid her bottom across the hot sand, coming close alongside him. She put her arm around his body, then snuggled against him and lay her head on his shoulder.

"Thank you for bringing me here," she said.

Mark did not reply, but ran his fingers through her hair and stroked her head. They sat that way, almost unmoving, until the sun orb fell below the lake and the light had faded to a deep red in the far western sky.

Now, Mark stood up. He gathered scattered pieces of dead wood from the surrounding scrub, formed them into a pile, inserted some dry grass and struck a match. The grass flared and burned brightly. Soon, the wood was burning fiercely, throwing sparks and bright splashes into the night sky. Mark found a packet of sausages in a cooler box, chopped an onion and fried the mixture in a pan, before adding in a tin of tomatoes. It was simple fare but tasted sumptuous after a long day of travelling.

They sat side by side, each eating with their own knife and spoon from the pan. When it was just juices left, he passed her a slice of bread. Each wiped up and ate the remnants until only an empty pan remained. He wiped the pan out with a damp piece of paper towel which he tossed in the fire before returning the pan to its box, along with the other meal things, saying, "Out in this place water is very precious. So, I don't waste it on washing unless I can refill the water tank. You never know when you might need it. One would be dead inside a day, on a day as hot as today, out here, without water."

Elin nodded for it made sense.

Mark said, "Ready for a moonwalk on the lake?"

Elin looked behind her. The moon had just crested the horizon, she remembered it was a day after the full moon, but still it made an almost perfect circle. In her mind, Elin was taken to other places of moonlight memory, nights in the Arctic winter when there was no sun, where a full moon made its way across the dark sky bathing the whole world in silver which gained an overpowering intensity when seen reflected off a snowy landscape. Then, it was so cold that every part of her was covered, here warm air played off her skin as it gently wafted in the night.

Mark found a coil of light, strong rope, the sort that climbers use, along with two webbing harnesses. He put one harness on himself and passed the other to Elin. She put it on following his lead. He clipped one end of the rope to her harness and, part way along, tied a loop in the rope which he clipped to his waist. He looped up the remainder of the rope which he also clipped to his harness. He took a big water bottle and also clipped it to his harness.

Then, he picked up a small, tightly rolled canvass bundle. "I thought we might sleep out there tonight, in a place where our whole horizon is only flat salt. We will have to walk for an hour to get that far out."

Mark passed her a hard plastic foam object, like a piece cut from a surfboard, about 50 mms thick and half a metre across, with a hand sized hole cut into one side. "This is for you. If you suddenly fall through the crust, lay this flat on the unbroken salt next to your body and fold your upper body to rest on it. It should be enough to hold your weight and stop you sinking down into the mud. Equally, if I fall through, stop and put it on the ground where you are, sit down on it and stay there until we work out how to get out.

As you are a lot lighter than me, it is probably better if you go first. Try to avoid places where the surface is a funny colour or looks different. If you feel the ground wobble, stop and walk backwards gently until you are half-way back to me before you try a different direction."

Elin nodded, she could feel the nervous energy course through her, filling her with a sense of intense concentration and excited anticipation.

They headed out. Twice in the first five minutes, she felt the ground move a bit. Each time she backed up, as instructed, and took a quarter turn to take a new direction. Then, the going became good and she fell into a routine, walking along carefully and steadily as she surveyed her route.

Mark and Elin went on that way for around half an hour. The moonlight bathed the surface in a sparkling glow of iridescent colours, innumerable tiny salt crystals each reflecting their own tiny point of starlike light. Elin felt as in a trance, captivated by fairy light beauty.

Without becoming aware, her attention drifted away from the close up watching required. In an instant, the world collapsed underneath her, sucking her down into bottomless liquid mud. The mud rose above her waist. It was midway up her chest before she mustered the presence of mind to put her plastic support into place. She felt fear washing through her. She tipped her upper body towards the float and rested her arms on it. She tried to raise her body slightly but the suction was formidable and she could feel the ground under the float wobble.

Elin looked over at Mark. He had sat down on the ground, body spread out, his back resting on his bed roll, and was now pulling in the couple metres of loose rope between them. She guessed he was about eight metres away. He was looking at her intently, gauging her courage and resolution to deal with this situation. He raised his eyebrow as if to say. *Well, what now?*

She knew it was a test. She could ask him to come and rescue her and, no doubt, he would. But, she did not want this. She must think on her own, see if there was some way for her to improve her situation and, maybe, get out.

Elin slowly turned her head and surveyed the salt surface which receded from her in all directions. Now, she could see her error. A seam of darker colour about a metre wide ran through the salt. It was like the meandering course of a river. She had fallen through two thirds of the way across this dark seam. Her plastic support was resting on the same unsafe surface directly behind her, its edge just tipping the harder surface.

Elin decided that she needed to move her support to the more solid ground, which lay closer directly in front of her, and see if it gave a solid enough surface to try and lift her body onto. Millimetre by millimetre she slid the foam piece across the wobbling surface, slowly rotating her body to stay over it. She was half way round when the ground gave a major wobble. Her heart skipped a beat but she calmed herself. She realised she had sunk another inch or two into the slime. The rope to Mark was now pulled tight, with him taking the strain. She was determined not to give up now and ask him for help. She steeled her mind to continue.

Slowly, Elin resumed the sliding movement. Now, she was three quarters of the way to getting her float to where she wanted it, her float corner was almost to the edge of solid ground. She squeezed all other thought out of her mind and focused on her task. Now, the float was ten centimetres onto the harder surface, then twenty, then at last it sat fully on it. She brought it fully in front of her and surveyed her situation.

The ground where the float rested seemed solid- but she would prefer to get it ten centimetres back from the edge. In that place, she would still be able to rest her upper shoulders on it and try and use this to lever her body out. So, she inched it forward, a centimetre at a time.

At last, it was in position. She bent her body forward as far as it would go resting over the foam, wrapping an arm around each side, resting them on the salt and crossing them above her head. He cheek lay flat on the foam. With conscious effort she blocked everything else out of her mind and focused it only on her body and its relation to the mud, making tiny muscle movements in her waist, hips and legs, testing for any places or spaces of give. One foot, her right, felt less tightly held than the other. She flexed her pelvis and managed to raise this hip slightly. Her foot slipped up, perhaps one or two centimetres, with a sucking sensation.

Now, Elin had to hold that gain before she tried to raise her other leg. She used her right arm and shoulder to inch this right side of her body forward until the suction stopped her progress. Now, she concentrated on her left side. Her foot felt trapped in a vice but, as she worked her knee around, she realised she could move it slightly backwards and forward. She did this several times gaining gradually increasing movement. Now, she must use this loosening to try and lift her left side.

Elin stilled her body completely and concentrated her mind only on that place; she would put maximum effort into a single movement to lift that hip. One, two, three, she convulsed her body. At first it felt futile, stuck in a vice. She redoubled her effort of lifting that hip as she struggled to keep the rest of her body locked in place. Suddenly, her foot gave and she realised she had gained five centimetres on that side. She felt a flood of exultation run though her body which was shaking with the effort of getting that one foot free.

She stilled herself again and regathered her strength to do it again, back to right side. She gained a further five centimetres. Once more she did it. Now the mud was only a bit above her waist and she was able to rest her body on her elbows improving her leverage. Now, she repeated her side-by-side movements with the support of her shoulders and upper body. Slowly, she slid free. Suddenly, she was out and lying stretched out on the salt, panting with exhaustion. Elin looked back at Mark. He gave her a wave and a huge grin. She felt ten feet tall. Her body was covered in slime, but she was still alive and her own efforts had made it so. Elin sat up and cautiously stood up, testing the surface. It felt solid. She took two steps further away just to be fully sure. She sat down again on her foam board.

Now, she felt light-headed as the adrenaline washed away. She pointed to the line of softness. "Do you see that? That is the bad bit."

"Yes, I can see it now." They looked in both directions, following its course as it snaked across the surface. It widened in one direction and narrowed in the other. The both started walking along the opposite sides, heading towards the narrowest place, after which it widened again.

Elin asked, "Should I come back to your side or shall we go on and you come to mine?"

"No going back," he said, "you managed to cross it, now it is my turn."

Elin walked away from the edge until she reached the end of the rope and sat down.

Mark walked forward until he was a metre from the edge. He lay down and wormed his way forward on his flat body, pushing his bundle in front. At the soft place, he placed the bundle on the other side to support his body as he slid it above the surface of this gap. Then, when his hips were across, he rolled onto his side and swivelled his legs across.

Now, they were both on the same side. She came to him and they gave each other a high five. They surveyed the horizon. In the mid distance, directly in front, they could see a slight rise. Behind them now the horizon was only endless undulating salt, as seen from their view.

They headed for the rise. It was a tiny relict sand dune, sitting about a metre above the surrounding salt. Parts of the surface were encrusted with white hard baked material which she realised was concrete-like: layers of dried bird poo, made rock-like from the baking sun.

Elin and Mark sat side by side on their little hill and shared a drink from the water bottle as they looked back to the faint line of the edge from which they had come, now a dark smudge behind the glistening silvered surface over which they had walked.

"I think this is a good place to stop and sleep," said Mark. "What say you? Is this to be our desert kingdom of the night? "

Elin nodded, lost for words. She felt a wild exultation at being in this place. It felt as if she had dreamt of it all her life.

In this faint glimmering of lights and shadows, she imagined that right here the gods and goddesses came down from the sky and walked on the land. She, too, walked amongst them, as did the man who sat beside her.

Moonlight glow lit her hair with flashes of silver and the palest gold. She arched back her body and with her hands fanned her hair out beyond her in a shimmering wave. She turned and kissed the God who sat beside her, in the billowing light, full on the mouth.

"That is a kiss of joy from the Elf Queen of the Vikings to the King of this Desert Land," she said. "This place is a union of the desert in your soul with my soul come fresh from the sea. Both are mingled on this vast plain. Today the desert is in the ascendancy but in another time the sea will rule again. In that time and from this place it will grow to cover the whole known world. I would like to come back to this place when the sea rules again and sail upon it with you. Then, I will be your Captain. Tonight it is you who rule."

Mark put his arm around her shoulders. He hugged her body, pulling it to him. "For now, you are my Elfin Queen of the desert. But one day, I will return and sail these waters with you," he said. She nestled in close to him feeling fully content to be his desert queen within this lustrous light.

Mark smoothed out a space on a flat patch of sand and unrolled his bed roll. Inside was a thin piece of high-density foam, with two thin light blankets of soft wool, perhaps cashmere. He took the piece of foam she had carried. He placed it at the end of the sleeping mat for a pillow, then spread one blanket to cover it in softness.

He indicated to her to come over to him where he sat on it. She walked towards him. As she came alongside, he stood up next to her and unbuttoned her clothes, sliding them to the ground. He took a hanky from his pocket. Slowly and tenderly, he wiped all traces of mud from her feet and legs, inch by inch, moistening it with the water bottle. Now, it was only her naked body reflecting the light.

Mark took off his own clothes. His body hair was dark although the moon glowed off highlights in his hair. She could see his member standing proud and erect in the silver light. It looked like the body of a Viking king, sword erect and she, his Viking queen, waiting to receive it.

Now, she lay down and gestured him to her, spreading her hips wide and arching her body towards him. The lovemaking of the hot day had been wild and exciting. This belonged to another world where only gods and goddesses dared to dwell.

Mark and Elin slept in their silvered world, waking in the earliest dawn glow. Far out the palest streaks of deep red were lighting the eastern sky as the moon lay low to the west. They watched the silver light fade as the red brightened to streamers of pink and gold which shot high into the sky. The lake bed glowed with a mix of both sets of colours. As they lay with bodies pressed together, their awareness of the outside world faded and soon it was only the two of them in their blanket cave in the soft dawn light: the Warrior Elfin Queen and the Desert King, bodies joined. They clasped together, his hands running through her hair. Her hands felt hard muscles and scars on his back. She had never really known any feeling for a man which compared to this before. She had found the one and would stay with him until it ended, that was enough. She told him these words.

He said he would write them down, record them for all the world to know, to tell of his and her joy of togetherness.

When the sun was fully risen, they rose too. They walked back across the lake bed following last night's tracks. They lit a fresh fire for breakfast and then drove on, she now sitting in close to him with her arm linked through his. Sometimes she dozed; sometimes she looked at his face and smiled.

They crossed a broad dry river bed with the name Coopers Creek on signposts, no water was to be seen. They kept driving, coming in the late afternoon to Birdsville, where Mark booked a room in the hotel for them to share. They showered and put on fresh clothes. Then they ate large steaks, washed down by beer.

In the late afternoon, just as the sun was setting and the day's heat was easing, Mark brought Elin to the Diamantina River, a channel with waterholes and high green grass. On the rocks on the other side, they sat on the hill of the Thutirla Pula or Two Boys Dreaming Place. Together, they imagined these black people of legend walking across the remote deserts of this land- another story and imagining which now resonated with each of their own. Mark told her of his crocodile spirit totem and told her that she was embodiment of the elf queen of Lord of the Rings become flesh- all he needed to do was add an F to her name for her to become Elfin.

They laughed together, then made love together in the soft grass of the riverbank. She puzzled at why she thought this man was dangerous, he was captivating and entrancing but she felt safe and secure with him. She had chosen to stay with him wherever life led.

However, Elin knew there was a broken part inside him that had broken when his own mother had deserted him and died. It was not very different to the part which had broken inside her when her own mother had died. He had told her the stories of his life: the good and the bad. Stories of his African lover, now dead, and their African son- even the stories of others he had killed. But, this only made her trust him more.

Chapter 18 – The Ending

Mark found himself surprised at how much this elfin slip of a girl had grown on him. He had been surprised when she had come to sit next to him for that Coober Pedy breakfast. As their eyes joined and minds connected, he had sensed something in her that was a kindred spirit to his. It was a wild fearlessness, the sense that all things were possible if one had nothing to lose. He read in her eyes that she also saw this in him, he also saw the reflected sense of danger she perceived in him.

He understood it- not that he would set out to hurt one such as her, but he had a capacity to create danger for others in his life, it was a law of unintended consequences. His sixth sense said he should walk away, that for her- he was danger, too, and she would be safer to stay well away. But he was as drawn to her as she was to him. So, really, walking away was a non-option. Instead, he decided to bring her with him and to share his wild ride through the world with her.

Their first lovemaking had been an adventure into the wild side, she did not cry out or complain at the prickles in her buttocks on the hot hard ground. She had also not sought his help to escape from the mud and had stood there, totally trusting in her nakedness, as he cleaned it from her body.

So, beginning in that first night of togetherness, Mark told Elin of his life with no details spared and she had told him equally of hers. She had told him her name was Elin, but almost from the outset he had renamed her Elfin, his Viking Fairy Goddess: she with the hair of gold and a willowy body, slim but full. Her head came only to his shoulder; when he lay on her, he covered all of her with his own self. But, there was steel inside that wiry frame. She, like him, would give no quarter when a fight must be had. He most loved the indomitable braveness in her, one who would go to any place and suffer all things without reproach.

Within two days, Elin had told Mark she preferred to stay with him than return to the ship: her life had moved on and she now wanted to be here, to be with him. He had said he wanted her to stay, too. Neither spoke the 'love' word but both knew that best described it. When he looked at her, he felt fiercely protective. When she sat nestled into his side, as he drove, he wanted to drive on and on forever.

But, in another part of his soul, he sensed that, as a fairy queen of the otherworld, she was only his to keep and hold for some short time. Then, she would vanish as if she had never been. He could see no clouds, he could see no danger, but his soul he knew that, for her, he was danger. She was too fragile for her bravery. Somehow, it would break her with he serving as its instrument. He knew he should leave her for her own safety, but yet he could not. He knew she would not let him even if he tried. It was a journey together to the end, whatever and wherever it came. He hoped it would come for them together- somewhere out in the wide ocean as she chased a Viking dream. Whatever life they had together, it would be life enough for him.

They were heading for an opal field in south-western Queensland, part of the Winton field, a vast area of former inland seas where opals had been laid down over millions of years past. Mark had been told of a mine out there, long abandoned, and given a map of it by an old timer in Coober Pedy. It was a place this man had always planned to go back to, having found a seam which promised great riches, but which he had been forced to leave by heavy rain and flooding, decades before. He had always promised himself he would go back. Now, he had admitted, his health was failing. It was beyond him to revisit the place he had not been to for almost forty years. He had asked Mark to do it for him- giving him a map he had scratched out, way back then.

Mark had promised him a half share of anything he found and made his plan to travel there in secrecy, when the heat of summer kept most other visitors away. He would reopen the old shaft and clean it out to a point where he could access the seam. He was told by the old miner that it was about 30 feet down and the soil was treacherous and would need careful propping, but that if he could manage it, the reward would be great.

Now, his Elfin queen was travelling with him, his partner in this search. Not only would he share half what they both found with the old man, they would share the other half equally between themselves.

He had not told this to his Elfin queen, but his mind was set that way. If the rewards were as promised, perhaps they would buy a boat together and go off and sail the world's oceans, wherever the fancy took them. He now promised himself he would be very careful, as her safety depended on it, and he wanted to share a future with her.

After Birdsville, where Mark met with old miner locals to get tips about mining the boulder opals of this country, he cut back east to come out onto the Cooper Creek system with its multitude of channels and flood ways. A New Year cyclone had come down the Queensland coast and gone inland around Rockhampton a month before. This rain slowly ran through the river channels and the flow was now filling the innumerable swamps. A wealth of waterbirds was now starting to breed in these wetlands.

Mark and Elin took their time as they came east, stopping to enjoy the isolated scenery. The days were still hot, but cloud was drifting down from the north east, offering the promise of a storm. This moisture in the skies eased the baking heat. They were heading for somewhere near the channels of the Bulloo River, where it spread out across its own mass of swamps south of Quilpie, a small town in far western Queensland.

Mark realised his knowledge of this country was not strong, but he bought the best maps available and matched them to the miner from Coober Pedy's hand-drawn document. As they travelled, he explained his mission to Elin. He made her promise that, if she came to help him, she would follow his directions with care as it would be dangerous work. She agreed- though he doubted she really meant it.

At last, five days after Birdsville, with only a few missed turns, they came to a place that matched his map. It was several abandoned mineshafts in a rough area of scrubby hills that lay between fertile channels and swamps fed by branches of the Bulloo River, with these good lands used by the surrounding stations. There was a waterhole on the river about a mile from the old mines which still ran water from the same rain which had run the Cooper. The mine area was fenced in to stop cattle from the surrounding stations from wandering over it and falling into a disused shaft.

It was a messy place covered in broken machinery, abandoned timber, hut remnants, a scattering of mullock heaps and other mining detritus. The mine of interest was abandoned decades ago when a big rain storm drove a wall of water down the gully it was in, destroying the mine and filling the shaft up with rubbish and silt.

At that time, the former miner was the only one still working on the site. He had told Mark that, by then, the other mines nearby were deserted. It looked like, in all the time since, nobody had done anything here. Now, it was just one of many old abandoned mine sites, a memory long lost.

There was little food for cattle here on a barren ridge and, with the danger from old shafts to man and beast, the nearby stations avoided this place. In the world of prospectors, opinion was these mines had never yielded much of value. So only a few people ever came to this place. Even fewer came in the summer heat.

Mark had stocked up with provisions, enough for a month, when in Birdsville. They could add to this with birds and animals from the hunt. Mark marvelled how quickly Elfin had mastered the skills of a bushman: snaring birds, shooting or spearing a kangaroo, anything he did she would attempt, too. She mastered things much faster than anyone else he had seen and did it with a mix of intense concentration and a fearless desire to improve.

Once at their destination, they built a bower shed of branches to shelter under, along with a second rough structure to cover the car- making it nearly invisible from air or the ground unless someone came close. Mark wanted no one disturbing them should their mining find good results.

On the second day after their arrival, with all their above ground preparations done, they started to work on the mine. They knew the shaft they were after, by its description and location. But, after almost four decades, there was little to show for it. Just some remnants of broken head timbers marked the top- part buried under a pile of refuse, branches, old tin, soil and the like. They started by clearing this all away, while taking care that the ground below them did not collapse. Even though it seemed safe to Elfin, Mark insisted they both wear a harness which was tied by rope a solid tree in the gully. As they began to clear away the rubbish, they found a portion of the side wall had collapsed and most of the shaft was filled with debris. Despite the water flowing down the river channel nearby, it had not rained here for a long time. This made the surface soil dry and crumbly, with parts breaking away under their feet as they walked near the mine edge.

Mark and Elin took turns, one excavating in the shaft while the other stayed above to haul the rubbish to the surface and carry it down slope out of the way. For the heavy items, Mark rigged a block and tackle. If needed, he could use the Toyota winch, but this had not been required to date. They scouted for new straight and strong pieces of timber to shore up the wall and roof once they were fully down. Mark had come prepared with a chainsaw for this purpose, but they would await what they found below before they started cutting. The first ten feet was done in a day, the next ten feet took two days and the final ten feet took three days, as they painstakingly cleaned everything away until they both stood on the solid floor at the bottom of the old shaft. It was a long way up to the light.

They built a bush timber ladder to make the coming and going easier. The uphill wall of the shaft was the part which had fallen in, whereas the downhill side seemed solid and safe to work from. They put the ladder there and hauled out the fill from this side, avoiding the upslope where the soil was very crumbly, with small parts continuing to break off and fall into the shaft.

They thought of trying to shore up the vertical shaft walls but it was a big job. So, they decided they would work carefully and not disturb the place where the soil was loose. After a couple days, the crumbling of the soil stopped and their concern about it collapsing into the shaft abated. To keep away from the sides, they made a lever structure which allowed them to swing the buckets of soil away from the shaft as they hauled them to the surface with the block and tackle. Each took a turn about, alternating between the top and bottom. It was good to break the drudgery of working in the near dark of the pit and stand in the fresh air, hauling the soil away, although this was the heavier work. A few times, they used the vehicle winch to haul up heavy objects, but mostly by keeping loads small they could do it by hand. After a week of work, they had an accumulation of debris on the down slope side of the shaft. They piled it up a starting a couple metres back from the edge.

After working nonstop for a week, they decided they were due for a rest day. It was a Sunday, a coincidence, but they laughed and joked that God had worked six days and rested the seventh, so after seven nonstop days they had outdone God and were having their own day of rest on God's day of rest.

This day, Mark and Elin swam in the river waterhole and hunted ducks for dinner. They would have started back the next day, but they had enjoyed their day of rest together so much that neither wanted it to end. It was agreed, over roast wood duck, that time was not of the essence, and they would treat themselves to a second day off as well.

Elfin had an idea for a boat to use on the waterhole, made from some old tin sheets and a timber frame. Mark grumbled at first: it was pointless to build a boat for a river in the desert which only ran one year in three. However, Elfin was at her persuasive best. By lunch of their second day, they had built a serviceable boat. It was not pretty to look at, made with old, rusted sheets of iron, nailed to a timber frame with unbent rusted nails. The seams were stuffed with wet clay. But it floated and together they poled it a hundred yards along their waterhole and back. Elfin announced that, for today, as they were on the ocean- not the desert- she was the ship's captain, Queen Elfin, and that King Mark of the Desert was her loyal servant. She named their boat "Ran, Goddess of the Sea," which Mark painted on the bow in wet white clay. In this manner, they passed an afternoon of play followed by a night of love before they awoke in the morning to start their work again.

The next week, Mark and Elin started on the side tunnel. By description, it was about as long as the shaft was deep before it came to the place of opals. Now, they shored the walls and roof as they worked. They would dig out a small amount, no more than half a metre, and then place in two wall pieces and a roof piece of bush timber, cut to length by the chainsaw and jammed tightly into place. The soil down here was also mostly dry and crumbly, predominantly sandy, with mixed pieces of mudstone, sandstone and ironstone. In some places, it seemed to be packed solidly together but, in others, it seemed like old seepage down the gully had hollowed out spaces and places which were a mixture of air and loose bits. The shaft ran away from the line of the gully into the side of the hill, sloping gently downwards. As they progressed, there was moisture in the soil, not wet but damp. It seemed more stable and less prone to collapse. There were also tree roots to cut away which seemed to have found this new place of soil and debris to their liking.

It took five more days until they had reached the end of the old tunnel and came to the face which the miner had described. Here, the ground changed into densely packed mudstone with layers of heavy ironstone nodules running through it. This was what they were seeking- the nodules accumulated here as this gully had filled over centuries and millennia with the soil washed away from the surrounding hills. Miners said these were the best place to find the boulder opal for which these Queensland fields were renowned.

Mark and Elin started working together, side by side on the face, chiselling away the pieces. Once they had a good pile, they would bring them above to sort and examine properly. It was late in the day when they first came above with a hoard to sort, two bucket loads of heavy nodules, with flashes of colour, under a patina of soil. They rinsed their load off and stared to chip the surface encrustation away to see what lay below.

Elfin was working with a nodule of stone about a handbreadth across, lightly tapping with a hammer to flake off the surrounding rubbish. She hit a little harder and the rock split through the middle, along a natural fault into two similar sized pieces. As they fell apart, she held her breath.

It was the most perfect summer blue, a Nordic summer sky tinged with flecks of gold and red as the sun lit up the highest clouds. She gasped as she saw what she had found and called Mark over. He was sitting with his own pile a few feet away He whistled with excitement, saying. "A stone truly fit for an Elfin Queen. It is marvellous to behold and, alone, it makes our whole trip worthwhile. As you are the first finder, this one is for you and for you alone. It will be yours forever."

Now, they both felt the excitement of a wondrous discovery flowing through the veins. They brought their collection together and, by the light of a gas lamp, worked through what they had found. It was extraordinary: another ten large pieces that all had wonderful opal colour scattered through them. They cleaned off the best of them and placed them underneath the end of the bed mattress they shared. They worked for three more days before this patch of colour ran out.

By now, Mark and Elin had several buckets full of wonderful opal pieces. Neither could grasp the true value- though Mark knew more from his work in Coober Pedy. The best he'd found before was far below anything here. These best pieces were each worth tens of thousands of dollars, maybe even more.

Both knew this stuff was fabulous! It was worth more than anything either had ever owned or held in their own hands before. They placed all the best pieces in a steel box that Mark owned and placed a lock on it, to deter any casual observers. It took a lot of effort from both of them to lift this box and place it on the back of the truck. Then, they took all the inferior pieces and brought them to a hole they had dug near the swamp. After that, they removed all the things they could find that indicated their presence from the site. Lastly, they started to refill the shaft with rubbish.

There knew there may be more to find here and they did not want to make it easy for any visitors in their absence. They discussed what to do now. Mark knew a gem trader he trusted in Brisbane, a thousand kilometres to the east, on the coast.

Mark and Elin decided that they would make another journey from here to there, following a leisurely and circuitous route, to ensure the place of their findings was difficult to trace. Once there, they would work out what to sell and what to do with the rest. Mark suggested they should not market it all at once as, so much material of high value, was bound to raise lots of questions. Rather, they should store it safely and slowly release pieces for sale. Once they had sold a sufficient amount, they could decide on whether to recover the remainder or just to bless their good fortune, cash in their chips and go travel to enjoy the world together from here.

Somewhere along the way, they would return to Coober Pedy and pass on the rightful share of the old miner- it was his just desert and they would do nothing to cheat fate.

Mark and Elin had now made an unspoken pact to join their lives together in a more formal manner, perhaps not marriage, but being together for as far as the future would take them with whatever followed- perhaps even children of their own. They had touched at the edges of this idea, walking around it on tiptoes, but had never gone to its core.

But first, they must leave this place of good fortune in a way that kept its contents safe. They decided to leave the side shaft alone but to fill the vertical shaft back to something like the way they had found it. They created a big pile of rocks, stones and rubbish, pieces of tin, broken timber and other debris just next to the lower side of the shaft. Their final act before leaving would be to pile it in on top of the dirt and other fill they had already returned to the shaft.

Mark was poring over his maps in the car, working out the detailed way to go from here when they drove away. He heard a little truncated cry. He looked around. No further sound came and there was no sign of his Elfin queen. He heard a little sound like a mewing kitten coming from over where the shaft was. He stood up and ran towards it.

As he came close, he saw that lower side of the shaft had crumbled away, the side of the rubbish, perhaps the side where Elin had been standing. The noises, like a kitten crying, seemed to be coming from somewhere down the shaft, under all the rubbish.

Mark realised Elin was down there! It had all come down on top of her! He called to her, trying to keep his voice calm, "Hang on Ellie; I am coming to get you, my Elfin Queen."

He worked furiously, clawing and tearing stuff aside as he fought his way down through the debris. Her voice seemed faint and sometimes it did not answer at all. An hour passed, and then another. Her voice had gone silent. Finally, Mark saw Elin, her golden hair shining in the pale light. She was lying with her body mostly buried under rubbish, just her face, shrouded by her hair, and one arm showing now. She seemed barely alive, breathing still, but without any awareness of what was happening to her.

With all his remaining strength, Mark pulled the pieces of debris from Elin. Finally, he had her uncovered except for one heavy stone, perhaps twice his weight, which pinned her lower body to the ground. He stroked her face and said, softly, "Hold on Ellie, one more thing to go until I get you out."

With a last huge effort, Mark rolled the stone to the side and lifted the broken body of his love into his arms. He carried her, as gently as he could, to the top.

The late afternoon light was fading as Mark laid Elin on his bedding mat. He stroked her hair and face. He did not really believe in God, but yet he prayed, nonetheless, that she would open her eyes one more time so he could tell her of his love for her.

Mark turned away to look for some water to clean and wash the dirt from her face. As he turned, he heard her call faintly. "Mark, don't leave me. I know my body is broken. I will not be here when the light is gone. Already my vision is fading. But, I can still see you and feel your touch and love. That is all I want to know and remember. Stay with me and hold me. When it is over, place my body in the boat, the one we made together. Bury it and me under the ground down by the billabong. Then, I can make my journey as your Viking Queen to another shore. Perhaps, one day, we can sail again in it, together."

So Mark returned to Elin and held her. She smiled a faint smile and touched his hand with hers. She told him, in a whispered breath, that something had made her climb to the bottom of the shaft, perhaps her soul knew it was her time. She thanked him for the happiest days of her life, the place where she had found peace and contentment with him. Then, she said no more for her spirit light was fading away.

Mark whispered into her ear that he loved her and she whispered back that she knew and loved him, too. Then, they spoke no more- the effort was beyond her and she just wanted to be held. He put his fingers in her hair and she rested her hand on his face.

They sat like this for a few minutes until Mark realised she was not breathing anymore and her blue eyes now were opened so wide that she could only see the sky in another place.

He stayed with her in the night, holding her cold and stiffening body to his and feeling the tears he had never cried for anyone before stealing down his cheeks.

In the morning, he carried her to the side of the billabong where they had hunted ducks in the reeds in their small tin and timber boat. He dug a big hole into the soft earth just back from the bank. He placed the boat at the bottom of the hole.

He took the two blankets from his bedding roll and wrapped her body in them. He laid her pack and her other things alongside her in the boat, that she may have her possessions for her trip.

Mark took out only her passport, it was the only photo he had to remember her by, and Elin would not need that in the place she was travelling. Then, he opened his box of stones and found the two pieces she had broken apart when they first made their discovery. He placed one inside each cold hand, to give her a fare to pay the ferryman. Then, he covered it all in, making a cairn of stones in the shape of a boat to mark the place where she lay. It was late in the day when he drove away, feeling as if his heart would break inside.

Chapter 19 - First Understanding

Anne had travelled to Stockholm yesterday. With the jetlag, she had spent last night in a hotel near the airport. She had kept herself awake for the long flight west from Australia but, with the extra seven hours added to the day, she was really tired by the time the taxi had brought her to her hotel. It was ten pm local time. The sun was low, but not yet set, in this mid-summer time. The light had a peculiar softness she associated with the northern latitudes, similar to the couple times she had gone with Susan to her aunt's home in Scotland.

It brought a wave of nostalgia for those lost childhood years which she realised they could never recapture. Life had been simple and joyful then. She found herself longing to see her own family again. They had visited her a couple months ago in Australia, but now she had that desire for familiar comfort: the bedroom of her childhood and her mother's cooking.

Well, she'd be there inside a week. She'd stop there after she left Sweden, before she went up to Scotland and then onto France to meet other families and in order to get to know about their daughters. She felt privileged to be given this intensely private access to these girls' lives.

Tomorrow, she was meeting Mr Axel Torborg, father of Elin, whose passport they had found in the box and who it was thought was the Elfin of Mark's diary. She would also meet his second daughter, Freya, who she hoped might also shed some light on more personal aspects of her sister's life, things like men friends which her father may not know.

Axel Torberg collected her from her hotel in the mid-morning. He was someone she had already met on his trip to Sydney for the Appeal. He was a tall, powerfully built, but slightly stooped, man, in his mid-fifties. He seemed to have aged prematurely amd now walked with a slightly shuffling gait. He brought Anne to the family home, where Freya was also waiting, offering a local cake called Pankaka with whipped cream, blackberry jam and coffee.

Axel's English was limited but Freya's was good, so she did most of the talking. It seemed that, with Elin's prolonged absence from the family, Freya had taken the older daughter role. After making polite conversation for a few minutes, Freya began to tell the story of their family.

They lived their early life in a village in the far north of the country until their mother had been struck down by breast cancer. At that time, Freya had been only five so her memories of her mother and before were not very clear-but both her father and Elin had been very devastated at their mother, Elle's, early death. Elin had been very close to both parents and had taken the loss hard. She had become quite wild after that. Here, Axel came in, with Freya helping with the translation

"She always was wild; I filled her head with stories of Viking ancestors, the heroes who sailed the world's seas. They were also a great love of my Elle. In the Arctic winters, way up there, for more than a month the sun never rises. On those days, when there was not a blizzard, I would take Eli out in the lunchtime half-light. We would tell of and imagine our brave ancestors venturing out from the Norse Coast to the furthest regions of the world. I would call her my Viking Princess, daughter of my Viking Queen Elle. We would imagine that one day she would be a queen herself and sail out to unknown places like her ancestors had done.

"I do not think those dreams ever left Eli. She lived a life where most of the world was a place she created in her imagination. As she became an adult, she tried to live that life, too."

Axel then handed Anne two photos. The first was a family photo of a time long ago. To the side stood a boy next to his father, similar but unremarkable. A proud young Axel, hair dark, without grey, stood with his arm around a truly beautiful golden-haired woman. In her arms was a small child, clearly grown into Freya, hair dark like her father's, with her mother's face of beauty. Between her parents stood a child of perhaps eight, flaxen golden hair the image of her mother's- though her face was sharper and more Elfin, perhaps from her father or an earlier generation. She was striking, if not with the classical beauty of her mother. And, already, she had the most penetrating eyes- eyes that seemed to be looking far beyond to somewhere all others couldn't see, to a place in another world.

Anne realised that Freya was talking to her, telling her who was who: a thing she already knew. Then, Freya passed her another photo: this was a recent one taken of an adult Elin and her father on the deck of a small yacht, their arms around each others' shoulders.

Freya said, "That is the last picture we have of Eli. She was home for a holiday from Greenpeace about a year before she vanished. She and my father, who both loved to sail, spent two days sailing out around the Stockholm Archipelago, one of the world's beautiful places, which they both loved. That was their shared passion. Unfortunately, I have never liked sailing so now my father sails alone."

Anne looked at the woman in the photo. No child now, she was truly striking, there was a resemblance to some movie character that Anne tried to place. It came to her: she was the Elf Queen of the Lord of the Rings movie, the role played by Cate Blanchet. Anne had seen and loved all these movies. She tried to think of the name, was it Arwen? No, that was the dark-haired one, a Freya look-alike. She had it now: it was Galadriel. Only Eli face was, if anything, more pointed and pixie-like. But, that golden cascade of hair which framed her face gave her the look, she really was the Elf Queen.

Now, Anne felt almost sure she had found the Elfin of Mark's diary. Small wonder he had given the name Elfin. She realised that both Freya and Axel were looking at her strangely as she gazed rapt at the picture. She turned to them and said, "I think I have read about her and what happened to her in this man, Mark's diary. She is the one he calls his Elfin Queen. Perhaps, I could give you both that part of the story to read and when you have done so, you can tell me if you agree it is her. It will be a hard story for you to read, but it is also a beautiful love story which I think you will be happier for knowing."

They both nodded.

Anne said, "It is in my bag, well, a photocopy. I am not really supposed to show it to you. But, if I was you, I would want to know. I have decided that I must give it to you. Perhaps I should leave it here now. Tomorrow, after you have read it, I will visit again. Then you can tell me what you think."

Freya took the sheets of paper, about ten in all, with a mix of tightly spaced writing and occasional other scribbles. She said, "I will need to help my father, his English is not that good, but it will be good for us to read and remember together, even to cry if we must."

Anne said, "I think it was written about a year after he met her, it is better if I tell you no more and let you discover it for yourself."

She said her goodbyes, then. She arranged to return for morning coffee at the same time the next day. In the afternoon, she bought a ticket to the port and took a sailing cruise out amongst the islands of the archipelago. It was, as Freya had said, one of the world's beautiful places.

She found the trip bittersweet, the beauty breathtaking, the image of the girl and her father sailing together poignant, then of her no more and him sailing only alone. Why had Elin not stayed here? Instead, she had gone to the furthest reaches of the world, the vast Antarctic Ice sheets, always putting herself in danger's way. And then, her final almost-sailing trip across the empty bed of the world's largest salt lake followed, a few days later, by a trip in a home-made boat along an ephemeral river which almost never flowed: now she was the Elf Queen of a Desert Kingdom.

When Anne returned to her hotel in the late evening, the concierge passed her a telephone message. It was from Freya Tolgron. It asked that she ring Freya and left a short message that she and her father would like Anne to come to their home village by train. The return journey would take three days.

She rang immediately and Freya explained that she and her father would like her to join them tomorrow morning for a train trip to Sweden's far north, a trip which left tomorrow evening and ran through the night arriving at the town of Gällivare the following morning. From there, it was a half hour by car to the town where the family had first lived. Freya said simply, "We'd like you to visit our home village. There's something to see to help you to understand."

Freya said it was best if she not to come around in the morning as they had other things to do. Instead, she arranged to collect Anne from her hotel at five o'clock in the evening and bring her with them to the train.

The next day Anne spent sightseeing, since there was nothing more to do in her search for now. She was waiting back at the hotel at the due time and, within half an hour, they were settled into their sleeper compartment.

Anne went to pay them for the fare, but Freya shook her head. "You have travelled across the world to help us find Elin. The story you have given us tells us it is so. Now, for this final part of your journey, you are our guest. As we travel, I will tell you more of my sister."

Soon, the train was sliding smoothly across the northern countryside. As it rolled away, Freya pulled out a folder of clippings and postcards: Elin arrested harassing the Russians, Elin in an inflatable confronting a Japanese whaler and being hosed with water canon, Elin on the Antarctic Peninsula amongst penguins and the final postcard she had sent from Adelaide. Across the back were scrawled some Swedish words which Freya translated.

"On my way across the bottom of Australia.
Heading for Albany and Perth.
Hoping to discover the Australian Outback.
Love to you all. Eli"

As they slid into night, Freya told her more of this girl and her endless series of brief liaisons, never finding anything beyond one night stands. Elin felt sex was just a biological act without any deeper meaning. Freya also told of her sense of fun and fearlessness, ever searching but never finding whatever it was she was looking for.

Anne found a real person slowly emerging from the pages and faces. At last she felt as if she could hear her voice and tell her story.

They talked for hours, until finally the yawning overtook Anne.

Just before she went to bed, Freya said, "My father found his great love in my mother, Elle. I have found a great love in my husband and children and in the joy in my ordinary work and life.

"As we read of Elin, the person who we saw forever searching, we knew she had finally found a great love. Even if it was short and not in the place and way we would have chosen for her, we are glad for her it happened. In the end, she found what she was searching for. We only wish it could have lasted longer, that we could have met him and that we could have seen her again. Even so we know she died happy. For that we owe you a great debt."

In the morning, they came to the town where they left the train and collected a hire car which they drove through the countryside. Anne wondered if they were going to visit their childhood house or something of that sort. Instead, they drove to a graveyard. They came to a patch of ground many times the size of an ordinary grave. On the ground, small white stones formed the shape of a boat.

Anne walked over to the headstone and looked at it. It had a picture of a boat, a faded photo behind glass and a symbol carved in the shape of an old Viking boat. Underneath was writing. She could not read the writing, but Freya and Axel came and explained it.

Axel spoke, with Freya adding the odd word which he could not find.

"Here is the place where is buried my Elle, love of my life. We knew each other as children in the village school and as adults we married and had our children, Theodor, Elin and Freya. Most of our courtship was spent in a timber boat I built, sailing the lakes and fiords of this land. Then, when our children came, they sailed with us, too. Those are the happiest memories of my life and they were the happiest memories of my Elle. There is an old Norse custom, passed down from our ancestors, that when a great sailor dies, they are buried in their boat so that it can forever carry them to the new and promised land.

"When my Elle died, I dug the hole below where we stand and buried my wife in our boat, as befits a great sailor. For more than a day I dug until I had made this hole. I would let none other help me. It was only for me to do this, as the man who loved her. Now, the boat carries her ever onward. until one day I join her."

He continued, "When my beloved daughter died, the man that she loved buried the boat they had made and had sailed in together. He placed her in it in the same way as I placed my wife in our boat. Now, my daughter too makes her journey to the next world.

"This man, who did this, must have loved her as she loved him. What he did was a great deed and is good. If he was alive, I would have truly liked to thank him. Now, you can tell his story and that of my Elin. Tell the story of my daughter, the Viking Elf Queen, and of the man who loved her, her desert warrior king, to all who would hear it.

"Such a story will live long after we are gone as do the stories of our heroic ancestors. It is enough and for this I thank you with all my heart."

Part 3 - Belle

Chapter 20 - Mountain Goat Girl

Isabelle's first memory was of following her goats walking in the hills of the Languedoc, in a small village in the mountains far away from the large and prosperous cities of Toulouse and Montpelier. Their family and those of her cousins were poor hill farmers, each with a small herd of sheep and goats from which they made a rich creamy cheese which they sold in the markets. Otherwise, they subsisted on the meat and milk, along with vegetables from their garden and the occasional food they traded with each other and those who lived in towns nearby.

As a child, Belle had few friends her own age and, therefore, had formed a close bond with the farm animals and with this land of rough and broken hills, particularly liking to go out with her goats and sit on a rock, dreaming as she surveyed the vast and barren vistas. She so loved to run with the goats, jumping from rock to rock, nimble and sure footed, imagining she was one of them, someone who could go anywhere they could, leaping from crag to crag.

She also loved to go to the village church. Despite the poor life of the villagers, somehow, they had built this beautiful place. It was not large but it was a work of art. She loved to sit in there, looking at the statue of the virgin, windows with pictures of the Christ child glowing in dim light, muted colours of the marble floor and the finely carved timber work of the posts and nave. At those times, she would talk to God, and it seemed he answered her back.

Belle was a bright child so, despite her humble beginnings, she excelled at school. She had a natural ear for music and languages. She readily picked up both Italian and Spanish which she learned from an early age in the local village, with its Italian and Spanish farm labourers, and then, as she reached high school, at the nearby town school.

Her musical talent was nurtured by her parents. By the age of ten, she was a competent player of both the aboès, the traditional oboe, which her mother loved to play and the bodega, a goatskin bagpipe, which was her father's favourite. She learned as a child at their knees, she watched and listened with rapt interest. Over time, they taught her simple tunes and helped her efforts until she became skilled too.

Later, she graduated to also playing the guitar which she used to accompany her voice. It had a deep rich timbre, a few people joked she was the new Piaf. She knew she was not in that class, but it inspired her to sing some Piaf songs when giving impromptu performances. She particularly loved, "Je Ne Regrette Rien". It suited her rich throaty voice.

Both her mother and father were talented musicians who played their instruments in a group which performed traditional French baroque music in the local towns and villages. Often, she would go with them and, in time, she too played alongside them on many occasions.

So, despite the family's relative poverty, Belle had grown up with an insight into the much wider world that lay beyond her home. When she finished school, she won a scholarship to the Sorbonne, where she studied Geography and Languages, while she also continued to progress her music, performing in a local group which mainly played the music of the south of France in the Latin quarter of Paris.

She was a top student at the University and gained top marks in her Geography Degree. In her studies, she developed a fascination for the French sailors of the Pacific and the colonies they had founded.

The following year, she applied to study in the University of French Polynesia, based in Papeete. With outstanding marks, she was awarded a scholarship which paid for her travel along with the tuition and living costs to study there for a year, as an early part of a research doctorate.

Chapter 20 - The Journey

Isabelle had never travelled beyond the bounds of her country. Paris had seemed exciting enough as a student and, in her free time, she had come home to her family with whom she was still close.

But now, she had caught the travel bug and was off to see the world, going to its furthest opposite side. She felt really excited as she flew across the world to discover this new land which was both familiar and yet so different. The language and the French culture had crossed the seas and still lived strongly in this place. But, alongside it, was a new people and new culture, where France and Polynesia partly existed side by side and partly fused into something else again. In this fusion, a unique new thing was created, with its own warm and embracing culture.

The year passed in a blur of fascination, as she imbibed and absorbed the Polynesian lifestyle and customs like a sponge. She had kept a strong religious conviction, loving the Polynesian singing at the local church. She joined in with gusto, bringing her guitar to accompany their singing and teaching them new songs. She soon was part of the island music scene.

Isabella gained great joy from this year of her life but knew, by the end, that this place was too small for her, that the wider world beckoned. Part of her wanted to return home to France to see family and friends, another part had caught the travel bug and wanted to see much more of the world, far distant from France.

She tossed up various options. She did not have a lot of money, she had saved very little of her small allowance. Her parents had none to spare for her, either. But she calculated she had just enough to support herself while travelling for a couple months on a low budget. She thought too she could always get some jobs to add to her store along the way.

In the end, rather than returning straight home, she decided she would like to spend some time in Australia. After all, but for a few days, a chance of history, La Perouse would have founded the first colony there and then, instead of speaking English, they would now speak French.

Isabella was also drawn by the idea of improving her English language skills. She was already fluent in French, Spanish and Italian and her German was more than passable. But her English was still weak and she knew the only way for it to get better was to live for a while in an English speaking country. Australia and New Zealand were both nearby choices. Canada also appealed, but with its bilingual status, she thought it may be a bit too easy to revert to French there.

She applied for and was granted a twelve-month working visa to Australia. She flew via Noumea and then on to Brisbane. Her friends said Sydney was the place to see, but rather than this encouraging her to go there, she found it motivated her to go elsewhere.

It was June when Isabella arrived, and after having spent a year in the tropics, the idea of going to the south of Australia in winter was not appealing. She drifted north and found work in a back-packers lodge in Cairns. This gave her a way to see the country, stay cheaply and meet people from across the world.

Her multilingual skills helped her get this job as she could talk fluently to many European visitors in a passable form of their own languages. In addition, when she did bar work at night in the backpacker bar, she would often bring out her guitar and sing a few songs. The extra tips from this added to her wages, so she found she was now saving money at a steady rate.

One visitor who stuck in her mind was a man named Mark Brooks. He arrived after she had worked in Cairns for two weeks with a pretty girl in tow. She had an accent that could be Canadian. They stayed there for two nights before the girlfriend caught a bus on to Sydney. They were obviously lovers, but in that casual way of travellers who meet and join together briefly before they go their different ways.

There was something in this man which exuded sexuality, a sort of wild devil may care look. She could not help looking at him as he danced closely with his girlfriend, clearly with one thing on their minds. The first night they stayed there together until late. The second night, however, it was not long before the level of passionate intensity between them needed to be consummated and they left. As they walked out, hand in hand, it brought to mind for Isabelle her own limited experience of that sort. She found herself remembering it in detail for the first time in the three years since it had happened.

Isabelle was not that "sort of girl." She had only ever had one man with whom she had become intimate. It had happened on a summer holiday in her village. This man, Francois, had known her since they were children. They had found themselves both home from Universities in different cities for a few days. He was two years older than her.

She remembered feeling a childish crush for him when she was about twelve and he was a much more grown-up and muscular fourteen year-old. But he had not noticed her then and she was too shy to give any clue. Then, their lives had gone separate ways. That summer, when she was twenty- one, in the second year of her four-year degree, they had re-met at a village party and both were on their own.

They arranged to meet the next day and go walking in the hills together- she with her goats, which she had promised to mind for the day, to give her little brother a day off.

Francois came another way to meet her, appearing to not want the village to know of their meeting. He found her in the high valley behind their village, hidden from village view by a mountain.

At first, they had sat side by side surveying the barren mountain. She had found herself telling him of her childhood crush on him. He was a handsome man and, as she spoke, she had felt that flush of early teenage emotion return to her and make her body tingle.

As she spoke, he lay his hand on her leg and stroked it gently.

"I noticed you, too," he said, "but you seemed too young then. Now, we are both grown up and can enjoy these feelings." As he said this, he slid his hand down her inner thigh, sliding it under the place where her skirt covered it.

His face was flushed and she'd felt her own face grow warm, too, as she enjoyed the touch. But, at the same time, she'd felt awkward with the intimacy. It was not something she had allowed to happen before, having always resisted the urgings of the local boys at the University.

Until this day, she had followed her mother's Catholic adage that some things were best kept until the time was right- in the marriage bed. She knew this touching was of that sort.

But his touch had brought her body alive in a new way. So she let his hand continue its slow, intimate journey, until it was stroking the place where her legs met, first over her panties and then from inside them. As he touched that place, she could feel waves of pleasure come over her.

Francois was obviously an experienced lover. He had gently stroked and fondled her body until it was fully aroused. After that, she remembered herself allowing him to undress her and lay her on a blanket he had brought along. It happened almost despite herself. Then, as he stroked her more and more in that place of pleasure, she became aware he had taken off his own pants and she saw his maleness aroused.

It was hard to stop his insistent touching and her body wanted more. She remembered how he had placed his body over hers and pushed her legs apart. Then, her feeling of alarm, not sure she wanted this, but not knowing how to stop him at this point.

When she had felt him try to push inside her at first, it really hurt! She tried to shake her head and push her body away. But, she was pinioned and he was too strong. The pain became sharp and she felt a place tear inside her. After that, the pain had eased. In its place, she remembered her sense of regret. It had been too cheap. But, by then, the time to resist, alone with him on a barren hillside, was past. She was powerless to make him stop.

She had allowed it to finish, lying still and unmoving on the blanket, flat on her back with her legs pushed wide apart. She remembered, as if a bird, watching, with a sense of sad perplexity, as his body rose and fell. He had groaned as he pushed in and out of her. For her, there had been a small amount of pleasure mixed with the pain, but it was not much. It did not override the sense of loss she had felt.

Then, when it was done, he had removed himself from her with a shuddering moan, leaving that part wet and bleeding. She had felt a sense of strong remorse at having done this thing.

It could not be undone- even if it was disappointing. It had given her little pleasure then and, even now, she felt short-changed. Soon after, he had dressed and left, suggesting they meet again soon for a repeat.

She had not responded. She'd known she would not do this with him again. For the next few days, she'd thanked him for invitations to do more things with her but declined. Then, he was gone. She'd not heard from him over the three years since. On that day, when it was done, she remembered how she'd also felt relief that no one else knew.

Since that time, Isabelle had very little inclination to repeat it with another man, religious beliefs aside. She still held to those religious beliefs, but they were not so strong now. She knew that almost everyone else her age, married or unmarried, did these things without second thoughts. They did not seem to feel any guilt. Now, she wondered was it really guilt and remorse? Or was it that she had done it with the wrong man at the wrong time and, with another man, it could be different?

As she wondered of other men, she found the face of this man, Mark, come into her mind. Now, he was doing this thing with another girl and not with her. So, even though she sensed a raw sexuality with this man, that made her tingle, she did her best to ignore it and push it away.

She expected Mark would leave on the same day as his girlfriend. Instead, he stayed on another night. She saw his name again in the guest list. In the afternoon and evening, she glimpsed him walking in the distance and felt a strange thrill despite trying not to notice. That night, she was rostered to serve in the backpacker bar. She took along her guitar. She had not played for over a week and felt a need to make music.

At first there was another girl behind the bar with her and, while she served, Isabelle played with her guitar and sang her bracket of Piaf songs.

As she started to play, she could see that Mark was sitting at a table at the back. She had not noticed him come in and had not served him a drink. But he had a drink in his hand and was talking to another man a few years younger, explaining something with his hands.

When her song began, Isabelle saw Mark turn towards her and put down his drink. She sensed his attention had locked onto her. At times, as she looked up, she connected with his eyes and sensed his admiration.

When the songs were finished, there was strong applause and a steady stream of tips which she split with her co-worker. Soon after that, most people drifted off. Now there were only half a dozen people remaining. She told the other girl she was happy to lock up, so her friend went off to bed.

At the end, before she closed the bar, it was only him and another couple left. This couple were only interested in each other. She fell into a conversation with Mark, discovering small fragments of his life, although he was guarded in what he said. She listened with interest as he told her of having worked in French Africa for a period.

She found that, notwithstanding his guarded way, she liked him and enjoyed his company. When the other couple left, he too made his excuses, though it seemed to her that he would have stayed on if they did. She would have liked to talk with him for longer.

She did not expect to see him again, such was the traveller's way. She felt regret as she watched his broad back walk away down the street. The following day, he was gone.

A month passed and she decided to move on. It was now the end of July. She decided she wanted to see the desert and booked a flight from Cairns to Uluru. She was now thinking that, after she saw the sights there, she'd go to Alice Springs and find another job for a month or two before she travelled on again.

When she came to Yulara, she saw a "Positions Vacant" sign at the Desert Sails Motel. A short interview gave her the position on the strength of the reference from Cairns and her multilingual skills. Again, living was cheap with a room provided and her days off gave her the chance to explore. After a fortnight of work, she had four days off. She caught a bus to Alice Springs.

As she left the bus and walked down the main street of Alice Springs toward the mall, she looked across the street. Her heart skipped a beat. There was that man, Mark, walking down the street. There was another girl on his arm, again acting very friendly. She felt regret that he was always with someone else, usually a girl prettier than her.

But then, he looked her way, saw her and gave her a huge grin. He brought his friend across the road and introduced this girl to her.

"This is one of my best friends from Alice Springs, Martha, who is a nurse in the hospital. I have not seen her for almost a year, even though I am often in Alice Springs, and here she is walking down the street."

Then, he addressed them both, "So, as I start walking along to have a coffee with Martha, what do you know? I discover another friend, Isabelle who I met over a couple nights ago when I stayed at a backpacker lodge in Cairns. She was a delightful barmaid who served me drinks late in the night, listened to my drunken stories when most other people would have told me to go off to bed, plays the guitar, sings like an angel and talks with the most delightful French accent."

Martha held out her hand in welcome, then they all walked along the street together before stopping at a cafe for a coffee and snack.

Isabelle found something really nice about meeting a person she already knew, and she also liked his friendly friend. They chatted freely, exchanging tales of the road and then talking of the goings-on in this bush town. The picnic races were coming up the next weekend. Martha asked Isabelle and Mark if either would be able to come.

Isabelle replied, "Regretfully, I cannot. I must catch a bus back to my job in Yulara in three days' time. Then, I must work for another ten days before I get my next break."

Mark also said that he had to head out of town this afternoon and would be away for at least two weeks before he returned. In fact, he must leave soon. He had just come into the town to get a couple things before heading out this afternoon.

After half an hour, he excused himself saying he had a long way to drive tonight as he was expected at the Granites Gold Mine, in the Tanami Desert, over 500 kilometres to the north-west, by tomorrow at daylight. As he left, he promised Martha he would call and see her when next in town.

Then, he turned to Isabel, took her hand lightly in his own and said, "Most sincerely, I hope to meet you, yet again, somewhere in your travels." He said it with such charm, she felt herself blush inside.

Then, he was gone.

Now it was just her and Martha left to finish their coffees. She found she really liked this girl. She was down to earth, good-natured and attractive in a well-rounded way, if not classically beautiful.

Isabelle could not help herself; she wanted to know what was between Martha and Mark. With Gallic directness, she asked, "Are you and Mark very good friends? Do you know him well?"

Then, she blushed, self-conscious at her prying.

Martha looked at her directly and laughed. "Oh, you mean, is he my boyfriend or lover? Are we shagging? God, no! The girls he picks up, those girls are much classier than me, much more your type, more often girls from other countries, people who want to see the outback. He often offers to show them, and I am sure he offers them much more than that. You know how it is, nights out under the stars, two of them in one bed. I am sure he tells them when it is cold that he will keep them warm," she said with a lascivious grin.

"Every time I see him, he has a different one on his arm. Not that I would mind trying it on with him, just a one-night stand would be fun, I am sure he is a great lover, you can tell it by the way he looks, so intense!

"But I have a regular boyfriend who works in the hospital laboratory. He is not as wild and exciting as Mark, but he is much safer. Now, he has gone away to Sydney for two weeks to see his family. That is why I am out on my own and at a bit of a loose end.

"Perhaps, if Mark stayed in town tonight and we kicked on, we would have a shag at the end of the night. I am sure he would give me a wild ride and one to remember, but that would be it. You can be sure I would never tell my boyfriend. But never so far, and we probably never will.

"Mark is just a good time mate. Someone to have a drink and a laugh with, a good friend- but not in the way you were thinking. It is better that way as, for mates, sometimes the sex thing gets in the way.

"I have known him for a couple years since I treated him in hospital one time when he cut his hand pretty bad. He is as tough as an old boot and his hand got better before you could blink. But we became friends and now I see him now and then, maybe once every six months.

"I know almost nothing about him. He seems to come to the Alice for a few days, every once in a while; it is like a base for him. Sometimes, when he comes to town, he rings me and invites me out for a drink. But then he is gone again and months go by until I next see him around.

"It was a genuine pleasure to run into him this afternoon and an equally big one to meet you. Where are you staying in town? Perhaps we could go out for a drink together tonight, instead."

Isabelle admitted that she had yet to find a place to stay; she had only stepped off the bus from Yulara five minutes before she met them.

Martha said. "I have a little flat near the hospital. It has a spare room, with no one in it. Why don't you stay there while you are here?"

It was agreed. Isabelle wanted to give her some money, but Martha would not hear of it. "No way, it would have been empty if you had not come. Tell you what. I have been promising myself a trip to the Rock for over a year. If you can squeeze me into your room, I am happy to sleep in my sleeping bag on the floor, that will save me some money in return."

The plan was agreed. Next weekend, Martha would come to the Rock and stop with Isabelle in return for the bed in Alice Springs.

They walked down the road to Martha's place and, after Isabelle was settled, went out for a drink. Their friendship grew from there.

Isabelle really liked the frank and open way that Martha talked about her life and loves. She had always kept her personal secrets much closer to her own chest, not that there was much to tell.

They got on really well over the next three days. While Martha went to work during the days, she told Isabelle of the places to see and the things to do. Each night, they met up for a drink and dinner- somewhere inexpensive, often with other friends of Martha's.

Isabelle found herself liking this town and thinking that, perhaps, in a month's time, she would look for a job here for a couple months. It was nice to make a group of friends rather than continually meet strangers.

When Martha came down to the Rock on her days off, Isabelle juggled her shifts to get a full day off. By the end of this, she felt she had made a real friend. They exchanged home addresses to keep in touch in the future and Martha promised to visit her if she came to France.

With Martha gone, Isabelle found herself strangely restless. She liked the desert, but she had more or less seen what was to be seen around Uluru and the Olgas. While she could return to Alice and look for a job there, she felt something beckoning her on, drawing her to go further.

One evening, Isabelle was chatting to a guest at the bar when it suddenly became quiet. He told her he lived in the town of Broome, on the opposite side of the country from Cairns but up north, too. He had a hotel in Broome and was always looking for barmaids and restaurant waiters. So, if she came there, he would be happy to give her a job.

Isabelle thought he might be sleazy to work for, but it put the idea in her mind as he told her about this town with its tourist resorts and sandy beaches. She decided she would like to visit Broome.

She had heard of guests at the Desert Sails talking of flying on to Broome direct. There must be a flight from here to there. Next day, she looked up fares to Broome and booked a flight at the end of her next batch of shifts.

Isabelle had the habit of sending a post card to her parents each week to keep them abreast of her travels- it was easier than ringing at the wrong time of day. So, after she made the booking, she put a postcard in the mail to tell them of her plans. She was starting to feel homesick to see her family again and told them that, after Broome, she may fly to Bali for a week, but then she was planning to head home. She said she was really looking forward to coming home. She knew they wanted to see her again, too.

Her last week in Yulara flew by. When she was at the airport she did a quick post card to Martha telling her of her changed plans. Then, she was on the plane flying across endless barren red sands before she came to a small town on a peninsula reaching into sparkling blue ocean.

Stepping out of the plane, the air was balmy and warm. She felt she had returned to the tropics although this was a much dryer place than Papeete. Its climate felt closer to the warm dry air of her home in the hills of Languedoc in the summer months, when the wiry hill grass was brown and dry and only in the river valleys was any green grass to be seen.

As she walked around the town, luxuriating in the dry air blowing from the inland, she felt more settled here than in any place since she had left her home a long time ago.

She soon found a job in a hotel in the main street of Broome and it supplied a tiny room out the back for her to stay. It only had a fan in the ceiling, no air conditioning, but the nights were cool. She did not care for the fancier resorts that were scattered along the beaches out from the town. There was something more honest about the locals who drank in her pub than the other tourist visitors of the upmarket resorts. She found their jokes and coarse humour, which she was beginning to understand as her English got more fluent, reminded her of the worker humour of those who lived in and around her home village.

It felt comfortable and good. They all called her "Frenchy" and mocked her foreign accent, but it was good-humoured banter. A week went by, then another and soon a month had passed. It was now

September. The weather was warming up and the drinkers were getting thirstier, telling tales of the ferocious heat of the inland and also of huge storms sweeping the coast when the wet season came.

Isabelle found this foreign climate and its weather patterns fascinating. It continued to remind her of parts of her hillside home. Each week, she sent another post card home- although as she was enjoying this place, she was now much vaguer about her return dates or plans.

She often did the late shifts as she was more a night than morning person. It suited her to work into the late nights, there was a peaceful solitude when it was just her and a couple last drinkers remaining and making polite banter.

It was a Tuesday night, over a month after she came, and there were only three drinkers left in the bar talking together around a table in the corner. The time was somewhere between ten and eleven in the evening. Eleven was official closing time and, with such a small number of patrons, she said she was happy to finish the shift and lock up. So, her co-worker went off to bed. She worked her way around the room: wiping down all the benches, stacking the bottles neatly and putting the glasses in the dishwasher to wash overnight.

She was bent down stacking glasses when she heard new footsteps come into the bar. *Another patron for a drink,* she thought. She stood up and found herself looking into Mark's face, opposite her at the counter.

She blushed, then smiled a big smile, delighted to see him yet again.

He returned a huge grin. "Belle, Can't believe my luck running into you again. Wherever I go to in Australia, I seem destined to meet you."

She felt breathless with the delight at seeing his face again. Three times over as many months felt like real friendship. It was like a strange destiny linked their travels.

After about ten minutes, the other drinkers finished their drinks and left. It was only them alone. He was perched on a bar stool, directly opposite her. They fell into easy conversation.

She asked him where he had come from and where he was going.

He told her that, after working for a fortnight in the Granites, he had been offered work on a station south of Broome, fixing windmills. It had kept him busy for three weeks but, today, he had finished the last mill. He had pulled up the pump, stripped it down, fitted new seals and made other adjustments. Now, it was working as good as new. He had called to the station homestead for a beer and a meal before deciding to push onto town. He figured he could make it for a drink at his regular Broome pub before it closed for the night.

He was now glad he had because, a couple times, feeling tired, he had almost stopped for the night and rolled out his swag- but the thought of a cold beer at the bar had kept him going.

She refilled his beer and replied it was good he had come tonight as tomorrow was her day off and, if he had not come until then, he probably would have missed her.

He said that really was a cause to celebrate. He would have hated to have missed her. He suggested she have a drink, too, his buy.

She agreed, said it was so nice to talk to someone she'd known a while. Then they had a second drink together as their conversation flowed seamlessly along.

She asked him where he was going. He said he was heading north, he had been offered a month of work at the Argyle Diamond mine south of Kununurra, up near the Northern Territory, but had two weeks until that started. In the meantime, he wanted to explore a remote place further north in the Kimberley that he barely knew.

Isabelle realised, as he paused in his story, that she'd enjoyed talking so much that she had forgot to finish locking up and shutting down.

She looked up. The time was now a quarter to twelve.

She stood up apologetic. "I'm sorry, I must close now. I have so enjoyed talking to you, I forgot the time. If the police come around now, I will be in trouble."

Mark got up, walked over, locked the door to the outside, and turned off the outside light. “That should fix it,” he said. “Now, they won’t ever know there is someone still inside.”

Isabelle felt a bit giddy and giggled.

Mark laughed, too. “Reckon, seeing as I have kept you talking long past your bedtime, I should help you finish the tidying and lock up. That way you will be finished sooner.”

She said, “No, you are the guest. I get paid to do this work.”

“It is an excuse to keep talking to you and I like helping you,” he said.

They worked side by side, with her explaining the tasks required and him doing them. After fifteen minutes, it was done.

She said, “I suppose I should let you out and then lock the door behind you before I go home to bed.” Then she added, almost as an afterthought, “I wish you were not leaving again and travelling on so soon. It has been so nice seeing you and talking to you. Every time it happens, I feel like you are gone before I have barely met you.”

Mark was looking at her quizzically. “I must admit, I have enjoyed talking to you tonight more than anything else I’ve done since I met you in Cairns three months ago. Why don’t you come along with me for the trip I am planning? That way we get to keep talking and telling the stories to each other that we both want to hear.”

Isabelle blushed, then she looked awkward. “I like talking to you and I like listening to your stories, but I am not very good with men. I don’t want to give you the wrong idea. I do like being with you and talking to you. But I am not like those other women, you know, that go with men, you know, that way.” Then, she blushed again.

Mark looked at her, even more curious. “Oh, are you one of those women who like other women, the gay ones?”

Now, Isabelle went really bright red. She shook her head furiously, feeling temporarily lost for words.

Mark touched her shoulder, eyebrows raised, questioning still.

"No, it is not that. I like men just fine, but I don't go with them the way you mean. It is hard to say why, perhaps I am just shy about that- I think being with men alone scares me. No, I really don't know what I mean, I am not scared of going with you, it's what you say, that I don't quite get that man-woman-in bed with stranger thing. It feels wrong."

Isabelle realised she was babbling, not making sense and should stop. She put her hand on her mouth, forcing herself to stop talking, and just shook her head as she collected her thoughts.

"I would love to travel to the places you talk about and to see them. But, I don't want you to think that means....." She paused, again stuck for words; she just could not say it. She felt light headed and started giggling, "You must think I am such a prude," she said.

Mark laughed, shook his head, and patted her arm. "Don't be embarrassed. I understand exactly what you are trying to say. That part doesn't have to be part of the deal. I do really like you- I won't pretend I don't find you attractive that way- I do. But I am happy for you just to come along as a friend, see the country and let me enjoy your company.

"That is, by far, the most important thing. Being my friend is more than enough. I don't want you to think that the other is a part of it. It should only happen when both people really want it to."

She found herself hugely relieved and excited. It filled her with a vast sense of adventure, the idea of travelling far out away from civilisation to see all these other places.

She said, "Thank you, Mark. I will come. When will we go?"

He winked and looked at her. "How about right now?"

She said, "But, what about my job? I must give notice."

Mark answered, "Don't worry about that, he will find someone else tomorrow. That is how it is in these towns. Leave a note to say you had to leave unexpectedly and ask him to post on your pay-check to your home. Oh, and tell him you have left the keys in the till. He will have a spare set to let himself in tomorrow in the morning."

Isabelle wrote out a brief note and showed it to Mark.

He said, "That should do just fine." It did not say where she was going or with who. It did not seem important and Mark did not suggest it.

They walked out into the street, pulling the door locked behind them. They got into Mark's Toyota. He drove around to her room.

In five minutes, she had packed all her things and they were on their way. Mark carried her bag outside and she carried her guitar as they left her room and locked the door.

It was a dark night with no moon as they drove away. After a few minutes they had left the town lights behind and the only sight was a huge mass of stars stretching out from the far horizon. Isabelle was spellbound watching them all. The view was much the same as at Uluru, but there the nights were cold and she had spent little time outdoors after the sun had set. Here, the night air was balmy, with only just a tiny edge of coolness.

She found herself thinking, *The universe is such a vast and empty place. I wonder if the God I have believed in all my life lives out there in some place? Or does he live in another place again, another huge but separate space that I cannot see?*

At first, they drove along in silence. Soon the signs of the town fell away and there was just a black emptiness. She became aware of Mark's occasional glance her way. She did not feel threatened by it; it was a friendly and inquiring look. After a few more minutes of silence, he asked her, "Penny for your thoughts?"

She did not instantly understand this English idiom. Then, it came to her, *he is asking what I am thinking about*.

She replied, "As I look out at this huge and empty sky, I wonder where is the God; the one who made it all? Does he live out there, in a place somewhere beyond all those many stars? Or does he live someplace else, another separate universe?

"What do you think? Perhaps you don't believe he is there at all."

Mark thought for a minute, used to making polite conversation with girls to try and charm them. But this was not like that; she was not making conversation for conversation's sake. It was the sort of question he often wondered about when he was on his own, looking at the vast immensity of the earth and sky.

He liked that this girl did not try and engage him with cute words, but was challenging him, trying to understand his deep thoughts. He drew breath and thought carefully before he answered. The pause went on and she looked at him again, inquiringly.

Finally, he said. "I wish I knew the answer. When I was only little, my mother, who was a Catholic from Italy, taught me to believe in God. She used to take me to church sometimes.

"But, when I saw the awful things my father did to her and how nobody helped her, neither other people nor God, because everyone was too frightened of my father, I thought God was either a coward, a terrible bastard or he was not there at all, if he chose to ignore what was happening. I think I mostly believed he was there and a coward who did nothing. That made him an even bigger bastard than my father.

"After my mother died, I had to look after myself and keep out of my father's way or he would hurt me, too. A few times, I felt like my mother was watching out for me. Maybe she was up there with God and God had done something good for her, to make up for all the bad from my father and now she was trying to protect me in turn.

"Then, they sent me to remand school and I saw the awful things that the men did to the little boys and there was nobody to help them either. At that place, I stopped believing there was any God, even a weak god could not be such a gutless bastard as to let what they did happen.

"At that time, I decided I had to take the place of God and to hurt back anyone who tried to harm me. When I killed the first man trying to hurt me, I was glad there was no God because it meant that, instead, I had taken his job to pay that man back for the evil things he did.

"Over the years, I have killed more people who have done bad things. Each time, I was glad it was me not God who was doing it. I liked doing it, taking responsibility for causing the payback.

"But, since I have lived out here and got to know the aboriginal people of this land, and the same in Africa where I also lived, I am not so sure anymore there is really nothing there. To them, God and the spirits are as a real as you or I are. They seem to gain wisdom and power from their believing.

"In the end, I thought it seems stupid for me to try and decide about God. If he is there, he is too big and I am too small for me to work him out like that. The more I see, the less I really know of the limits to what is out there. In a place where so much is beyond my understanding, I think it would be very conceited of me to tell a God-thing how to do his job.

"Instead, I find a part of me wants to believe there is something out there, something keeping the balance of the universe.

"But I do not think it has much to do with the world down here. I think it is mostly up to us to do the good things and right the wrongs of the bad people. Most people can see the good and bad and know how to choose to do the good. But, sometimes, bad things take them over. Then, I think they become like a sick animal which can spread its disease to others. Whenever that happens, it is up to each of us to stop them, in whatever way we can.

"I don't believe it is for government to do this. It is for the people who see it and know it has happened. That is the best place for justice. I think God has left us alone to sort out our own messes while he deals with the bigger stuff of running the Universe. I am happy it is that way."

Isabelle looked at him in amazement, half shocked that he talked so openly about what he had done, the killing of other bad people, and half in awe at his honesty.

She said, "Do you normally tell people things like this, so honestly? I am not sure I could be that brave."

"Normally, I do not tell people anything about me, not even my real name. But you are different. You asked me an honest question and so I gave you an honest answer. It is like when you told me the truth about how you are with men, you did not make an excuse- you just said what was in your mind. That was brave. Perhaps it helped me to be a brave and truthful with you. I think you are a true brave person. I most like brave people, particularly those who think deep thoughts."

In that moment, a real and a deep friendship was born. It was the first time Isabelle could remember being with a man who she thought was a true friend. She'd had girlfriends, but could not remember a real man friend. And he clearly was a man, he exuded strong "man feel." But that seemed of far lower importance- the thing that mattered was that he was her friend, a person who, like her, thought deep thoughts.

After driving for a couple hours, with odd fragments of conversation, Mark turned down a side track off the main road. After a couple minutes, they came to the side of a small creek.

He said, "We both need to sleep. The sun will be up in four hours. It is less than an hour's drive to Derby where we get some breakfast before our real adventure begins. I will fix your bed, then I will fix mine."

He lifted a wire frame off the back of his truck, placed a sheet of canvass and thin mattress over the wire, then covered it with a blanket and put a pillow at the head, saying, "It is not quite hotel class, but it is good to sleep off the ground around here- there are things that crawl around that you would not want sharing your bed. I will say good night now as I need to sleep, too."

He made a space for himself on the flat tray at the back of the truck, unrolled a bedding roll there, and then climbed up.

Isabelle said, "Thank you, Mark, and goodnight."

As she stretched out on her bed and looked at the endless stars above, she felt a tiny regret he was not lying beside her. She would like to know what his body felt like.

Chapter 22 - A Barren Wildness

When Isabelle woke up the next morning, the sun was just above the horizon. The air was still cool, but she knew it would soon be hot. Mark was sitting on a rock looking over the creek, writing in a small book with a battered cover. She rose quietly from her bed and walked over to him with her softest feet, stepping carefully to avoid causing the crackling of twigs and leaves.

She loved walking with bare feet. This memory came from her earliest childhood in the mountains, taking her shoes off and running free. Since she'd come to the tropics, she wore sandals when needed but the rest of the time she had bare feet. Her feet were so hardened that the boss at the pub told her she had feet like a "blackfella." She could walk on sharp gravel without flinching, although in the midday, the melting road bitumen was too hot even for her.

Mark seemed unaware of her. She approached without any noise, taking pleasure in her total stealth. She put her hand on his head. In one second, she was standing above him, the next he was not there anymore, but was towering over her, hands poised to strike. It was a blur and for a split second she was immobilised with fear. Then, his face recognised hers and he relaxed.

She found herself laughing, she could not say why; it was a sort of nervous relief. "My God," she said, "that was like a Foreign Legion movie, one second you are sitting, the next is like a tiger strike. I am glad you realised it was me before you killed me."

Now, Mark laughed, too. "Sorry I scared you. You gave me a start. I never heard you coming. I didn't know anyone could walk so quietly."

"I just came to say, 'Happy Good Morning.' I am sorry I startled you, but you were so absorbed with your writing. What is it, a diary?"

He went to close it quickly, as if embarrassed. She placed a hand on his arm. "I'm sorry; I did not mean to pry. When I was a little girl, I often walked in the mountains with my goats. I took a book to write my thoughts and poetry. I described the things and people I saw: the way a falcon would dive for a rabbit, the way the sun lit the hills. I did not have many people as friends. Instead, my thoughts and writing were my company. Perhaps your writing is something like that."

Mark looked at her with intense eyes as if amazed at her insight. "You read me like a book. I am mostly alone. This is the place where I keep my thoughts; all those words inside my head that I never get to say get written here. I write poems and tell little stories which amuse me.

"I was writing about meeting you last night, how it was the third time and how I knew your shape before I saw your face. Then, as we came away, you asked me whether I believed in a God. It seemed an important thing, your question, not my answer.

Isabelle sat down on the rock where he had been sitting. She wrapped her arms around her knees. She looked up at him towering over her. She reached out, took his hand and pulled it down.

"I would like it if you would sit down beside me and finish your writing. Then read it back to me, just the bit about me. I have never had anyone write a story about me. I would like to see myself through your eyes. I will not try to see what you say. I will look at the scenery and try to imagine what your words might be. Then, when you read it back, I will see me as you see me."

She could see Mark hesitate for a few seconds, torn between his wish to keep a private, separate world and a desire to share it. She tugged his hand again, more insistent, "Come on, try it."

He nodded and sat alongside her, almost touching but not quite. He closed his eyes, as if lost in thought while long seconds passed. Then, when he opened his eyes, he began to write.

Isabelle looked away. There was a small, red coloured bird nearby in the creek, moving from branch to branch. She turned her attention to it. It was flitting here and there. She imagined it as her, jumping from place to place on a barren mountainside, flashes of light, like a bright butterfly. She felt wonder in its moving freely, the way these creatures could.

She realised Mark's writing had stopped. She turned to him.

He looked towards her, saying, "Would you like me to read something I wrote about you?"

"Yes," she replied.

He began, "Hair dark, back turned to me, at the bar. She sees me not, absorbed in work. I know her, the curve of her neck, that shape of her shoulders as they move with grace. She looks around, dark eyes sparkle in faded light, face bright with smiling delight. She sees, knows me, familiar in a land of strangers. I say, Come with me? She hesitates briefly but then agrees.

"We drive into the night. Our talk is of Gods and the Universe. She asks me where God lives. I try to answer truthfully and tell her things I have not told others. Her mind is like a soaring eagle looking from on high. She moves like a wallaby, leaping from rock to rock, tiny flashes of bright light reflect. Yet she is silent like a cat. A strange gracefulness is hers, moving over life's surfaces without ripple."

He closed the book and looked at her, questioning, a strange uncertainly in his eyes.

She said, "Such words are to be treasured. They are of me and of you. I like the way you tell it. Tomorrow, I would like to write something of you, perhaps it will be in French. The music of that language will speak of your essence, stillness which blurs into movement."

Soon after, they were packed and drove on. They came to Derby after an hour. Over breakfast, Mark pulled out a map and explained the route he had planned. He told her he wished to go to a place where few others went, a rough and barren place, a place where sheer rocky mountains joined a sparkling sea, a place where the hills held their own treasures as yet undiscovered.

He said he wanted to go there before he started his next job. If she could spare two weeks, he would bring her there. The place was deep in the rugged Kimberley Coast, and they would go via the Mitchell Plateau, a place of spectacular waterfalls and a wealth of wildlife. From there, they would head up to the area near where a crystal creek ran out to the sea and spend their days fishing and exploring around the coast.

It was something Mark had always wanted to do. He told her he had worked on the Mitchell Plateau helping biologists do fauna surveys a few years ago. Then, he had flown over much of the area in a helicopter. This had whetted his appetite, as he had never explored further north on the ground. Now, he wanted to return and spend a week exploring this new area. The travel there and back would take the rest of the two weeks as the road was slow and bad.

While lots of tourists visited the Mitchell Falls to see the aboriginal rock art from antiquity and the wonderful waterfalls, cascading over three levels to the river below, very few made it right up to the coast, other than by boat or helicopter. Now, at the start of the build-up season, with its ferocious heat and humidity and with huge thunderstorms gathering, where the moisture of the sea met the heat of the land on the far north horizon, the tourists had dried up to a trickle.

Mark expected to have this place almost empty of others- which suited him fine. He did not want national park rangers or tourist guides trying to direct where he could and could not go. They would travel unobtrusively and park the vehicle out of sight from the air once there. They would use their feet to explore both the rough and barren hills, creeks and the seaside below. They would bring fishing lines and a light rifle to help support themselves by living off the land and sea. But first, today, they would stock up with provisions bought from the town. Tonight, would be a last night spent in civilisation before departing early tomorrow on their trip. Isabelle agreed to come with delight, it sounded like a wonderful adventure and the two weeks away would not matter.

After they finished breakfast, Mark booked two rooms in the Spinifex Hotel, a local Derby icon. He insisted on paying for a separate room for her- even though she said that, if they were travelling together, they might as well share the room and, anyway, the room had a second single bed. But Mark politely insisted it be this way.

With that done, they visited the store where they filled up a shopping trolley with food and other necessities. Mark asked her to choose some food that appealed to her, suggesting that she could cook something that she knew from her homeland- a food from her culture. The choices were limited, but she took garlic and fresh herbs to give flavour to an unknown dish.

It was now the heat of midday and Isabelle was yawning. Mark suggested she have an afternoon siesta in her room. A bit reluctantly, she agreed. In the cool and dark of the room, she had barely laid her head on the pillow before she fell into a deep sleep.

When she woke, the sun was low. Mark was sitting on the verandah outside his room sipping a beer. He offered her one and she declined, thirsty for a glass of water. He suggested they spend an hour seeing the sights of the town, now the day's heat was easing. They visited the boab prison tree, a tree shaped like a bottle with strange scraggly branches that almost looked like it had been uprooted and placed upside down with its roots waving in the breeze. This particular tree had a huge cavity hollowed out of a massive trunk which was reputed to have served as the local jail in the town's early history.

After this, they walked out along the wharf. Derby was said to have the biggest tides in Australia, rising and falling up to twelve metres. Now, the tide was low and the walk carried them far out over what seemed to be miles and miles of mudflats. They watched birds feast on tasty morsels as fat mudskippers bounced across the mud.

They returned to the hotel in the dusk to shower and change for dinner. Isabelle found a fresh light dress which she wore with sandals; Mark wore light coloured calico pants and shirt, in the style of an English safari suit.

She thought him very handsome and said so. He admired her, too, but it was in a friendly, almost asexual way.

They ordered a selection of courses from the menu and the food was good. Then, they played pool in the bar with some others until a country and western duo sang some songs of the outback. The audience joined in. At first Mark was silent, but Isabelle sang with gusto. She encouraged him to sing with her. She found he could sing well, if a bit hesitantly at first. She liked the way their voices blended together.

Then, softer ballad music came on and she got up to dance. She asked him if he would join her, but he was reluctant. Another man came up and asked her for a dance. She agreed because she felt like dancing. As she took to the floor, she turned back to look at Mark. She would have rather been dancing with him, even though this man was a good dancer and had her flowing around the floor in an effortless way.

Mark had turned his body away. It seemed deliberate and she felt disappointed, wondering if she should go back and stay with him. At last, the dance ended and the man asked her to continue. She decided she would rather go back to sit with Mark, even though she loved to dance.

He was still looking away, so she walked right up in front of him, forcing him to look at her. "Come on. I know you can dance. I saw you do it in Queensland."

He looked up with a lopsided half-smile, "You are a far better dancer than that. I thought you would be dancing yet for hours."

She answered, "The man wanted me to. He is a good dancer and I love to dance. But I decided I like your company even more, so if you are okay with my being here, I decided would rather come back and sit with you. Some other night I will teach you some of the dances from my homeland for us to dance to."

Now, he gave her a genuine smile as he said, "I would like that."

An hour later, it was Mark who was yawning. Isabelle picked up his hand and brought him out into the clear night air. "Now, it is you who needs to sleep," she said.

She led him back to his room and opened the door. On tiptoes, she kissed him lightly on the cheek with her body slightly brushing his.

Mark ran his fingers through her hair as she stood there, saying, 'You are so beautiful. I will call you Bella, woman of true beauty. It feels right."

She nodded, feeling a great urge to push her body up against his, to know how it felt to be folded against him. Just as her mind decided that it would be good and right, he pulled away and went inside.

After his door closed, she sat on a chair on her verandah, looking across to his room, hoping he would come back out and give her an excuse to join him. She felt a great desire to tap on his door and ask him to bring her in with him. But it was just her and the dark night. At last, she too yawned and went to bed.

They drove off early in the morning, just as the sun was striking its first shafts on the scraggy trees alongside the road, lighting them with orange light. They drove through featureless scrub, sometimes crossing open grass plains, their edges dotted with scattered boab trees. It seemed to Isabelle the trees were watching as upside-down sentinels.

The dirt road was flat and straight. They roared along with a cloud of dust following, passing an occasional opposite way car, with which they exchanged dust plumes. After an hour, Mark took a turnoff to the north, declaring it was time for breakfast and a cup of tea. He followed minor tracks until he came to the banks of a tree lined river with dark silty water, the May River. A dry creek with odd pools ran into the river at one side. Birds flitted down to its water to drink as the morning heat grew.

Mark put two folding chairs side by side and indicated to Belle to take one, handing her an icy can of lemon squash from the fridge. She sat in the shade and sipped her drink while Mark gathered dead branches. Soon he had a fire going under another patch of shade. She watched as brightly coloured birds flitted above the water, seemingly darting hither and thither in some random pattern. One landed on a twig near her for a minute. It had amazing colours: a mixture of blues, greens and golds. It was so small she could have cupped it within the palm of her hand.

Mark looked up and she pointed to it. He nodded and grinned. In a second, it had flitted away. He said, “It’s a rainbow bee-eater, beautiful, isn’t it? They catch small insects on the wing over pools of water.”

Soon, the billy was boiling. A pan of bacon and eggs followed quickly. They sat in the shade eating bacon and egg sandwiches, their seats now turned to face the big river below them. It was a time for eating and watching, not talking. As they were finishing eating, there was a small splash in the river below. Mark put his finger to his lips and Isabelle looked towards the sound. Slowly, a head emerged. Two eyes surveyed its surrounds. After a minute of stillness, the eyes came towards the bank. From the water emerged a creature of scaled markings. It was about as long as she was tall. She knew this was a real crocodile, every shape and pattern of its form arranged in picture book symmetry. It wriggled itself around in the sun until it had found the right place, then lay still. Bella watched in fascination- it was so immobile. After a couple of minutes, it opened teeth covered jaws to smile at the sun.

Mark nodded, pointed at the car and smiled too, enjoying Bella's wonder. He began to stand up. As he moved, the crocodile scuttled down the riverbank and disappeared from whence it had come.

Soon, they were packed up and driving on. Mid-morning, they came to a turnoff signposted, 'Windjana Gorge and Tunnel Creek'. They turned south following the sign. Now, rocky hillsides rose to the east, "the start of the broken hill country of the Kimberley", Mark told her. They passed by the turnoff to Windjana Gorge, Mark promising to return this way as it was a good place to stopover and camp for the night.

It was ferociously hot when they emerged from their air-conditioned car at Tunnel Creek, looking across to a sheer red-orange and black cliff face that bordered the road they had driven along. Mark filled a backpack with two torches, water and things for lunch. He led the way to Tunnel Creek Cave which he said would be much cooler and was a good place for lunch. After the car park, they came to a place where the dry sandy creek bed plunged down into a series of clear pools of water with a huge cave entrance coming into view. As they came into the shade of the rocks, it was suddenly cool.

Mark put down his pack, took off his T shirt and strode into water up to his chest. Then he plunged under, coming up with water streaming down his face. He said, "God this feels good, why don't you come in?"

She waded in up to her knees. She was wearing a T-shirt and shorts only- she had dispensed with her bra in the heat. There was no one in sight and she felt self-conscious, alone with him in this place.

She asked, "Should I get my bathers, they are in the car?"

He shrugged, "Up to you, but I would take off your shirt and keep it dry as it is pretty cold deeper in the cave. I won't mind if you come in topless and there is no one else here to see you at the moment."

She took a deep breath, feeling both prudish and shy to expose her body, yet not wanting to walk back in the heat to the car. She shrugged in reply. *In for a penny, in for a pound,* she thought.

She pulled off her T shirt with her back turned, then decided it was silly to be shy and removed her shorts- now only wearing a pair of plain black panties. She thought of taking them off, too, part of her wanted him to see her fully naked, but caution rose- she'd be giving him a good eyeful anyway and some modesty was required, particularly if others arrived. *Well, it is now or never,* she thought. She turned to face him.

As she walked towards him, she felt self-conscious that her breasts were small, she was sure he liked women with bigger breasts.

She could feel his eyes on her as she walked into the water and found herself too self-conscious to look up. She kept walking- her body tingling as the cold water rose to cover her hips and knickers. Now, she was in water up to her waist and she looked up.

He was gazing at her intently, his eyes savouring her. He looked at her breasts and she felt her nipples tingling under his gaze. Even more self-conscious, she lowered her whole body into the water, the cold of the water shocked her and she stood up again. Now, her nipples were tingling even more and the cold had brought them into sharp points. She looked up and Mark was looking intently at her.

She gave him a self-conscious shrug. “I am not used to this sort of thing, swimming without clothes. I’m embarrassed to have you see me.”

Mark grinned, “No need for embarrassment. All I can say is you look sensational, the body of a mermaid.”

He splashed her and she splashed him back, now laughing with relief, it felt fine to be here with him like this. She flung herself at him and grasped him around the waist, trying to pull him off balance. He went with it, dunked them both. They came up spluttering and still laughing.

Now, he was standing right in front of her, his body almost touching hers. He reached down with his hand. He touched and caressed a nipple. She crushed her body against his, pushing her thighs against her leg.

Then, he pulled back. “I promised not to try and seduce you, just to let you come along for the ride. Here I am, wanting to do the sex thing with you when our trip has barely begun. I don’t want to spoil our trip and friendship by going there unless it is something you really want, too.”

She did not want him to stop touching her that way. Yet, she also understood what he meant. This friendship was something very precious and it might become much more complicated if they kept going.

Now, the spell was broken. She nodded, “I like you touching me that way, very much. But, perhaps you are right- the friendship is more.”

He nodded, turned away and then dived under the water. He surfaced at the opposite side of the pool, where he climbed out, shook himself dry and walked to where his T-shirt lay and put it back on.

She came back to the place of her clothes and dressed, too, feeling an ache within that was frustrated and unsatisfied. She was on the point of calling out that she had changed her mind, that she wanted it all now, not to wait for an unlikely better time.

The words were on the tip of her tongue, ready to call out, when she heard a distant noise. It was another car coming into the car park. In five minutes, another couple arrived and the moment had passed.

These people were friendly New Zealanders and after a chat about their respective trips, they all found a shady place beside a pool where they spread out and shared their lunches. It was somehow a relief for her to have someone else to break the tension of the moment and distract her. She guessed a part of Mark felt the same.

The day passed exploring the fantastic cavern, almost a kilometre underground where the creek had carved a huge tunnel through the limestone. Their torch revealed stalactites and stalagmites in a rainbow array of colours from the softest whites to the deepest purples and almost everything in between. Along the bottom ran a clear icy creek. As the cave air was cool, they had little desire to plunge in, toe-dipping sufficed. They shared the exploration with the Kiwi couple and in the process became friends, with offers to meet again in the Shaky Isles. They parted in the car park to go their separate ways.

That night, they returned to Windjana Gorge and watched the dozens of crocodile eyes in the remaining pools of the river that flowed through the gorge, now a late dry season waterhole. "They are only freshwater ones which are not dangerous," Mark assured her.

They sat and talked as they watched their campfire burn down to the merest glowing embers and above them the stars grew ever brighter. There was something beyond breathtaking in the night sky as they talked and shared all the untold stories of their lives. He told her of many things that he had done- some good and some bad. She told him of her own travels and of the one man who had taken her body and how she felt cheated, thinking there must be something more and better than what it had been on that day.

As Isabelle spoke, she leaned into him. He rested his arm around her slender shoulders, saying, "Yes. Next time you give your body to a man, it needs to be truly wonderful- you deserve no less."

She said, "Much of me wants that man to be you. But you have had so many girls. I do not want to be just another one. Still, I think I could trust you. Do you want to try it with me?"

He said, "No man could look at you and not want to make love to you, but that is not reason enough. There is still a part of you held back from being fully ready to trust me. When you do, you will tell me and, until then, I am your friend. Now, you should sleep, for tomorrow we have far to go."

The next morning, they headed off into the true wilderness of the rugged broken hills of the Kimberley. Mark told her where they were going, but for now it was just words. He talked of a place called the Mitchell Plateau, sheer red gorges, lots of unique Australian wildlife and incredibly ancient aboriginal paintings, dotting the caves and rock faces which were scattered all over the area.

After that, she understood they would head up to the coast, following a track known to only a handful of locals. Mark told of a cliff top paradise, where a spring fed creek cascaded over the broken hills into a sapphire sea below, so clear you could see every fish. A place of huge crocodiles which could be surveyed in safety from the cliffs and a place of innumerable other treasures and delights to explore.

Mark said he was searching for gemstones. This place was so remote that past surveys had been minimal, just an occasional early foot prospector passing through, leaving odd, small, abandoned diggings, but now the big companies were interested. They had opened the Argyle Diamond Mine to the south and were lobbying for access to the beautiful and remote coastal country with many competing claims from local aboriginal groups. For himself, he was not greedy, he just wanted to poke around on his own and see what he could turn up. He had found this to be rewarding many times before.

He had a collection of wonderful stones which he showed her. He hoped that together they would find something special. If they did, a half of any find would belong to her as her own special memory of this trip.

Now, they were off to this wilderness place together, just the two of them, sharing it in friendship and, increasingly she hoped, sharing a much more intimate thing. She would let that happen in its own time but, in her mind, she was making up love songs to sing to him and woo him with on her guitar.

She would also teach him how to dance and let his feet take flight, to know the joy of that flowing movement to music. She would tell of this by writing it in his diary and her own little notebook, phrases of the passion she felt, written in her own French words.

She wrote,

"Mark, mon ami et maintenant amant.
Nous sommes ensemble pour toujours avec joie"
Together forever with joy.

Chapter 23-With the Crocodiles

Mark felt so gutted as he returned to Katherine- the place where he had a flat in an ugly building in the town. He wondered what it was within himself that destroyed everything he loved.

He had loved Elfin without reservation. While it had started more slowly with Bella, by that final day, when he made the impossible choice to end it for her, his love for her had grown to something similar. In a way it had become even deeper: the way they shared their stories through both writing entries in his diary, the way she had taught him to play simple chords on her guitar and to sing harmonies with her, her voice like drops of gold, his more guttural but it had a resonance and timbre that seemed to blend with hers so that the whole was more than the parts.

He especially remembered the way she had taught him to dance as she sang the music for their feet to move to. They had practised on the flat ground next to the campfire. She had sang a waltz and patiently taught him the steps, doing it over and over again until his body flowed alongside hers in a perfect synchronicity. She had recognised a shyness in him on that night in Derby, the man who no one had taught to dance properly and who thus had been deprived of one of life's great joys. She had decided to fix that and give him this legacy even after she left- not that he planned for her to go as the days unfolded.

Dancing with her was like the joy he felt in riding a horse, two bodies moving in effortless flow, two wills fused. Except with her, it was more wonderful, bare-footed in the dust, infused with a gorgeous dark-haired woman-child who flowed in his arms, whisper light, she slid and brushed past him. It was endlessly enticing to be so close to her without consummation. He knew if he had tried to ravish her, the magic may have broken- she would have not resisted, but part of him wanted it to go on and on forever, both their bodies trembling in anticipation. He remembered that wonderful second last night when they joined their bodies, after a week of circling around in increasing desire, both wanting it to happen, neither quite ready to make the first move.

It had been in the aftermath of a glorious song into the sunset, sitting together perched on the cliffs above a Kimberley Ocean that it had finally happened. Their bodies were touching as they sang, as if the song had given them permission to press ever closer against each other in a wordless embrace. Then, as the glow of light had faded, they had stayed sitting that way for a long time, neither wanting to break the spell.

Finally, she had nuzzled her face into his neck. He had found himself kissing her. From there, all the rest was inevitable. It was something they both wanted so badly. It was as wonderful as any other moment he could remember in his life, the joy he felt as she held him tight, her body open to him and the wonderful release that came for both of them together.

The next day, Isabelle had been like a frolicking goat as she bounded from rock to rock and cliff to cliff, so confident and fearless. She said she had grown up in hills like this and, now that they were lovers, she wanted to sing and dance for joy. Their one full day together had been wonderful as they explored the coast, cliffs, rock pools and caves around the place of their camp. During that day, they had made love more times than he could count, in the hot sun, in cool caves and pools and during much of that last glorious star-filled night, with only their two bodies in a wilderness of stars.

But what was even more precious to him was the way they had talked. She had told him all her hopes and fears and he had done the same with her. No secret was hidden by either from the other, their souls were bare. He had promised to come back with her to meet her family. He had spoken of imagined babies with her and her singing them lullabies. It was as if they were soulmates even more than lovers and this was the most precious thing. She was his Bella, his most beautiful one with the beautiful dancing spirit and a voice to charm the angels.

But she was gone now. He felt now he should have dived in to be with her in that final moment, so clearly imprinted on his brain. Him:

sitting in the shade of a tree in the midday sun, as she cavorted on the cliff edge, dancing above a blue ocean as five large and lazy crocodiles circled below, hoping for more of the small lumps of leftover meat they had thrown to bring them in close.

Then how, as she danced by the edge, enjoying his eyes on her body as a prelude to more love making, the rock had crumbled under her ankle. A brief second, as she wobbled on the edge, her little shriek and then, she plunged out of sight, two seconds of silence and the splash of water as she landed below. When he reached the edge, he saw the five crocodiles, initially startled, now converging with her in the midst.

He ran back to pick up his rifle, only a 22 with small bullets, shorts, good for shooting the rock pigeons of which he was collecting a brace for their dinner. There was no time to run back to the car for his heavy rifle. He saw the terror in her eyes as she saw what was about to happen. Her cry to him for help tore him deep inside. He first considered trying to shoot the saurians; perhaps he could deflect one. However, his gun only had the power to sting something this size, not harm it.

He remembered the desperate look on her face in that last second, with the closest crocodile less than a metre away. Then, his sudden knowledge of what he must do, even as that thought broke his heart.

She must not suffer, his beautiful Bella, she must not know and feel their teeth, the terrible tearing of their mouths. That final split second, as she looked up at him with an unfathomable hope and trust; and he brought the foresight into line with her small white forehead. The flat crack and her body slumped in the water, knowing nothing more. He had turned away, unable to look below as they tore her body apart.

He willed himself to try and merge his soul with hers, to be in whatever spirit place she now existed. As long hours passed, he felt as if he achieved a sort of fusion between his spirit, hers and those crocodiles who had taken her within them.

He sat there in the full sun, still, unmoving, with no tears to cry, until the sun came to the same place as on the first night of their lovemaking.

Then, as the wild dogs howled their hunting cry, he had howled his rage and grief to the endless, empty sky.

After the stars came out, Mark gathered all her things and found a small cave, hidden under the cliff at the back of their first love making place, a safe and dry place. One by one, he placed all her objects into this place, holding her clothes to his face for a long time so he could absorb and remember her smell. Her guitar came last- he strummed its strings one last time before he left it. He filled the entrance with large stones, to deny any other creature's entrance.

He drove off into the night, rage still burning in his soul and tears un-cried. He drove all the night and most of the next day until, finally, he found himself coming into the town of Kununurra. Here, he bought a hotel room and a bottle of overproof rum. He finally succumbed to alcoholic stupor. He stayed for three days, consuming bottle after bottle. Finally, on the fourth day, he woke up almost sober but with the mother of all hangovers. He fed himself for the first time since Bella died.

He was due to go on to the Argyle diamond mine soon, but he could not bear to do this work without her. Instead, he drove slowly back to Katherine, the nearest thing he had to a home at his empty flat. As he unpacked the car, mechanically going through these meaningless motions, he found her passport. It was funny how these things refused to die and lie with their owners: he still had the Elfin one which also should have been left behind to mind its owner. But now that he had it, he could not cast it away. It was far too precious as it bore her image. He found a small tin box and placed the two passports side by side in this box-mementos of these two lost loves. The box went behind his car seat to travel on with him to wherever he came to next.

A month passed, then another. Life had lost its flavour. Only a sense of the crocodile spirits remained and, in a strange way, he treasured them. He could not blame them; they were his totem after all. He found a small comfort in the togetherness of his soul and hers, linked through the crocodiles. Increasingly, his mind turned inwards to this place.

Chapter 24 - Anne in France

Anne looked back on what she had understood from Mark's diary thus far. It was the most heartbreaking story she had ever been part of, she had read plenty of awful stories in books, but here was an immediacy to living out the scribbled words penned in that far off place. He described tragedy with banality and it felt like someone had pulled her heart out.

It was a patchwork of fragments. It was only when she had come to France and met with Isabelle's parents that it had begun to make real sense in her mind. There were many French passages in this diary part, some in a lovely flowing cursive French script which Isabelle's parents had said was Isabelle's own hand. They seemed so familiar from the memorabilia of her bedroom, these notes in her own hand the incontrovertible match to her diary writings. Other parts were in simple, unadorned English in Mark's hand. Some parts were written awkwardly in constructed French. Here, it appeared that Isabelle had sat alongside, helping Mark to find words and phrases to express his emotions- a voyage of joint discovery which spoke of friendship and growing love, a shared poetry of togetherness.

Of her own notebook, to which she referred to in a couple places, there was no sign. It must have remained with her other things as the repository of her most private thoughts. But there was plenty in the diary in her hand. It spoke of her infatuation with this man, and equally of his with her, telling of the many kind things he did for her and little gifts he gave her. It was first told with the sense of ever deepening friendship, and then through eyes filled with the intense passion of new lovers. In scenes which told of the singing and dancing were places of pure magic.

Then, came those final flat sentences where Mark told of her fall and the end, redolent with grief.

He told of his act with the rifle, an act of kindness, but it was a finale so devastating- she and Belle's family had tears flowing over their cheeks.

He told of his remorse that he had not brought a bigger gun; he talked about how his 308 or 243 could have kept the crocodiles at bay. He told of his similar remorse that, in that split second of decision, he had not flung himself in the water to try and use his body as a shield while she swam to the bank. But there was no going back from that second.

She could see that, in this reading, both Mark's and Isabelle' words had brought some closure to Isabelle's parents' grief- not removed it, but it at least had given them understanding. A sense that Mark had taken the best bad choice, better than the awful fear and pain of the alternative. But, still, it was so hard to read and know the truth.

After this happened, Mark had descended into a very dark place. There were few words in his diary in the next year, but what was told spoke of the void in his soul with the loss of this girl, his friend and lover.

Mark seemed a man marked by an evil finger of fate, his upbringing and this series of misfortunes, deaths for which he could not really be blamed but which still destroyed some part of his soul. If was as if this day marked the true start of his descent into inhumanity.

If only that day had been different, she had little doubt that Mark would have returned with Belle to France. He would have met her parents and married this girl. By now, they would now most likely have had children of their own and have forged a new, happy future together far away from the previous darkness and tragedy. And, but for this, the rest would never have been.

She could picture the man and his dark-haired girl in a French village, him using his skill to make and fix things, she using hers to teach the local children. Evenings filled with laughter, dancing and singing.

Perhaps they would have travelled the world together, going to faraway places in French Polynesia or French Africa. Yet it was not to be.

Where her final resting place was, the place of the cave of her things, was little more than guess. Anne had surveyed the vastness of this wild place on the map, but there were few clues of an exact location in the diary- it was hundreds of kilometres of possible coast. Perhaps that part would never be known, or perhaps, with local knowledge giving a better guess, a search could be made.

In the meantime, she felt she had closed one more chapter of Mark's life with a degree of understanding. She feared to read on in detail, her previous limited reading gave a sense this story would be much darker from here. But, to do justice to the other lost girls, read it she must.

Now, she must say goodbye to Belle and her family and travel on.

As she went on, she must try and discover another girl. An unknown emergent from shadows, she was not a known person, J, perhaps Josie, was her diary name. She appeared but briefly, like a moth drawn to candle flame. Like a moth it seemed to end badly.

Part 4- Interlude

Chapter 25 - Desert and Crocodile Families

After Belle was gone and he had got part of his mind back, Mark flew to Thailand for a couple weeks- spending time with a succession of girls in the hope the sex act would fill the emptiness he felt inside. He tried a lot of varieties over two weeks. Even though his body performed its part with mechanical precision, no loss of potency and climactic pleasure, it was as if these joinings were soulless encounters.

A few of the pretty girls tried to talk to him, wanting to practice their English, and he tried to humour them. He really did not want to talk to strangers. What he wanted was friendship and companionship, a place to unwrap and leave his aching heart. He wondered if he should travel on to France. He knew he could locate Belle's parents from her passport, tell them the awful story, he knew they would grieve with her vanishing and that she would have wished to spare them this.

But, he could not bear the thought of facing them and telling them how he had failed their daughter: how she had entrusted herself to his care and he had entrusted himself to mind her in this place of wildness. He had known he needed to be more careful after what had happened to his Elfin. Yet, in the passion of love, his caution got lost.

Mark could not bear to tell them this, it was not an admission he could bring himself to make. The words in the diary which told of it were enough, he could not bear it be relived yet again in his mind. Yet the pull to see those who were of her, to see the faces of which she spoke with affection, was very strong.

For two days he sat in Bangkok airport, watching the flights to Paris come and go, wanting to buy a ticket and with it some closure, but he could not. Finally, tired of his unusual indecision, he returned to Darwin and drove on down the highway, passing through Katherine and heading on, not able to bear the thought of even a night in that empty flat. He had no plan to go anywhere in particular- he would drive on and allow the empty space of the land to open up before him.

Mark had known Vic for a few years and had met his mother, sisters and brothers at various times when he had worked in the Alice. He would not say the rest of the family were close, but Vic was like a brother. He had not seen Vic for months. He knew, only, that he was working on the Barkly at the moment as the last of the cattle season was in full swing.

As he came to the desert, he found a small healing in its emptiness. Each day he would find a place in the afternoon where he could sit on a ridge, nursing his OP rum bottle. As the sun fell low, he let his spirit travel to a remembered place with Belle- until his friend, OP, brought darkness.

A week passed until one day he found himself sitting on a McDonnell ridge, looking west from the town of Alice. He was unwashed and unshaven, but he still had this friend, OP, for company. At least OP did not answer back when he did not feel like talking.

Into this mist a voice called his name, "Dat you Mark, what for you sit here, just with drink. You stink, you need wash, you need proper tucker, you come with me."

The face of Vic's mother penetrated the mist. She took OP and tipped him neck down, so OP wet a small patch of baked earth. Then, she took Mark by the hand and led him back to her house where she gave him a towel and fresh clothes and pushed him into the shower.

For five days Mark stayed with her. Each day she made him get up in the morning, walk with her to the town to shop, and then help with the preparation of the day's meal for the rest of the family. It was simple mechanical work that he found satisfying. In the spaces between, she talked to him as she would a child: telling stories of Vic and her other children, their successes and their failures, her pride and heartbreak.

Slowly, he began to tell her of himself, not of Elfin or Belle, but of the mother he once had and other small parts of his life. He even told her of being a mercenary in Africa and of a woman he had loved there. And he told her of his crocodile totem and his other family, like hers in Gove, how they too had brought him in.

She also taught him how to cook, until then his menu was limited to steak and sausages, but she enjoyed the cooking and creating and made him learn as she worked. She brought him out with her gathering bush tucker and taught him how to find those things that were good to eat in this land. It was what she was doing when she found him.

It was a week of simple companionship. Mark began to get his mind back, to see the world beyond again and bear to be in it. After a week, she said to him, "I have helped you as much as I can, now you must go and sit with those old men of your crocodile totem, perhaps they too can help, it is like there is a bad and unhappy part of your totem, you must find special medicine that makes it quiet again, or it will eat you up."

So, he went to that place and sat in the dirt with his totem elders. Together they watched the coming and going of the crocodiles, he held the carved object of his totem and brought it away with him. It did not heal him, but, when he held it in his hand, it was as if his spirit and it were joined, and it gave him a measure of peace.

Chapter 26 - Travels in an Empty Land

Anne read of the barrenness in this man's soul and the empty land in which he had travelled and felt a need to see it for herself, so as to help her understand. It was now the start of September and, after a month away discovering two people who lived in Europe and parts of a third who came from Scotland, she felt a need to come home and be with David again.

In her mind, Australia was now her home as David was there, even though all her roots and most of her possessions remained in England. She needed to both spend time with him to replenish her own emptiness and to travel and visit the places of which the diary told. The places to which Mark had travelled in his empty existences, so as to try and understand, to allow the telling of his story to merge with the places.

David found the time to take three weeks away from work. They flew to Uluru and hired a car from there, retracing part of the journey Susan and Mark had made, without trying to find all the back roads. They spent a night in Kings Canyon. Then they headed on via Henbury Meteorite Crater and Chambers Pillar for a night in Arltunga, before heading up to the Gulf via Heartbreak Hotel and Borroloola. They did not try and relive the trip of Mark and Susan but, still, seeing these places brought the words of Susan on tape and in Mark's writing to life.

In Borroloola, Vic met them and took them on a helicopter flight to give them a sense of the sort of country he had shown to Mark and Susan. From there, they came back across to Top Springs from where, after some hours talking about Mark and Susan with Michael Riley, they continued on to VRD station. They stayed a night with Buck in a stock camp and spent a half-day out mustering cattle with the other stockmen. Anne rode an old quiet horse- she did not have Susan's riding flair though David had been instructing her on their farm behind Sydney. David rode a spirited gelding which he handled with ease.

Then, it was on to Timber Creek. Here a boat owner took them on a night trip, spotlighting crocodiles of the Victoria River, giving them a sense of the silent power of these creatures.

They travelled on west towards Kununurra, accompanied by the local Timber Creek policeman. Just before they crossed from the Northern Territory into Western Australia, they stopped and parked on the side of the highway at a small turnoff heading north. From here, they travelled in the police vehicle to the likely campsite of Mark with the shadowy J.

They walked the return trip from campsite to highway, following the twists and turns of this road in its winding course through the valleys and low hills. It was a clear, dry September day, hot in the sun, but with a light breeze in their faces. For a while, they walked side by side down the dusty track. Then, Anne said, "This does not feel real. It did not play out like this." Anne backtracked walking to the side of the road and retraced her steps trying to make out the footprints she had left in the dusty soil. She pointed them out to David. He agreed it was a similar sign to what J may have made.

It was something but not enough reality. Anne said, "I need to imagine I am her with someone following. I need you stop for half an hour and then for you to try and follow me from my tracks. Sit still and wait for thirty minutes, then follow using only my footprints.

Anne walked ahead, rounding a curve between hills until she was out of sight. A hundred yards further on, she stepped off the road and walked across to the side where the hill rose up. She found her way up between the rocky boulders and found a space between two boulders with a bush in front where she was hidden from view from the road but could survey the traffic below. She sat and waited with a nervous anticipation, wondering whether it was possible to hide from a follower. At last, David came into view, moving slowly, regularly checking the ground as he came forward. At the point where she had left the road, he went on for a few yards before stopping then coming back and retracing her last steps. She could see he was searching for the place where her steps had vanished.

He cast around on both sides of the road in increasingly wider arcs until he finally found something which prompted him to walk towards her hillside. She could feel her heart pounding as he approached. He did not know where to look but, she must have left enough clues to suggest she had come this way. Even though she was not being hunted, she knew a moment of real fear before she stood up, called out and waved to him.

David had a look of relief on his face when he saw her, and she felt her own delight in his smile. Now, Anne finally had a sense she could try to tell a real story of the person known only as J, having lived a part of her last journey as the prey pursued by the hunter Mark.

They returned to their car, thanked the Timber Creek policeman and went on their way, stopping for a night in Wyndham where they surveyed the crocodiles, looking out across mudflats and vast steamy ocean inlets.

From here, they travelled on towards Derby and Broome, via Halls Creek with a side trip to Tunnel Creek and Windjana Gorge. Anne said she needed to travel part of the road of Belle and Mark, so as to tell their story with her own sense of its truth.

She and David had camped next to Tunnel Creek Cave and swam in the pool where Belle had first shown her body to this man. That night, they made love under the stars of a Kimberley night sky and talked of how it might have been for this other couple, whose story lived in their minds from the pages of a diary. It felt much closer to reality when experienced thus.

As they lay in night stillness, the cry of hunting dingoes sprang out across the night air. There was a predatory sound to their music. They would hunt, kill and feast- that spoke to them of the many journeys of Mark in a way that no words ever could. And, as their song passed out of hearing, all that remained was the endless empty night through which his soul had travelled.

In that place, she could see with his eyes to continue her story.

Part 5-Josie

Chapter 27 - The Meeting

One day Mark was walking down George St in Sydney. Sydney was not his home town, but as of late he came here with increasing frequency, now money was no longer an object- as it was an expensive city to visit.

A scrawny-looking girl came up to him and asked him for five dollars. At first, he was inclined to refuse, as one dollar or perhaps two was the going rate. He went to brush her off and walk past. But she walked alongside him and, with a touch of desperation, offered to come with him to a place of his choosing to give him the works for fifty dollars.

Mark looked at her more closely. It was not clear if she was a druggie, a call girl down on her luck, or just a street bum. He had first thought she was fourteen of fifteen, but now, as he looked more closely, he saw she was older, seventeen or eighteen was more likely. A malnourished look gave her an apparent frailty, making her look younger.

He stopped. He was not that poor he couldn't help someone else who was down on her luck. He'd been in this same place in his early life. He asked her what she wanted the money for.

She said, "If you gave me five dollars, I could get a cheeseburger from Macca's. I was not really trying to get fifty in one go, but it was worth a try as that would give me food for a few days."

He said, "I'm a bit hungry myself. How about I come with you to Macca's and buy us both some lunch? That way you can order as much as you want. Or we could go somewhere else with much nicer food if you prefer. What is your favourite food?"

Mark could see he had taken her by surprise. She appeared unsure what to make of his offer. He decided he would not torment her further. If she just wanted money, he would give her money. He opened his wallet and pulled out two fifty-dollar notes, saying, "It's fine, if you want to do your own thing and eat alone, then you can have this."

She shook her head emphatically. "No, that's too much. For that, I would give you a full night. Maybe it would be nice if you were to buy me lunch. I really like Thai and Chinese food. But, what I most like is the Spanish food they bring on little plates with lots of different things, they call it Tapas, I think."

Mark gave her his best grin. "Tapas it is. I saw a place, a street back, just around the corner. Shall we go there?"

She gave him a genuine smile and it lit up her face, making her look almost pretty, as it pushed away her street girl desperation. He could see that, with nice clothes and grooming she could have been a looker, she had good features and a kind face hiding behind her scruffiness.

He said to her, "I suppose, if we are going to have dinner together, I should introduce myself. I am Mark. My surname is unpronounceable, so everyone calls me Mark B. Is there a name I can call you?"

She replied, "I am Josie." She did not proffer a second name and Mark did not ask. Everyone was entitled to their secrets.

He held out his hand and she somewhat reluctantly took it. "It is nice to meet you, Josie."

She merely nodded in reply.

They walked down George St, side by side, not really talking. When they came to the restaurant, the doorman looked at Josie's scruffy clothes and face, as if to refuse entry. Mark passed him a twenty dollar note and winked. The man nodded, minimal thanks, and let them pass.

They went inside and were shown to a corner table, in an unobtrusive position. The waiter asked what they would like to start with. Mark indicated a beer and raised an inquiring eyebrow to Josie. She mumbled, "Coke."

The waiter returned with their drinks and two menus, handing one to each of them. Mark took his and looked at it for a minute. Then, he looked across at her. She was gulping her drink, not looking at the menu. He caught her eye, inquiring, "Do you want to order something?"

She shook her head. "No, you can choose, I don't know what half these things are. I can't read too good. I only came to one of these places once with a man. He chose, but I liked it and him."

Mark chose a wide selection from the menu- he was hungry. He figured, if he ordered enough for two, that would be plenty.

Once the food came, Josie started eating with a ravenous intensity, taking double what he ate. She had said nothing further. Soon, all the food on the table was gone and they were waiting for more to come.

Mark looked up and asked her. "Did you enjoy that, Josie?"

She just nodded.

He asked her, "Would you like another drink?"

She nodded again.

He reached out and put his hand over hers.

She looked up, curious. For a second, it seemed she would pull her hand away but stopped.

He said, "Josie, I am trying to be your friend. It would be easier and would make our dinner more enjoyable if you talked to me as well. If you don't want me here, why don't I just pay the bill and leave you to finish the food? You can keep the change." He placed two hundred dollars on the table and started to push back his chair to stand.

Her face looked suddenly vulnerable, as if she did not know how to react to his unexpected kindness.

She looked at him with something more than defensiveness. "OK, Mister, I am not real good at talking, when I am not asking for something, but I will try. I don't have much practice making polite conversation."

Mark said, "How about I tell you something about myself and you, in turn, tell me something about yourself."

She nodded, so he continued, "My father was a drunk and a bully. He used to beat up my mother. She committed suicide when I was seven. Then I learned how to survive by stealing from shops until I was caught when I was twelve. They sent me to a remand home, which was like a prison, only worse, and where the warders did awful things to lots of the little boys. I ran away when I was thirteen.

"At that time, I learned how to survive on my own by being strong and tough and never letting anyone put something over me.

"Now, I have plenty of money and just a few good friends. Mostly, I live far away from here in the outback, in a place called the Northern Territory. Have you ever heard of the Northern Territory?"

She replied, "Everyone has heard of the Northern Territory, Duh!"

Mark continued, "I told you something about me, now's your turn."

He looked at her face. There seemed to be a struggle going on inside. Then, her face hardened again. She stood up, spilling drinks. "Thank you for the food, Mister. It was really nice. And I know you are trying to be kind. But I learned long ago to tell nothing to nobody. So, I will just leave now and say thank you."

Josie tried to step to the side, feet tangling with the table legs and spilling more drink.

Mark reached out and took her wrist, "Josie, you can leave in just one more minute, but, first, you made me a promise to tell me something about you, anything you like; it's up to you. Now, you need to sit back down for that minute, keep your promise. After that, you can leave, or I will go if you prefer."

Mark watched another struggle play out on her face. It ended with her sitting down again.

"OK, fair is fair. My Mum is a drunk and druggie. I ran away from home when I was eleven. She used to make me do sex things with the men who came into our home, so they would give money to her. Mostly, it was things like sucking their dicks. But one day, a man gave her a lot of money, said she could keep it if he could fuck me, proper. He said he liked it doing it much better with a fresh young girl like me than with an old bag like her.

"She took the money and he told her to go away for an hour. He brought me into the bedroom, told me I was not to cry out so other people could hear, or he would hurt my mother. He made me lie on my back with my legs apart, while he pushed and pushed until he managed to get his dick inside me. It really hurt; I was bleeding and crying when my mother came home. She told me to have a bath and get over it. She was high with drugs from the money.

"After that, she would let other rich men do it to me as well. It always used to hurt me. My body was not properly grown and I only had tiny little breasts. My mother called them pimples, though they seemed to really turn the men on. I hated it. One day, I left and never came back.

"Since that day, I have lived on the street making money any way I can- mostly doing that same thing with men. At least now, I get to keep the money and, if they try to hurt me, I hurt them back worse. I don't take drugs or get drunk like my mother did and I try to make the men wear protection, so I don't catch any diseases. Sometimes they won't or they offer too much money to not make them do this. However, I think I am still clean that way. Maybe, when we finish eating, I can pay you back that way. I don't like to take something for nothing; at least, I don't take more than the cost of a burger without paying it back."

After that, the conversation moved into more comfortable places. Mark told her funny stories of life in the outback and Josie told him funny stories of life on the streets.

As they talked, Mark kept ordering food, amazed at Josie's ability to consume. He had eaten his fill and she had eaten double again. He pushed back his plate and ordered a coffee for him and some small pastries. On second thought, he added a coffee for her, unasked.

He asked her, "You seemed really hungry. When did you last eat?"

She shrugged, "Even though I don't stay with my Mum or much like her, I still try to help her. Yesterday, I had one hundred dollars from the night before, a single shiny note. I decided to give it to her. I put it in an envelope and put it in the post, using the last dollar in my pocket to buy a stamp. I thought I could soon get some more money. Instead, yesterday was a bum day. I only got one fifty cent piece, not enough to buy anything, everyone else pretended I wasn't there as they walked past.

"This morning, as I was really hungry, so instead of asking for a dollar or two, like I usually do, I decided to ask for five, it would give me enough to buy a cheeseburger in one go. I hate begging. I had asked maybe twenty people before you came along."

At last, the meal was done. Mark paid and left a good tip. They walked out into the street. As they walked along, she asked him if he wanted her to come to some place with him, so she could pay him back in her own way.

Mark shook his head, "No, Josie, I did not buy you lunch to get that from you. I bought you lunch because I liked you, and then, as we ate and you told me funny stories, I liked being with you. It is good for a man and woman to be friends without there having to be sex."

She said, "All the other men I know only want that one thing. And once they get it, they are not really interested in me anymore, I can tell. I always make them pay first, that way later when they don't want me anymore, I don't have to threaten them to get the money. But, just now and then, I meet someone I like and then it's a nice thing to do, it's not about the money. That is what I was offering you."

He turned to Josie and said, "I understand that and part of me thinks it would be really nice. Another part of me remembers how it was when I was poor and had to do almost anything to survive. What I most wanted then was people who were my friends, people who liked me without me having to do something for them. That is what I would rather do, be your friend. Perhaps, I could help you get away from all this.

"Here, let me give you some money so, at least for one night, you can stay somewhere nice and don't have to beg." He took five hundred dollars from his wallet and handed it to her.

She shook her head.

He insisted. "Josie, I told you my story. I have been down on my luck, poor and with nothing to eat. Think of this as an investment in your future. You must have dreams of things you would like to do one day."

He handed her a card with a phone number on it. "Why don't you get yourself cleaned up and try and find a place to live? Maybe you could go to TAFE and get a qualification so you can earn some regular money.

"I would like to help you. Think of this money as the first step to helping you do that. Once you work out how much you need for a flat and some money to live off, not working in the game, ring me. I will arrange to send you the money. If you want to pay it back, it can be a loan which you can pay back one day with interest."

He could see her face thinking about possibilities. Finally, she took the money and the card and put both inside her bra for safe keeping. "Thank you, Mister, I might just do that."

Chapter 28 – Re-meeting the Unknown J

About a month later, Mark was in Katherine collecting mail from his mailbox. He had a small flat in the town which he stayed in for a few days a year. He used Katherine, more than any other place in the NT, as his base. It was at the crossroad between the Kimberley to the west, the north-south road between Darwin and Alice and it was not far down to the road to the Gulf and to Queensland, heading east. The road to north east Arnhem Land, where he had first gained his crocodile totem, also turned off not far down the highway, heading up through Mainoru and Bulman and on out to Gove. Also, it was not so far from here to the good cattle country of the Barkly and VRD where he did a lot of contracting. All in all, it was a good place for a base, as he often passed through this town on his way to other places.

After he got the opal money, he had decided that it would be good to have a few places he could call his own. He was not much interested in bigger blocks of land that someone had to maintain. A flat that could be locked up and left, without anyone to care for it, suited him. So, when he was in the NT, he had places in Katherine and Alice Springs which he used when he needed them. The rest of the time, they gave him a place to store things. He never rented them because his things were private and he did not want others snooping around. Since he had found that big stash of opals, he had money aplenty without needing to get rent. He did not need to work but he liked the purpose and satisfaction it gave him.

Mark had got to Katherine the day before yesterday and last night was his second night here. He planned two more nights here before he headed out to the VRD and on to Halls Creek for a series of jobs. His post office box in Katherine was the place where his phone bills and other business correspondence came.

Not having checked it for more than a month, he thought he should call and clean it out. There was a man he paid a few dollars to do this when he was not around, but today he would attend to it himself.

He almost tripped over a girl sitting on the steps of the post office; she must have been half asleep the way she was sprawled out, part blocking his way to the boxes at the side. She sat up with a start. As she did, he realised with a jolt it was Josie. He knew this was no accident. Somehow, she had tracked him down here. He remembered a couple missed calls on his mobile from a few days ago. No messages, he did not recognise the number, and when he had called back there was nothing at the other end. Perhaps that had been her trying to ring him. He had given her the card with his mobile, Post Box address and the name Mark Butler on it. So, she had come to find Mark Butler at the only place she knew.

He had known all along she was resourceful. He was not really surprised she had tracked him down, even if she had crossed the country to do it. He looked her over. She had cleaned herself up, cut her hair and was now wearing a nice dress and sandals. She actually looked good, easy on the eye. He felt a wave of affection for this girl: she had started off hard with a tough life, so much like what he had lived as a child. He decided that, if she had come looking for his help, he would give it gladly.

He sat down on the step next to her, saying, "Well, fancy finding you here, not by chance, come from the other side of the country, I assume."

She sat up straight and smiled at him, an almost dazzling smile. She said, "I wondered whether you would remember me, and if you did whether you would even speak to me. Part of me thought it was a bad idea. But you seemed to like me and be kind. I thought, *Sometimes, you just have to go hard for the things you want.*

"I tried to ring a couple times and you did not answer. I thought, then, my best bet was to come here and wait until you showed. I have only been here for three days so far. All in all, that is pretty good. Plus, as a city girl, I wanted to see this place called "The Outback" that you kept telling me stories about. It took four days of hitching from Sydney but, here I am and here you are."

Mark stood up and reached out his hand for her. She took his hand and he pulled her up. "First things first, I don't know if you still have that great appetite from the last time, I saw you, but I am famished. I decided to call here before I went up town to buy breakfast. That way, I could sit and read my mail over a cup of coffee. I'm hungry for a big plate of bacon and eggs, what about you? After we eat, you can tell me your news."

Josie nodded, "Sounds real good, Mister."

Mark looked at her and smiled again. This girl brought out kindness in him. "Josie, my name is Mark, please call me Mark. That's the name my friends call me, or sometimes MB or Mark B, but none call me Mister."

"OK, I will try and remember to call you, Mark."

Over breakfast, Mark told her his news. He had spent three weeks working in central Queensland fixing up broken houses in an aboriginal community, then a week at a mine in Tennant Creek. He had arrived the night before last. Then he looked at Josie, "Your turn now."

She said, "When you told me that story of how you made good it got me to thinking. I realised that I don't need to run and hide from my Mum anymore. Sure, she made me do some real bad stuff, but now, I am grown up and I can look after myself.

"I moved back with her except I don't do the men things for her anymore. But, at least, I can take some of her social security money each week, buy food and cook it for us both. There still is some money left for her grog and other things- no point me trying to stop that.

"I started to look at courses I could do, like you said. I read about TAFE courses and how to get a proper job, one where I have money for myself without being on the game. That way I don't have to do the sex stuff with men except those I like. I even used some of the money you gave me to buy new clothes.

"I found a fashion course that I want to do, like in TAFE but in a private college. It starts in a bit over a month from now. Only trouble is, it costs ten thousand dollars and I don't have ten thousand dollars. Sure, I could make it on the game, but I don't want to do that anymore either.

"That is when I remembered about your promise to help me, just to lend me the money until I can pay it back from a real job. I tried to ring you. Maybe I should have sent a text or left a message, but it was from my mother's phone. I didn't want her knowing about it or her getting her claws into you- she would try if she thought you had money. Her phone almost never has credit, but I bought twenty dollars and for two days she did not notice as it had been left in the drawer. Then, on the third day, she found it and used up the rest of the credit so I could not ring again.

"After that, I thought, rather than keep trying to ring you, it was better if I came and found you at the place where your card said. I did not know it was so far and, a few times, I felt a right dork for coming. But, once I started, I could not bear to go back without trying. So here I am."

Mark laid his hand on her arm, "Of course, you must have the money for your course. I am happy to give it to you to keep, but if you prefer it to be a loan that is fine, too. I am glad you have gone back home although I think you might be better off if you rent a place of your own. It might be hard to study if you are staying with your Mum and she gets drunk. How about I organise to rent a small flat for you, somewhere not too far from where your Mum lives? You can stay there until after you have finished your course. Then, you can decide what you most want to do from there."

Josie nodded, "That would be real kind, Mister, Mark"

With breakfast finished, Mark told her he had to do a bit of business in the town. He asked where she was staying.

Josie looked a bit shamefaced. "Well, I used up my money getting here, so the last couple nights I found a place down on the river. There were some abos camping there. They shared their food with me and let me sleep near the fire. They even gave me an old blanket to cover me so I could take my dress off, cuz I only have the one good dress and did not want to get it dirty before you met me.

Mark found himself amazed at the pluck of this girl, to travel across the country with almost nothing. It was foolhardy, but admirable. He looked at her: she had an awkward shy smile as if waiting to see what he said. He patted her arm again. "Josie, you did great. I am proud of you."

She beamed with pleasure, realising she had done alright.

Mark said, "OK, now I need to take you shopping. There is a spare bedroom in my flat. You can stay there for the next couple nights while I am in town. And we must buy you some more clothes. I don't know much about women's clothes but there are quite a few shops in the main street so I am sure we can find someone there to help."

By lunchtime, she had a new wardrobe and he brought her back to the flat, showing her to her room and also where other things were.

He said, "I must go out for a few hours but will be back before dark."

He gave her a key and told her directions to the main street where the shops were. Last, he gave her $100 and told her to spend it on anything she needed as there was not much in the flat. He suggested she make herself at home, she could even think about something for dinner if she wanted, although he was happy to eat out.

As he went to leave, he called back, "Josie, don't run away on me. I am looking forward to our dinner and you telling me more of your plans."

She smiled and waved and even blew him a playful kiss.

As Mark drove away, he had to head down to Mataranka for the afternoon, he found himself wondering about the way this girl had just breezed into his life. She was an enigma, both shy and confident. There was a hard edge to her which he had yet to plumb but there was also a kindness, particularly for someone who had grown up on the wrong side of the street, very much like he had done.

He really wanted to help her make a new and good life: it was as if he was acting like the uncle she'd never known and giving her a leg up. She was also much prettier than he first realised, not quite beautiful, but with a lovely smile which lit up her face.

He realised he actually liked having her around. Never before had he allowed anyone into his place and, yet, he had instantly given her the keys with no restrictions and without a second thought. It was strange to trust someone he did not know, but in a way, he felt he'd known her all his life, a sort of kid sister who had come up the hard way, just like him.

The next two days passed in domestic harmony. Josie cooked meals and went out around the town during the day, coming back with both food and other little treasures with which she decorated the flat: some flowers, a painting from someone in the street who was trying to support themselves and some brightly coloured stones she put in a bowl in the middle of the table.

He found he liked having her around, she was good company and easy to talk to now that she had relaxed in his company. And with her nice clothes and makeup, she was also seriously sexy. He knew she was aware of that part of herself and was enjoying him becoming aware of it, too. He kept trying to think of her as his kid sister, but it was getting hard.

On the third night, he fell asleep in his chair after dinner, tired after a long day out. She woke him up after a while and took his hand and led him into his bedroom. She climbed in beside him, taking off her clothes as she did, and then unbuttoning his shirt and undressing him, too. In that way, they become lovers and it was surprisingly good. She was not the soulmate Belle had been but joining his body to hers felt good and she was experienced in many ways to pleasure a man.

He also marvelled at her creative flair. She had taken to drawing pictures and had a real gift for it, mostly of beautiful ladies with beautiful clothes. She bought fashion magazines and improved on the pictures she saw there. She also started to make little things out of pieces of fabric: mixing colours and shapes into exquisite little objects, some clothing-like, some decorative. He gained a strong impression that this girl could go far, she had such an obvious flair for colour, design and creating beauty from whatever was at hand.

He stayed for an extra two days in town enjoying being with her. It was in his mind to give her the money she needed and send her on her way, telling her to get on with her life in the city. He felt she was a city girl at heart and needed to return to where she belonged. On the fifth day, he brought her into the bank, set up an account in her name and deposited fifteen thousand dollars in it- along with an instruction to transfer five hundred dollars a week, for a further year, from his funds into her account. He figured that would give her enough to allow her to live comfortably for the year and it was better to give her the money in a steady stream, lest her mother somehow got hold of it, if it was all in a lump sum.

As they walked outside the bank into the hot Katherine midday sun, she thanked him with tears in her eyes, saying, "You are the kindest man I have ever met. I really want to stay on here in Katherine with you, not to go back to Sydney. Don't you like me staying with you?"

Mark put his arm around her shoulder; he felt great affection for this waif of a girl. "Josie, I can't pretend I don't like having you around and I particularly like sharing my nights with you. You are really something and with so much ability that needs to be given the chance to grow. You are like the kid sister I never had, and I so much want to see you get on with your life. I want to see you succeed and still stay the best of friends.

"But I am a boy from the bush and you are a city girl. There is nothing for a girl with all your ability out here. I think you should grasp the opportunity to make a new life in the city, go to fashion college, get a qualification, then get a job that pays good money and get on with living.

"I will look forward to coming to see you every time I get the chance to visit the city. In time, you will meet a man who is much better for you than I could ever be, get married, have children and live in a nice house. You can have all this if you set your mind to it and work hard."

As he spoke, Mark could see a hurt look come into Josie's eyes, a wild animal look, as if that trusted hand that fed it had now rejected her.

She replied, "Could I not just stay on here for a while? I know you need to go bush and do work and I would love to come out with you and see these outback places, maybe even help you. The rest of the time, I would be happy just to stay here, make your house nice for you, cook nice food and give you pleasure in the nights."

Mark glimpsed real pain in her face; she was getting in far too deep, getting attached to him. He liked her and wanted good things for her. But he was not ready to share his life with her. She was too like him, a wild animal, used to treating life as an adversary and dangerous if she did not get what she wanted. He knew her idea of living here with him would not work. In a month, or two, or maybe three, it would become boring. She needed to take the chance he offered and make good.

He said, "Josie, it just would not work, you staying on here. I am almost never at home. These last five days are the longest I have spent in this place in more than a year. I would come and see you more in Sydney than if you stayed here, and you would be learning there- using all your creative flair to make a life that you like and find interesting."

As he spoke this time, it was as if shutters came down over her eyes, she had offered herself to him on any terms he would take her and now she understood he did not really want her at all.

She pulled herself together, trying to cover the hurt, stood straight and smiled brightly, "Well, at least you must take me bush for a few days before I leave. Having come all this way, I still want to see the outback. I will not get in the way if you let me come along for a few days."

Mark thought, *what the hell*, she was good company and he liked being with her. He was due to go out to the southern VRD, doing work on Wave Hill and Kalkaringi for four days before he headed up the Duncan Highway, through Rosewood Station to Kununurra for two days before he came back to Katherine for a night before heading east to the Gulf.

It would not hurt to bring her along. He knew she was smart and would not get in the way and she would give him pleasure in the nights. He nodded and grinned. "OK, deal, I have a week's work out west. You can come along so long as you promise to jump on a bus or plane to Sydney to do your course once we get back to town."

She smiled and nodded her head. Her smile seemed too bright and brittle, as if covering hurt, but he hoped that would pass.

Chapter 29 - Trip to Nowhere

The next morning, they headed away early. They stopped in the late morning at Top Springs for a beer with the bartender, Mick, before driving on. Mick was a fey Irishman, always good for a yarn. They chatted and exchanged many stories for half an hour over the cold drinks before heading on.

Mick, always one with a sharp tongue said, as they were leaving, "Well, it is good to see you back with another pretty girl on your arm, Mark. It has been long months now since you brought one this way.

"This one is a kindred spirit to you, I see. You should take good care of her. Otherwise, she could be nearly as dangerous to the world as you are. Treat her right if you want her to stay nice."

Somehow, the words jarred with Mark, even though Josie gave Mick a bright smile and blew him a kiss.

Their trip was mostly enjoyable and Josie proved to be both a capable camp cook and good company. She also went out of her way to pleasure him with her body, arousing him in ways he had not yet discovered. He found he treasured her company, not love- like what he had for Belle- but she was a good and practical companion.

But, where before she had a bright smile and been pleasure to be around, now there seemed to be a dark place in her soul that sat next to the emptiness in his.

He wished he could take it away. It was as if the part of him that had become one with the crocodile had also created a dark place in her.

He wondered if it was jealousy, that she had grown attached to him and, at the same time, now resented there being a place in his heart which he had reserved to love others. Once or twice, he tried to go there in his midnight conversations, but she always moved the subject on- as if unwilling to confront this part of the person that was her.

On the fifth night, after a day on which Josie and Mark had travelled north through Rosewood, stopping for a few hours to do some work there, they came to secluded camping spot in Keep River National Park. It was a few kilometres north of the main road to the west, the Victoria Highway which ran between Katherine and Kununurra.

Tomorrow, they would drive into Kununurra for a half day of work and an afternoon of shopping. He told Josie that he planned for them to have a night together sharing the best room in the best motel in town before they returned to Katherine for a final night together. This would be the last night before Josie returned to Sydney and Mark went south east, heading down to the Gulf for other work.

Mark's affection for this girl was undiminished. He knew he would really miss her once she was gone. It was not love, but it was a bond between two people who had a dark place in their souls and yet could share life's pleasures together, or so he thought.

Part of him felt he should offer her something more- perhaps allow her to stay on with him in Katherine until the end of the year. She could always go to fashion college next year. Maybe they could try the "living together" thing for six months. He thought that he could come back to town for a night or two most weeks, and sometimes, he could bring her out with him.

Mark knew this offer would make Josie deliriously happy, that it was what she wanted, and he would have liked to make her more fully happy. But he found a part of himself was unable to compromise with this offer. It felt as if he would be giving too big a part of himself, and he was unwillingly, to go so far with her. It felt untrue to offer it, unless he was fully sure it was what he wanted.

So, no offer was made. He could feel a dark kernel of bitterness continue to grow inside her. He hoped he could make it up to her with a night of pleasure together at this waterhole in the wilderness. Then, two more nights living it up in civilisation before they went their separate ways. He hoped that, once she was on board the bus to Darwin, followed by the flight to Sydney, she would start looking forward to her future life and what she felt as the pain of his rejection would soon ease.

They ate supper by the waterhole and took pleasure in the animals and sounds of the night that were gathered around.

Mark had seen pig tracks in the mud at the edge of the billabong last night. He told Josie he wanted to go off in the dawn and try and track one down- suggesting that she should enjoy an extra hour of sleep.

She agreed, it seemed a bit too readily, but then she did like being in bed- even without him. They made love and slept. Later in the night, he woke and saw her looking at him with her eyes dark and hurt.

He asked her, "What is it?"

She said, "Who is Belle? Last night, when you were making love to me, a couple times it seemed like you whispered her name. Then, you kept saying her name in your dreams. You have been tossing and turning in dreams for the last half hour and you have been saying her name over and over again. Is she the reason you don't want to stay with me? Is she the person you really love, but pretend does not exist?"

Mark turned away, -he could not bear to hear Belle's name spoken. The wound was covered in six months of scarring, but it was still too raw. A peculiar malice resonated in the way Josie spoke the name. It tore away the thinly healed scab, opening a raw bleeding place below.

He wished Josie would stop but she was insistent, "Tell me who Belle is, or I will find out some other way."

Mark could feel a slow rage burning and building inside him. He would not cop this from anyone. He turned to her with anger in his eyes and spat out, "Josie, for once in your life, shut the fuck up! Don't ever mention that name again! It has nothing to do with you and it never will!"

With that, he turned his back on her, pulled the pillow over his head and willed himself to empty all from his mind.

Mark had a vague awareness that Josie was gone from his bed, and he was glad. What happened felt like she was trying to prise open a place in his heart that belonged to another. He would not share these memories with anyone. He knew his words had hurt her, but did not care, when she spoke the name Belle with malice, his mind turned it back on her, magnified seven-fold.

As he drifted back towards sleep, he felt that his body was now one of the crocodiles that consumed his beloved- at one in spirit with her and them. He and they would protect their own; there was no space for any other. His reason tried to tell him that here was madness, but his crocodile mind would not listen and did not care.

Mark awoke with the first glimmers of dawn, he would hunt a pig and feed it to his crocodile spirit brothers. They were to calling him from the billabong nearby, seeking sustenance from him.

Josie was still not in his bed, he rose to look for her, now feeling some shame at his cruelty to her in the night. In this morning light, he did not really want to hurt her, but he could still feel the anger of the night sitting just beneath his skin.

He found her asleep in his Toyota cabin, clad only in a T-shirt and sprawled out across the front seats. She looked so young and vulnerable. He felt tenderness for her, not his love for Belle, but affection for another damaged soul, not so unlike his own. He felt a desire to run his fingers through her hair and reassure her, to rebuild affection between them. But the anger was still there, too, and it stopped him.

Instead, he took his gun from the back, a 223, along with a pack of bullets and went pig hunting. He followed fresh tracks from the water out into scrubby wasteland. Then he went down into another dried out swampy place where the pigs had been rooting for tubers. They had gone far but he followed their trail, blocking out the memories of the night and focusing only on the hunt- sharing his soul with hungry crocodile spirits.

By the time he returned, carrying a pig large enough to make his shoulders ache, after the miles he had walked with it, he found the camp deserted. He called out Josie's name- nothing.

He carried the pig to the billabong, there was no sign of a crocodile, yet his own crocodile spirit was alive to a presence. He lay his gift at the water's edge, it would come when it was ready to carry it away.

Now, he must find Josie. They needed to pack up and drive on to Kununurra. He called again, loudly- no sound returned. He checked his swag; it was as he had left it last night, undisturbed by her hands.

The doors of the car were closed but he could see she was no longer inside. He decided to look in more closely, going first to her side. The small overnight bag which had rested at her feet when they travelled, holding her few things, was not there. He looked to his seat. There was a sheet of paper on it. It had writing which looked like hers, it certainly was not his. Perhaps it was a message for him.

Mark,
You are a rotten bastard. I know your dirty secret. I found passports of Belle and Elin and read in your diary how you shot Belle. No wonder you did not want me to know about her. I bet you killed the other girl too.
I have done plenty of bad things, but I don't kill people.
Yesterday I would have done anything for you.
Today I can't wait to get even.
I found a big pile of jewels which I am sure are worth lots.
So rather than take the help you offered I will just help myself.
If you try to mess with me, I will send your diary to the police to see what they make of it.
Enjoy the rest of your miserable life before the police come.
I hope you go to jail for a very long time.
Then we will see who is laughing.
J

Chapter 30 - Rage

Mark read the note with a numb mind which slowly transformed through sadness into rage. *Why had he ever agreed to letting her come with him?* There was a part inside her that did bad staff, so like what was inside him. The two of them together just did not work, despite what he had started to feel for her, affection and perhaps the start of something more. Hell, he had even thought of letting her stay around, to see how things worked out. Well, that would not happen now.

She had proved herself jealous and incapable of trust. Now, she had taken his most private possession and was threatening to give it to the police. And she had taken his precious stone collection, something he really treasured, both for its value and beauty, but most for the good memories it held. She assumed she could just keep it or else.

It did not work like that. He would not be bullied. He would not be blackmailed! She would wish she had never started down this path.

He could feel the crocodile spirit taking full possession of his mind and transforming his rage into a primal hunting instinct. He would follow her until he found her. He would take back what belonged to him back. If she tried to stop him, he would finish her.

He picked up his rifle again, chambered a new round and started to cast around for her tracks. She was a city girl; she would not be much good at hiding herself in the bush or avoiding him. He saw the sandal impressions in bits of soft dirt; so he knew that was what she was wearing on her feet this morning.

Sure enough, the footmarks headed down the track he had driven in on yesterday. He wondered why she had not taken the vehicle; the keys should be in the ignition or on the driver's seat. Then he remembered, one day she had told him she did not know how to drive- it was not something a city girl who lived on the streets did.

He looked carefully at the road going out. It was a two-wheel track that only locals knew. It had seen light traffic since the last wet season, enough to break up the hard crust and leave plenty of patches where the soft dirt gave clear imprints of her sandals. Mark suspected Josie would just follow this track back to the main road, then hitch a lift from there.

He knew his geography of this place pretty well. The road wound around through a gap in the hills and then came out the other side two hundred metres from the main road. Following the track, it was about seven kilometres to the main road, but as the crow flew- it was between three and four. There was a hill of a few hundred feet high, followed by a second one, that blocked a direct path out. It was easy enough to walk over, though the big broken rocks prevented driving that way.

He did not know exactly how long she had been gone, but thought an hour earlier at most. She was probably half-way back to the road, three quarters at most. She was not that fit that she could do it like a marathon- even if she was trying to get away.

He tossed up driving after her or going on foot. If she heard his vehicle coming, she would run into the bush to hide, and it was hard to keep track of her footprints while driving. But, at the same time, he would have to travel pretty fast to cut her off on foot, even if he took a shortcut. Perhaps he would drive part way and then cut over the last low hill- it was only about three hundred metres across but saved the best part of two kilometres on the road. That way, if he had not seen her from the car, he could come out alongside the track about two hundred yards from the main road. He was sure he would be in front of her there. From there he could work back, checking the road for tracks if he did not find her first. If she had turned off, he would soon run her to ground.

Once he caught up with her and talked to her, she would surely give his things back and drop her threats, if he showed her he really meant it. Surely, she was not so foolish as to try and run from a man with a gun.

He walked over to the car, checking for keys. The keys were nowhere to be seen- neither in the ignition nor on the seat. He checked the floor lest they had fallen out. They were not there. He really felt angry again.

She must have taken his car keys to stop him following. It made sense, she was clever that way, but it made him angrier.

Well, she had chosen the path he would follow. He would hunt her on foot, like a wild animal. He would go quickly to get in front and then set an ambush. His mind went back into predator mode.

Carrying his rifle, a light but powerful 223, he set off at a jog up the hill by the shortest route.

Mark would have to move fast to catch Josie before the main road, though even if she beat him to it, he reckoned the odds were still well in his favour of stopping her or hunting her down. He thought she would head to Kununurra as it was closest.

Yes, he was nearly certain she would go that way, knowing its proximity; they had talked about that yesterday. She would be easy to find in a town that size, people remembered strangers and there were not many travel options on from there unless one kept hitching, or had a big balance credit card.

Even if she went back the other way, he would soon find out from the roadhouses along the way. The car carrying her would surely stop at either Timber Creek or the Victoria River Roadhouse to break the 500 kilometre trip. All he needed to do was ring these two places from Kununurra. He knew their staff; they would let him know if she came through. Then, he could grab a charter plane and be back in Katherine before her to greet her on her return, just when she least expected. She had a key to his flat and most of her things were there. He was almost sure she would stop there to collect her things. It would wipe the smile off her face if he was sitting there waiting for her.

All in all, he was confident in his ability to run her to ground and give her a simple choice: whichever way she went, his things back and nothing further said, or else. Surely, she was not stupid enough to still defy him if it came to that.

By the time Mark had run these options through his head, he had reached the top of the first rise and was breathing hard. He stopped and carefully surveyed the road below. It wound through the valley and then crossed a creek before it came around the point of the next low range which hid his view of the main road. There was no sign of her down there so he loped down to the road at a jog, cutting it at right angles. Here there were footprints in the soft bits, the same flat sandals. It appeared she was pushing herself to go fast: he saw places where she ran as well as places where she walked.

Mark needed to shorten the distance. It would take too long to follow her directly from behind. He headed cross country to the next hill at a faster jog, starting to breathe hard. His annoyance with Josie was rising for putting him through this. It was not a burning anger but something colder and more implacable- the hunting crocodile was alive and living in his mind.

He came to the last hill and pushed himself up it, his chest and legs feeling the strain. He crested the rise finally. Below him, the road turned sharply away from the hill and headed straight for a bitumen strip a bare two hundred yards away.

There she was, a hundred yards in front of him with another hundred yards until the black strip. He settled himself, took two deep breaths and called out her name, loud and clear, "Josie, Stop."

She turned and looked back at him, seeming temporarily unsure. He gave her his best friendly wave, hoping to reassure her, willing her to stop. But she turned her head away and started to run.

There was a distant noise; it was a silver car which had crested the rise about a kilometre away. It was coming fast towards them. Josie had seen or heard it, too. She seemed determined to get to the road in time to hail it, confident in her girl ability to stop it.

Mark could see Josie was running as fast as she was able, legs and arms flailing. Now, she had a bare 50 yards to go. Twenty yards in front of her, trees hid her from the main road, past them was open ground in full driver view.

He brought the rifle to his shoulder, steadied himself against a tree on the ridge. His gun was zeroed to this distance. Despite her running, it was an easy shot. Her head and shoulders loomed large in the scope, trigger pressure. He could stop; let her go, then find her again on another day if he wanted.

But, crocodile hunting eyes filled his mind; now was his moment to take her- his prey. He pulled the trigger back. Bang!

The car roared past, unknowing.

Mark walked to the place where Josie lay in the dust, suddenly so small and broken. He saw the round indent of the entry point where her neck met her head, through her parted hair.

The crocodile was gone from his mind. Overwhelming sadness remained as he looked at this broken body. He picked her up in his arms and walked with her back to the car, trying not to look at her face. It felt like he was carrying his little sister, she was so light.

Mark knew he had done something truly terrible, far more terrible than anything before. Despite her threats, he could have let Josie go. Even if she took all his precious stones and his diary and vanished- it did not need to come to this.

Yet, he had chosen to make it so. In that moment, he knew he'd lost his last shred of his humanity. All that remained was his crocodile soul.

He buried her deep in a sand drift down on the edge of the desert, 300 miles south, after an all-night drive.

It was just as the sun was rising. This was a special place for him. Rain had made this patch of desert into a carpet of flowers. He picked them by the armful and laid them over the disturbed sand. Mark knew Josie had loved flowers for their beauty. She was always bringing them to his flat, "to brighten it," she would say, "for they are really one of God's most beautiful things."

They would wilt and shrivel in a day or two- like her body already was. But it was the kindest thing he could think of to do for her.

He hoped her soul could find a happier place than his in whatever future existence followed.

He could not seek her forgiveness- it was long past that time.

Two days later, he came to the Top Springs Hotel. He was not the crying type, but decided to drink a rum or two and remember her as he had liked her best- that street urchin he first found in Sydney.

He was joined at the bar by others, the drinks passed around in good humour, beers with rum chasers.

A loudmouth from Josie's hometown joined in, a man who always talked about how it was so much better down there than up here. Mark had seen him a few times before when he was in the company of other girls, ones who had gone on their own way.

He had also been there, drinking in the corner, that lunch time when he and Josie passed through- a bare week before. There was something resentful in this bloke's manner, as if her begrudged Mark's success with the girls.

This man decided to make a joke at Mark's expense. "How is it you are always with a fresh girl? Why do you keep changing them? What do you do, root them, shoot them and chuck them in a hole?"

This man laughed at his own joke and looked around, expecting to have his audience join in. There was silence.

Mark picked up his drink and flung it in this man's face. The killing rage was burning in his mind, he could barely contain it. He spoke in a measured voice through gritted teeth. "If you ever say something like that again, I will kill you. If you think you are a hero, meet me outside."

He walked out the door leaving silence behind him.

Now, he could hear raised voices. He waited at the edge of the light. A minute passed; the talking ceased.

The door swung open. This man stumbled out. The man's eyes found his as he swore, he cursed Mark, then said. "Can't take a joke, no one treats me like that and gets away with it. I will teach you some manners."

Mark put his hands in his pockets, taking a fist full of coins in each. As the man came close, he hit him twice with each hand: a left and right to the body and then, as the man folded forward, with a left and right to the face. All the power of his rage went through to his fists

The man crumpled to the ground with barely a sound.

Mark walked over to his car and drove away.

Part 6 - Amanda

Chapter 31 - A Woman in Control

Amanda could barely remember her father from when she was little. But she did have a couple magical memories of when it was just her and her Dad alone, with her Mum away somewhere. When her Mum was at home, she bossed her Dad relentlessly. One day, her Dad must have had enough. He walked out of the house and was not seen again for years.

Now her Mum turned to bossing Amanda around and this worked for a while until, one day, she had enough, too. She packed her bag and left home, just like her father had. The police picked her up and brought her home, two days later: an eleven year-old, walking the streets of Newark, with almost no money left.

After that, she and her Mum lived out the rest of her school years in an uneasy truce: her Mum largely left her alone and did not push too hard as she realised this was one person she could not control with her voice and empty threats. It was like a battle of wills where she had bent her mother's will to her own, using her mother's fear of losing her.

At that time, Amanda had learned her own first big life lesson: if you did what you wanted, even if other people did not like it, they were almost completely powerless to stop you.

By the start of University, she had perfected this technique and used it to get what she wanted, almost all the time. She knew she had a very pretty face and a good body. That helped, too, but most came from being clear and determined in getting what you wanted.

Even so, it was amazing what you could get people to do for you with promises based on that physical thing- even if you did not intend to carry them through. Though, at least sometimes, you needed to. She supposed most people would call her selfish and self-centred, but really it was just making the best of your opportunities, because if you didn't no one else helped you- that was her life experience at the age of nineteen.

Amanda was a bright girl who got good marks with very little effort. Once she completed school, she had her choice of local Universities and posh colleges as well as some New York options. In the end, she accepted a place in her hometown campus, not because she really loved the place but, because here, she was a bigger fish in a smaller pond with more opportunities for advancement. She knew in New York the competition to get to the top would be a lot tougher. First and foremost, she had worked out she wanted to achieve success without excessive effort.

Amanda cruised through her first year at University, doing almost no work, but enjoying the social life. Somehow, she passed all her exams-just! She got no credits, just a bare pass grade average. In second year, it slowly dawned on her that her status was on the slide, all the boys she knew now had a new crop of fresh-faced students to focus on and she did not have good enough marks for any special privileges.

She also found that some of the courses she had wanted to do this year were not open to her. They required credit grades in last years' exam subjects for acceptance. Added to this, her money was tight.

Last year her father, weak and useless man that he was, had come back into her life. He had done well for himself in the last decade since he disappeared. When he returned, he had a well-paying job.

She worked herself back into his good books as a dutiful daughter, charming him with a mixture of her vivacity and his guilt for many years of abandonment. It worked so well that he had taken her on a shopping trip to Paris and had given her the money to buy lots of nice clothes.

Best of all, he gave her a generous living allowance for her first year in University, along with paying the expensive course fees.

However, as the year ended, so too his fortunes were on the slide. His work was based on commissions and the work volume was way down. With this, down went his pay.

To allow her continue into her second year, he just managed to cover the course fees, but there was nothing left for her to live on and without this she felt dirt poor, like someone from a trailer park.

Her mother came up with a little bit of money to help with her living costs. But it was barely food money, the total was a poverty allowance, enough for a shabby room and basic food to cook, but nothing to meet her social aspirations as a good-time girl.

She supposed she could move back home. It was across the other side of the city. It was even more drab and boring than the place where she lived now. She was not yet desperate enough for that.

Chapter 32 – Blackmail

Amanda thought about how she could improve her situation. She realised she would have to reinvigorate her effort to charm others at University. She wanted to find someone rich who would be generous to her, but who did not demand much from her in return. She might also have to do a bit more study this year to get her marks up again, but it would be a pretty dull year if lots of study was all there was.

She started to evaluate the options, both among fellow students and the academics for a generous benefactor- or at least someone who would help with money if the right pressure was applied.

Some of younger lecturers were dishy, but they were early in their careers and still too poor to be of much use. She had yet to discover any students with super rich parents who were not total losers, so this seemed not much of an option; many were too childish for her taste. She had found that older men were generally more rewarding as companions, they did not just want the sex bit. They had seen more of the world and could also hold an interesting conversation. There were a couple old-fart lecturers, who gave her lascivious looks. But they were too old and doddery for her taste; she was not that desperate yet.

There was one man who did appeal to her, a rising star, a professor in his mid-forties. He drove a hot red sports car, dressed well and obviously had good taste. He was also obviously married, as a couple times she had seen him walking around, affectionately holding hands with an older woman, somebody at least his age, and now starting to show a bit of wear and tear.

This woman was stylish, like she came from moneyed stock, and she was clearly well groomed. But it seemed like age was no longer her friend, whereas the Professor was genuinely good-looking. That may give her an opening.

Amanda found out the timetable for his courses, one was a small class with only 25 other students. She went along and sat in the back, deciding to ask him for a private meeting as he was packing up to leave at the end of the lecture.

That was her first break, she did not have the marks, but he arranged an appointment to see her. She spent a day learning all she could about his subject field, and then turned up on the day modestly-dressed- but still with enough on show to make him aware of her femininity.

She constructed a hard luck story about how things had gone badly for her last year, things outside of her control. Now, she was back on track and was really interested in this subject. It must have worked because the next week her name got added to his course admissions.

She knew she had to move slowly at first, apply herself to learn the key facts and build up her knowledge in this field. She had to work as a diligent student for at least a few weeks before she made her moves in her other main game.

After a month doing the course, she stayed back one day at the end of a lecture to ask him a serious question. She dressed modestly apart from wearing a low-cut top. As he sat at his desk working through the detailed answer to her question, she bent forward to write notes as he spoke. Carefully, she positioned herself so, as she wrote, it gave him a close-up view into her open topped halter in which her breasts were well outlined. They were directly in front of his eyes. She knew it was working as several furtive glances were directed that way.

Determined not to overplay her hand on day one, she asked whether it was OK, once she had worked through some examples on her own, for her to come back to see him next week after class- to check her answers and see if her understanding of the questions were correct.

She could tell his interest to see more of her was aroused. He checked his diary, saying, "Next week I have a social engagement after this class, however we could do it the following day if you like. My last class ends at five. I could see you here just after the end of class. I am planning to work for a couple hours to catch up on a few things."

The day arrived. It was a hot, late spring day. Amanda decided that a light and filmy summer dress, cool and almost see through with the lighting at her back, was the best thing to wear. That way, when he was sitting at his desk and she was standing in front, her own body silhouette would be impossible to miss.

She tossed up what underwear to put on or whether to skip it, so the outline was most revealing. She experimented, looking at herself in the mirror with only the light from the window behind. In the end, she decided to skip the bra, that way her breasts and nipples were highly visible, standing out in a side on silhouette. From the front, the curves and spaces of her hips, legs and thighs were highlighted for him to see.

On her bottom, she wore brief black lace panties. Their colour, which contrasted against her pale skin, could not be missed as she stood in front of him. She knew that from there, she would be showing him almost everything except the small parts her knickers covered.

Amanda would use the heat of the day to apologise for the lightness of her dress, knowing this would draw his attention to it even more. She timed her arrival for fifteen minutes after the lecture finished, figuring this would give time enough for any slow students to leave, but for it to be unlikely that he would have gone off somewhere else. This was in case he had forgotten the appointment.

She saw he was still sitting at his desk near the front of the room as she came in. It was dark and cool at his end of the room away from the windows. She approached from the front of a big bank of windows which cast light from directly behind her.

He looked up at her footfalls. She paused to convey a level of anxious timidity, saying, "Sorry to keep you waiting. It is so hot out there. I hope you don't mind my wearing a light summer dress; it was far too hot for me to wear jeans."

As she spoke, standing a body length back from his desk, she made a little luxuriant stretch, half raising her arms with her legs apart. She could feel her dress hem slide up to her mid thighs as she raised her arms above her head.

She spoke in her throatiest voice, “It is so lovely here in the cool, it feels so good to have that cool air wash over me.”

She knew in that instant he had seen a full view of her almost naked body shimmering through the dress, it felt like she had sent a little current of electricity to him as his body reacted.

She now came right up to the front of his desk, putting her written sheets to the front of his work papers.

“I hope it is still OK if I ask you to check these,” she said.

His eyes went down to her work. As they did, she turned her profile sideways, moving half a step across to the side. She leaned in towards the front of the desk, knowing that way her breasts were clearly seen side on, illuminated by the light of the window behind her. She felt them hanging forward from her body. She held her pose for several long seconds, surreptitiously watching his eyes being drawn to look at her.

She straightened, pulling her body taut and pressing her nipples out against the filmy dress, knowing they were now the focal point, saying. “Sorry, I must be blocking your light.” She walked behind him and stood leaning over his shoulder, allowing the curve of one breast to slide against the top of his shoulder, moving it slightly to maintain contact and increase his awareness. It also heightened her own arousal.

She knew from her biology studies, that her body was pumping out pheromones which were going straight from his nose to his brain. In this position they stayed for a couple minutes, he forcing himself to read her work- though it was clearly a struggle.

He pushed back against her, making full contact with his shoulders to both of her breasts, a seemingly deliberate motion. He appeared to be about to speak.

She pre-empted him, saying, “Thank you for taking the time to read my examples. Your kindness really means a lot to me.”

She rested her hand on his shoulder. As if abstractedly, she ran her fingers through his hair.

He spoke with difficulty, "Actually, you seemed to have really grasped the key concepts very well."

He paused as seeking to go further before the situation overwhelmed him. Now, she felt his hand go around her waist and work downwards, beginning to caress her buttocks.

She said, "I am glad you like it, but I am finding it very hard to think about my writing, when you put your hand there, it feels so incredibly sexy and delicious. I can't help it. I am getting a super aroused feeling inside me with your touch."

She put both arms around his neck from behind and pressed her full body against his shoulders while she ran both her hands through his hair and down the front of his chest, nibbling his ears as she did.

From there it was a cascade of hands touching, lips connecting and clothes discarded, until they were naked together on the floor.

After it was done, they dressed. She decided to play the bashful maiden once more. "I am always a sucker for serious, handsome men in suits. I did not mean it to come to this, but you looked so sexy sitting there. I found I just could not help myself."

"Me neither," he nodded, ruefully. "I am not in the habit of seducing students. But when I saw your almost naked body outlined with the light behind you, I felt something come over me."

She said, "Well, don't feel bad, I really liked it! The feel of your strong body over and inside me. I hope we can do it again some time. That would be really special. Though here is probably not the best place- in case someone walks in."

They started their weekly assignments, mostly on a Thursday afternoon when he had established a tradition of working late. Now, however, little work was done. The next week, it was in his office with a locked door. The week after that was in a hotel room near the University. By the fourth week, she was ready to take it to the next stage.

By this time, Amanda had mapped out his life and assets in their post lovemaking conversations. He was clearly still attached to his wife and felt guilt at what he was doing. But, at the same time, he found himself powerless to stop the affair.

From her point of view, he was a mediocre lover and, while he gave her little gifts like perfume and minor jewellery, they were of no great value to her. She wanted something substantial as the result of this affair. She knew that to get this, she needed some real bargaining chips.

For the fourth week, she arranged to meet him at a friend's place, someone who was conveniently out of town for a week. Amanda had suggested she use the place for a night or two to improve security, so the friend left Amanda with the keys, giving her unfettered access.

Amanda set it up the day before, packing up all her friend's personal effects and substituting things of her own: a framed photo of her with her father from last year, a similar one of her and her mother from a couple years earlier and a third one of her with her Mum and Dad when she was little. She added a couple knick-knacks to give a personal feel.

Hidden in room corners, she carefully placed cameras giving views from two angles in the bedroom and another camera giving a view of the lounge in the living room to capture the preliminaries. She checked the recordings. The noise volume was too low so she added separate audio recordings in both rooms. All were set up to run with a single quick flick of a switch on his arrival.

When all was ready she showered quickly, put on a bathrobe, sprayed her body with perfume and part dried her hair, knowing her visible nakedness underneath would quickly arouse him.

Now, all she had to do was to wait for him to buzz the apartment entrance door for her to let him in. She set up two wine glasses on the lounge table and poured herself two inches- a nerve steadier.

The doorbell buzzed and she spoke through the intercom, "Come on up, second floor, first door on the right after the stairs."

Amanda greeted him with a kiss on the lips and brought him to the couch where she poured his wine. As he sipped, she let the bathrobe slide partway open over her thighs. Now, his hand was caressing her all the way up, pushing the robe aside as he stroked her intimately. She glanced at where the camera was positioned, knowing it had got a full view. Then, his mouth was on her nipples and working down to the bottom of her naked belly.

She pulled his head back, saying "The bed will be so much more comfortable, let's go in there."

He picked her up and carried her through the door, setting her down beside the bed while he took off her bathrobe and then stripped off his own clothes. Now, he was on top of her grunting and groaning. She looked up at the two tiny camera lenses and smiled, thinking, *This is truly perfect, these pictures will tell an amazing story*.

Then, before he could come, she flipped his body under hers and worked herself up and down over him like a gymnast while he smiled unknowing at the camera, his face clear for all to see.

That night, after he went home to his wife, she replayed it all, both the video action and the sound. It was perfect; the game, set and match to Amanda in Round 1 against Mr. Professor.

She thought she should feel sorry for him about what was coming his way. But all she felt was contempt. It would be easy from here. It would cost him big time if he wanted to keep his job and his marriage. Plus, she felt entitled to have him pay her to use her body: it was like a rental transaction, he was really only an ordinary lover and there had to be other compensations.

She skipped seeing him for a week, wanting to heighten his desire and anxiety. In the interim, she had two copies made of the video and audio recordings. She also had three little sample bottles which held three cotton buds with his DNA. They were taken from his sperm which filled the condom he had removed and left in her bin. Her sample collection and bottle labelling process was also on videotape lest he try and claim they had not come from him.

The next week, she agreed to meet him in his office an hour after lectures finished. That way she would ensure there were no other uninvited guests around, when she laid it all out.

As he was pouring her a drink, she placed the USB stick with the video recording in his office TV and switched it on. When the memory stick was installed, she watched as the file loaded and then pressed the 'play' button. His back was turned.

She called to him, "You might want to look at this."

He turned to see Amanda sitting on the lounge as a back view of a man showed with him sliding apart her robe and moving his hand and mouth over her body. There was a period of silence as his mind slowly absorbed the evidence.

He was shaking his head in horror and disbelief.

She decided to play with him before her ultimatum, now opening her top and baring her naked breasts.

"Do you recognise these?" she said, with her sweetest smile, "They are here now for you to play with, though after today the price has gone up. Tonight is to be your last free taste. Next week on the price will be $10,000 a month, payable at the start of the month, all in cash of course.

"That will give you access to continue this fun one night a week. If the money does not come on the due date, I will be sending one of these little USB things to the University Chancellor. The week after, another one will be sent to the local paper. I think it is obvious what follows."

She had to give it to him, he was cool. He knew his goose was cooked but was determined to keep eating while the course was on offer.

It seemed the heightened stakes improved his lovemaking, giving an edge for them both, knowing they were now playing for so much more.

The next week, before he got down to business, he handed her a sealed envelope with the ten thousand dollars. Their life continued peacefully for a further month with ever more wild and adventurous sex.

And then the payment was due again. She reminded him and, even though she could see this time it was really hurting, the money came again the next week. Another month rolled by.

This time, when she indicated the date was due, he shook his head, "You have cleaned me out. I have given you all that I can give. I can't pay that much anymore. It will have to come back to $1000 a month, $2000 max- that is all I can afford from here."

As she kissed him goodnight after their best sex yet, he looked at her, almost pleading, "You know I really can't pay what you are asking."

She shook her head and turned away, "Well, you know what comes next; it is all downhill from here. Goodbye career."

Chapter 33 - Fugitive

Amanda returned to the Professor's office at the same time next week. She had not seen him in private and he had avoided her eyes in class-which was unusual as normally he looked at her way too much. It made her uncomfortable, like he was seriously sweet on her. For her, it was just profitable sex, though she had started to increasingly look forward to her weekly trysts for the pleasure they brought her. She would sometimes think of him privately with affection remembering these times.

It would be nice if he could find the money to continue, she could not cave in on that, better to move on to another person. She already had two other possible candidates in mind.

She would play hardball if she must, not full and immediate exposure but a trickle. First releasing less-incriminating bits to keep him nervous and give him a chance to find at least part of the money that would buy more silence. *That would be best*, she thought.

She found she was unusually nervous today, not her normal super-cool self. She wondered if she had a premonition of a problem as she lifted a hand to knock on his door.

She paused and undid the top two buttons on her blouse, still feeling a desire to keep the sexual thrill going; it was more pleasurable doing it for high stakes than simple lust. Perhaps he was still trying to assemble the money. If so, she would give him another free sample to keep him keen. She found this thought turned her on, big time.

When she knocked, she heard a muffled, "Come In," but the voice was strange; it sounded pained.

He was sitting at his desk, still not really looking at her, his face drawn. He pushed an envelope her way, it seemed skinner than usual.

He spoke, still not looking up, "You need to take that money and get out of here. My wife found out about you and the money: she checked my accounts and demanded to know where it had gone. I ended up telling her about our affair and that I paid you because you filmed us and threatened to release it. She confronted me last night. She had been suspicious and asking me questions all week.

In the end, I told her as it seemed the only way to save our marriage and for me to keep access to our children.

"She called the police today to tell them I am being blackmailed by you. They came and met us this morning and questioned me. I told them what happened. They asked when I would see you next and I said I expected to meet you tomorrow. When that time comes, they will be here to arrest you, to charge you with extortion.

"As a result, I expect to lose my job and you are likely to end up in jail. My job is as good as gone, but I do not want to see you in prison.

"On my way here, I got a small amount of extra money that my wife does not know about. It is here for you. It will give you enough to cover your travel and living costs for a couple weeks.

"I strongly suggest you leave town and go somewhere far away-overseas would be best as they are more likely to trace you and arrest you if you just go to another state.

"Provided you are not here tomorrow, I can say I do not know where you are or where you have gone. If they cannot locate you elsewhere, it might just go away for us both. If they arrest you, I will be forced to give evidence against you. That will be bad for me and even worse for you.

"The funny thing is, despite knowing what you are like, someone who uses and manipulates people, I find myself very fond of you. You are very bright and have great ability. I don't want you to end up in jail like any other convicted criminal.

"Part of me wishes I had enough money to set you up in a nice place and let you enjoy a good life. Maybe that person would have become a better you, someone who lived up to all the potential you have within.

"However, that time is past. This is the only help I can give you. You must go and go quickly. Even now, you need to be careful. The police may already be looking for you, although I think they have yet to seek an arrest warrant. I understood that this afternoon they were going to try and trace the money, to see if you deposited it. If they get information showing you have received large sums of money, I think they will arrest you without delay.

"I suggest you go back to your house unobtrusively and collect anything essential, like a passport, and vanish. It would be even better if you could ring a friend from your house, ask them to get a few essential things for you and meet you somewhere, make up a story that sounds plausible and perhaps meet them in a local bar or cafe.

"Then, as soon as possible, you should leave town. Perhaps take the Airtrain to JFK where you will have the best choice of airplane options to faraway destinations."

Amanda found herself struggling to take it all in, to comprehend how quickly her world had turned on its head. She had thought she was clever; now she was a fugitive.

He was right. She must get out of here quickly. Unexpectedly, she felt sad about saying goodbye to this man. As lovers, it had started ordinary but had become increasingly good. But what moved her was his unexpected kindness. She knew that what he had done today would not benefit him. It may make his situation even worse if it was shown that he had helped her.

Yet, despite her using him in a "get rich quick scheme," and him knowing it, he had treated her with unexpected decency. She felt tears forming in her eyes at his goodness. It made a tiny chink in her otherwise hardened soul.

She stood up and walked over to him. He put out his hands, took her hands and pulled her to him and held her against him, stroking her head like a favourite daughter for a long minute. Then, with apparent regret, he pushed her away.

"Go now! Perhaps, one day, you will realise this was a good life lesson and remember me with kindness. Perhaps you could send me a postcard from a far away and exotic destination. I won't promise to come and meet you, but you never know."

She reached forward and kissed him gently on the lips, a kiss of affection rather than passion, saying as she pulled away from him, "Thank you, -you have been good to me. I will send a postcard when I can, signed with a big 'A,' carrying with it all my affection."

She walked out, wondering what she would do now with the rest of her life. Suddenly her future did not seem so bright.

Chapter 34 - Pickup

Over six months had passed. Amanda found herself working on an island resort in the far north of Queensland.

Fortunately, she had kept the money that she had been paid by her Newark professor in cash, not having lodged it into a bank account.

In the late afternoon, when others were off having a drink, she had slipped unobtrusively into the shared house and gone to her room: quickly packing an overnight bag with her best clothes, other valuables, her passport and cash, still over fifteen thousand dollars, plus another four thousand in the envelope.

She made a snap decision, as she was packing, to head for Australia via the West Coast. She booked an evening flight from Newark to LA. In LA, she bought an open return ticket and arranged a working holiday visa for twelve months in Australia. She found it was easy with her US university student status. By lunch time the next day she was airborne, flying across the Pacific Ocean, knowing that in another half a day her next touchdown was Sydney. It had all seemed so easy it was hard to believe that there could be any problems following her, but still she knew she must take care.

She only stayed a week in Sydney, it was an expensive city and she wanted to ration her money. So, first she went down to Melbourne, the other main city, and got work in a bar for a couple months. Then, when Christmas came, she returned to Sydney for the fireworks show, meeting up with a few casual friends she had made when she first came here. She stayed in a backpacker hostel near Bondi Beach, during the long hot days of summer, doing odd jobs as they turned up.

By February, with the heat of summer easing, she decided to go north and follow the sun- that was the way the other backpackers talked of it. She worked her way up the east coast, stopping here and there and taking more short-term jobs as needed to replenish her money.

Learning to dive interested her so she booked a diving course on the Barrier Reef in Queensland. It was at a place called Airlie Beach. With her qualification in hand and using her friendly manner, inside a second week she had a job offer at a nearby resort at a place called Hamilton Island.

It was an hour and a half by ferry from the mainland town. Amanda had now worked here for two months and found it easy and enjoyable. There was usually the chance to practice her diving in the afternoons or when tours were going out and they had an extra space to give away.

Her job was in customer service: booking local tours and island activities for overseas visitors, particularly the rich world of an American traveller clientele. Her American accent always ensured good tips when she gave service with a smile to her fellow citizens. She also had a good story to tell of an American student, on a gap year, seeing the world.

Now that she had a stable address, she sent a post card to the Professor as well as a letter to her Mum telling of her decision to make an Australian trip and defer her studies for a bit.

Her Mum wrote a letter back which came two weeks later, telling of the local news. It said nothing about the police or other authorities looking for her. Perhaps, with her gone and no money to trace, it would just fade away, like she and the professor both hoped.

She would like to know, she decided. She could stay here for another month or two but, ultimately, she wanted more from her life than odd jobs in holiday resorts. She needed to know if there was an arrest warrant or open criminal investigation that would cause future problems should she return home.

She tried to ring the Professor, but the University receptionist merely informed her he longer worked there. She would not provide information on where he had gone: only that he left unexpectedly late last year. She realised this was due to her and felt a bit sad about it.

Amanda was starting to find life dull on the island. She had done most of the tours and activities and had added an additional $3000 to her bank balance since coming here. She had also tried very transient affairs with two other tourist staff, but all-in-all it was becoming boring.

One night, a mid-week night, when business was quiet, she was sitting in the resort bar where she worked, having a drink with a Canadian girl who worked with her. There was something comfortable in their accents and backgrounds that made each enjoy the other's company.

She noticed a man in his thirties buy a drink, a rum and coke. He took it to a corner table, in the furthest corner away from the bar. There was something incredibly self-possessed about him.

He was not exactly handsome, quite weather-beaten looking, tanned from many long days in the sun, but there was a sense of physical power and toughness that she found appealing. His body had that hard look of a person doing manual work.

She tried to catch his eye, to see if she could draw a smile. It was as if he sensed her interest and avoided it. She felt her interest piqued in turn.

She asked her friend if she knew who he was, very few came to the island as 'unknowns' except for tourists and he did not look like a tourist.

Her friend replied, "He just arrived today. I think he is here for three days to do maintenance on resort machinery, maybe the air conditioners. I heard his name was Mark, Mark something. That's right, he was talking to the Resort Manager when I was working on the front counter and he was introduced to our head of maintenance as Mark Brown."

Amanda said, "Let's go and introduce ourselves to him. If he's here on his own, he might be looking for company. God knows, interesting men, who are not jet-setting tourists, are few and far between."

They went across and said "hello," smiling brightly in their best girlie way. He nodded politely but evidenced little interest in keeping them company. He was not rude, but it seemed as if a dark spirit sat on his shoulder, giving him a serious demeanour and little ability to smile.

He sat and talked to them in a low-key way for a few more minutes while he finished his drink and then said, in a quaint and almost courtly way, "Well, nice meeting you ladies. Got a big day's work tomorrow, replacing several air conditioning units in the west wing, then the same the next day in the east wing. So, for this evening, I wish you good night."

Amanda felt her interest doubly drawn. He had the edges of a nice smile that she had almost glimpsed a couple times, as if in response to her obvious pickup lines- which he clearly saw through. It was like he was saying. *I have been around lots of bad places and tough motherfuckers. I've seen it all before*. There was an edge to his manner. It spoke of challenge and maybe danger. She refused to accept his brush-off.

He was there in the bar again the next night. This time, he stayed for two drinks, though he refused her offer to buy him one and did not offer to buy her one in return.

However, Amanda sensed that she had intrigued Mark too, just a tiny bit, but he was now conscious of her and intrigued by her interest. He told her a small bit about his work as a jack of all trades across the vast open spaces of Australia. She told him she was at college in New Jersey, just the other side of the Hudson River from New York, and had decided to take a gap year and travel to see the world. For now, she said, she was enjoying life in Northern Queensland and was wondering about where to go next.

She knew, as she spoke, he had seen through her shallow lies, not that he seemed to care, but his manner told her he had a nose for scenting out things that were not fully truthful.

He said, "We all have our stories; I have given you a tiny bit of mine, true but telling nothing. You have given me a tiny bit of yours, part true and telling even less. That's how it goes."

With that, he stood up and left again.

The next night he was not there. Amanda asked around and found he had departed to the mainland on the last ferry. She felt disappointed that he had left without her knowing or saying goodbye.

A week later, her Canadian friend left, too. Now, she had no more drinking partners and there was no one else she found interesting at the resort at present. She decided she needed to do something to pass all the empty nights. She went to the bookshop and bought a novel with good reviews. It had stickers saying it had won a major prize, something called "Man Booker." It seemed like a big deal prize in England, not quite a Pulitzer but still a seriously big something.

Hopefully this book will be OK, she thought as she settled in to reading it, while nursing a drink on a corner table of the resort bar.

She realised a person was coming to sit at her table, so she looked up. It was the man, Mark. This time, he was carrying a drink for her as well as one for himself. He had ordered her regular mojito and she wondered how he knew what it was. Clearly his eyes were sharp and little went past him.

Amanda looked him up and down appraisingly, wondering if tonight would be her lucky night, the start of something new and exciting. She was confident in her ability to bait the hook and catch the fish from here.

Chapter 35 - The Wrong Man

Amanda and Mark talked for maybe an hour that night. When he looked at her, she felt like she had his total attention, his eyes looked at her with such penetration. It made her a bit giddy and breathless, she decided she would not let him get away tonight without something more.

She asked him what he was doing back on the island and where he was off to next. He said he was just back for a day to service the new air conditioners he had installed a week ago, make minor adjustments and to ensure that all were working well. Tomorrow, he would return to the mainland once finished. After a night in Airlie Beach, he was off, early next morning to go prospecting for opals in central Queensland, a place he'd been told about which was promising. He would spend ten days to two weeks out there, the length depending on what he found. When that was done, he would go further west, across to the NT where he was booked to do a few weeks of station work, contract mustering cattle.

She kept asking him questions about his life and what it was like out in "The Outback", as he called it. She wondered, *Was it something like the American Wild West?*

Finally, after about her tenth question, he turned to her and looked at her with eyes that bored straight into her soul.

"If you really want to see it, you can come with me for a week or two. It won't be exciting. I will be digging for opals. It is hard work. And once I leave here, I won't be coming back this way anytime soon. If you get bored, I can take you on a four-hour drive to the local town to catch a bus if you want to leave. Or, when I am finished, I can take you on to Mount Isa from where you can catch a plane to another place. Or, if you really want to stay on longer, you can come on with me to the NT and see a couple real cattle stations at work. When that is finished, I will bring you to either Alice Springs or Katherine- which are the nearby towns. By then, I am sure you will have had more than enough of the Outback and you will be more than happy to leave from there."

There was something implacable and hard in his eyes when he said those words that it gave her a little shiver. It was as if he had laid down a challenge to her, a challenge for a trip and a challenge for control. She liked challenges and she liked control.

Amanda nodded, now exerting her own control. It felt interesting. "What do I need to do if I decide to come?"

He shrugged, dismissive; as if now regretful he had made an offer, but not willing to go back on his word if the challenge was accepted.

"I will be catching the last ferry back to the mainland tomorrow. If I see you on the ferry, I will take it you are coming with me."

With that, he stood up and nodded a good night.

Amanda sat there for a further five minutes, feeling wildly exhilarated, thinking how the strangest things in life came when least expected. She was determined to accept his challenge; she would be on the ferry. She would give notice tomorrow saying she was leaving at the end of the day, that a job offer had come up on the mainland that was too good to refuse and that she needed to start immediately. They would make up her pay by the end of the day and she would be gone.

Amanda would say nothing of her plan to travel to the outback with Mark. It would be fun. She knew, despite his challenge, that she could control him, the same way as she had always managed with other men.

The next day, the ferry was well over halfway across the water to the mainland before she saw him. She was starting to wonder if he had done this just to tease her. But, sure enough, there he was. He looked down at her gear in her bag, picked it up and carried it to the car deck, dropping it onto the back of a white four-wheel drive.

"That is my car. I assume this means you are coming with me."

That night he booked them into a five-star resort at Airlie Beach. He did not ask her whether she wanted to share. He simply told her of his plans for them to enjoy a final night of civilisation before heading out the back of nowhere. He carried her bag up the room, a palatial apartment looking far out across the beach to the islands in the distance. It had a huge bed, a separate lounge area, a bathroom with a Jacuzzi and a wide terrace with a table and chairs.

He took two beers from the fridge and offered her one.

She nodded and thanked him.

After they had both had two drinks and were feeling mellow, he suggested she might like a bath and that, after that, he planned to go and eat in a new restaurant in the town if she would like to accompany him. It was not quite a dinner invitation, more of a take it or leave it offer, he was going and she could come along, too, if she wanted to.

She accepted with alacrity and decided that tonight she would "wow" him with her sexiest dress. She asked if he needed to use the bathroom for the next half hour.

Mark said, "No, it's all yours."

Amanda took out her favourite soft silky dress, bought on her trip to Paris, turquoise colours that shimmered as she walked. She did her make-up to blend and match it. Then, she slipped the dress over her head and walked back out onto the terrace.

He looked up, she could feel the sexuality exuding from herself and knew it hit him full in the face as she stood there.

"Wow, I wonder who the lucky man will be who gets to take that dress off you at the end of tonight."

She gave him a lazy smile and said, "I thought that might be you."

A week passed. The sex, beginning with that first night, was wild. This man was insatiable and brought her pleasure beyond what she had known before. And she knew she turned him on big time, too.

However, the trip itself was not at all exciting, truth be told. It was something like the badlands of America; at least the way she had seen them on TV, as she had never really been to those places.

The first day had been the best. They had driven down the coast to a town called Mackay, then turned inland through hills. After a few hours, they had come to a town called Emerald. Mark told her it was in the heart of the good cattle country of the Great Divide of Queensland.

It was a pleasant bustling town. They stopped there for night in a local hotel, where they had taken a room and resumed their sexual romp, along with having beer and steaks for dinner.

On the first night when they had come back to their apartment at Airlie Beach, after undressing Amanda and fondling her in the most sensual and intimate way, Mark had produced a condom. She decided she did not want this, so she had told him she was on the pill and it was not required, even though it was not true. Not that she thought she'd get pregnant, she was pretty sure it was past that time of the month.

But Amanda wanted all the leverage she could get if it came to a battle of wills with this man. It occurred to her there might be leverage if she was to fall pregnant or even claim to be, that was if she wanted to get real control of this man. She was not quite sure yet but the thought of keeping this man and bending him to her will, seemed exciting.

Mark had her captivated, he was so goddamned sexy and wild, not just in bed but in everything he did. She had felt a lump on his arm one night and she had got him to admit it was from a bullet wound, it came from a time when he was a mercenary in West Africa, he told her.

She asked if he had ever killed someone. He said, "Yes, quite a few times." She found that fascinating, too. There was a ruthlessness to him that was unlike anyone she'd been close to before. It gave her little chills at times, but she was sure she had his measure.

Mark was consistently kind and gentle. So far, she had not asked him to do anything major as a favour. However, he had anticipated and done lots of little things for her, even before she realised she needed them. He had done them with a smile as if he liked doing things to please her.

Amanda liked this kind and gentle way he treated her. She felt sure, if she insisted, that he would fall into line with her other wishes.

The day they left Emerald they had visited a little town called Ruby, named after the gems. In the town, he had gone to a shop that advertised things bought and sold. The man who worked there was an old miner. He had made Amanda a cup of tea while he and Mark talked alone at a corner table. After a while, the man started showing Mark small things that must be gems, although from where she was sitting, she could not see them properly.

At first, Mark shook his head, but after being shown more he nodded and pulled out a roll of money. It looked like lots. He counted out a big pile and gave it to the man. It looked like several thousand dollars.

Then, Mark nodded to her that they were ready to go. As they walked out Mark showed her what he had bought, two rich red rubies, each the size of a large pea. The colour of them was like the glow of a fading sunset or a dying coal from a fire, a very deep red.

Their beauty was striking. Amanda could imagine one set on a chain between her breasts. This thought made her smile as she looked up at Mark. He was looking at her intently and said, "Perhaps I will give you one of these when you go; the colour matches the fire in your heart."

Amanda smiled back, thinking, *That's good. I would like that, but I do not plan to leave you anytime soon.*

Mark put the rubies in a little pouch of other stones. She could not see what was in there. But, it rattled and looked heavy: as if there were lots of other jewels in there, each worth lots and lots of money. That was good, too. That would give the money for their life together- which she had started to plan.

She just had to bring him back to a city, civilise him a bit and dress him in good clothes. After that, he would really "wow" all the people they met. She decided it was her life's mission to rescue this man from the Outback and turn him into something civilised. It felt like a noble calling. But, first, she must build more trust and affection with him. She needed to have this in place before she tried to direct him to the places she needed for them to both go.

Amanda had heard, back in America, that when one first caught a wild horse, one needed to smother it with love and affection until it trusted you. Then, once you had its trust, you could take control.

That was her sense of how it would be with Mark. She was glad she had been driven to come to Australia as, without this, she would never have met this amazing man.

She was not sure if it was love, there was certainly lots of lust. But she really did feel something deep and special for him.

The only trouble was that, after they left Emerald, they had come far out into the middle of nowhere. Now, it was getting boring. She was not sure how many more days she could stand of being out in this wasteland.

Amanda did not mind helping a bit, but the digging work was hard. She soon got sore hands and, a couple of times, little blisters started to develop. After that, she stopped digging. There was not really anything else to do out here. She had gone for a few short walks, but there were no proper footpaths, the grass was spiky to walk through and full of prickles and there was nothing exciting to do out there.

Mark had warned Amanda to be really careful where she walked, as the country was full of old mine shafts, some of which were really hard to see in the long grass. He said he did not want her to fall down one and injure herself. She felt indifferent to this danger, but even when she went off walking, wherever she went the scenery did not change: just more horrible rocky hills with stunted trees and dead grass. No paths, no views, knees scraped and toes stubbed on rocks and rough ground was all she got. So now, she mostly sat in the shade, trying to pass the time.

Mark seemed happy enough to let her rest, it was not really hot, and he had set up a comfortable bed and chair for her to use. But there were so many hours in each day to pass, and they never seemed to end.

She was tired of birds in the trees that squawked, and she was tired of no hot showers to wash herself properly- just a tin of warm water from the fire and a cup to rinse with. She was tired of the same boring food cooked in a frying pan on the fire every day. She had already read the two books she had brought. Mark did not seem to have any interesting books, just a few books about Australia that looked more like textbooks. She could not even get onto the internet out here to amuse herself. It was way past any place where there was an internet connection for her tablet and she was tired of just playing games with herself on it.

Amanda checked the date. It was now seven days since they had left that last town, Longreach, not that it was anything, a flat and dusty little hole. It must have taken three or four more hours of driving southwest from there until they came to this place. She could not name any other places of civilisation that she had seen nearby since then.

All that was here were scrubby tree things that Mark called mulga trees, other non-descript scrub and endless rocky hills. The only signs that other people had ever been here were the old mine shafts and bits of abandoned equipment, rusting in the sun.

The first day she had thought it was beautiful in an arid, 'badlands' way. Now, she was over that kind of beauty. In truth, it was ugly. She had also not understood, before they came here, that no one else lived here.

Mark told her the nearest places with regular people were two cattle stations each about twenty miles away from them in opposite directions. He did not offer to take her to visit. They occasionally sighted another prospector in the far distance or saw the dust of a car or truck on some distant road. But that was it- the total of humanity.

For the rest of the time, it was just him and her, stuck in the middle of this endless empty desolation. As fine as the collection of opals was going, and Mark said it was going really well, she was over it.

Mark was giving Amanda progress reports each time he came up to the surface, usually every two to three hours. He told her the hole he was working in was not quite a bonanza but it had a lot of good stuff. He now had a four-gallon drum half-full of the bits of rock he dug up.

They did not look like much to her, but he showed her flashes of colour amongst a dark rock he called ironstone and said that, when these bits were cleaned up, there was plenty to sell in here. At a conservative estimate, there was at least ten thousand dollars-worth here already. Last night, he had suggested that it would take another three or four days to finish his digging. Then, he would head north-west to Mount Isa.

That was all fine and she could see it was good money for a week's work. But really, rock was just bloody rock and it was getting seriously boring! She thought they should stop now, cash it in and go back to the coast. Then, if he wanted to come back out and dig up some more, Mark could come while Amanda stayed and minded their nice place by the sea. She had pictured the place they would buy, a place with lots of other people for her to talk to.

She decided that, when he had finished work tonight, it was time to start to exert control. To demand that he bring them both back to the place from whence they came, that they must leave tomorrow, not drag it out for another week to two.

He had told her a couple times that if she got too bored, he would take her back to Longreach and from there she could catch a bus.

But, Amanda could not let Mark just leave her there and vanish from her life. He needed to stay with her and continue to mind her in the way he did so well. That was where a baby would be really useful. She did not have one growing inside her yet, but she decided she would find a way to convince him that one was on the way. Even though it was not yet quite true, it could be so by the time it really mattered.

Of course, there was one other card she could play, too. It was to say that she would go to the police and cry rape and abduction. That she had gone to Airlie Beach and met up with him and had innocently gone back with him to his apartment, only to be raped. Then, she was forced to come with him in the dead of night to this God-forsaken place.

It was bluff- but he did not know that. So, if he tried to leave her somewhere, that would be her fall back. She had his name and his license plate number, she could tell him it would be easy for the police to run him to ground if he left her and tried to shoot through.

Going to the police was the furthest thing from her mind; Amanda did not want any risk that they would contact the Americans to find out about her. If they did that, it could result in them deporting her to face charges back home. Still, Mark did not know about that. It was yet another lever to pull if she thought he would try and give her the slip.

Of course, she did not want to go there- to use threats. She liked him and wanted to stay with him in a nice place, to keep having him around. So, the other was last resort stuff, to have in her back pocket should the need arise. Meanwhile, Amanda felt confident Mark would listen to sense and it would not come to that.

She felt so sure of herself, certain she could control this situation. But, at times, she saw glimpses of danger in his hard, implacable eyes and there was a tiny seed of fear in her, too.

Chapter 36 - An Uncertain End

Anne had read Mark's diary, had talked to Amanda's parents and, most usefully, she had talked to the Professor- now living on his own with a much- diminished status. He had lost his prestigious college post in Newark, as a result of his affair with Amanda. He had lost his wife and family, too. He was now living in Canada, as a research scientist on a much-reduced income, with only the memories to sustain him.

Despite great pressure from his wife and the county police, he had refused to testify to her extortion. Without that, they had no case. So, it was only him who wore the consequences of an affair with a student: his dismissal from his post.

Anne imagined that, if it had happened the way he told it to her, she would have been aggrieved and bitter. But, instead, he said he was just sad that this beautiful but misguided girl had met an untimely end.

Despite him telling Anne the tale of her seduction and manipulation of him, he refused to speak ill of her. Instead, he told of a person that needed to be dealt with using both strength and love. In their long conversations, he said that Amanda had revealed a joyless childhood, one with little real love and affection. She had come to a place where she substituted control as her purpose in life.

The Professor seemed to carry a burden of guilt that his advice had led her to leave America and driven her into the arms of the wrong man, thus leading to her demise. He had hoped that, after the lesson with him about the danger of abusing control, she would not have repeated this mistake. That she would no longer believe that her over-inflated sense of power would always get her what she wanted. Perhaps it partly worked; she had become cleverer in hiding her fatal flaw. Mark seemed to have an inkling of this character trait and had tried to warn her off, but, ultimately, her overconfidence made her reckless.

Everything about Mark made him the wrong man; so, so much the wrong man. He was a man who hated to be bullied. He was kind to a fault when asked for help without coercion. But, alongside this, was a deep and burning rage, a rage at all the people in his life who had tried to trick, misuse or bully him. Her trying to coerce and control him was destined to be a recipe for disaster.

As the years had gone by and Mark had his series of doomed affairs, that hole of anger inside him seemed to have got ever darker. His diary, in its second half, told about a far different man to the earlier years. There was this restless, brooding spirit which he called his crocodile demon. It consumed his soul and could break out with less and less provocation, doing awful things with no normal human restraints.

At those times, Anne felt as if she had peered inside the mind of a hunting predator. But then, even after these events unfolded, some parts of his humanity would come bursting back.

At some point in this relationship with Amanda, out in the opal mining place, something had snapped inside him. His diary did not say that in so many words. It told of his caution in first meeting her, that she was really pretty and sexy but she had something eating her up inside, a thing a bit like the devil in him. He saw within her a mirror to his crocodile spirit companion, in her soul was her own controlling monster creature.

His diary told how she had virtually flung herself at him, seeming to be determined to have him as one more conquest. It told of how he succumbed, despite making his rules clear and trying to warn her off.

His diary then told of a lovely and happy week with lots of affection and wild sex, even though, more and more as the week passed, the sex seemed to become a substitute for real love for both of them.

Then, it told of Amanda's increasing unhappiness in the isolation, of his offer to return her to Longreach from where she could catch a bus back to the coast. It told of her demand that he drive her back, over 1000 kilometres each way to the coast, and of his refusal to do so. Then, it told how it escalated into threats of pregnancy, threats of crying rape. That is where it ended. His diary simply ended her story by saying:

"A is really doing my head in. She is so angry and keeps trying to boss me. Today, she spat at me when I would not do her bidding. I slapped her face so she came at me with a knife. I hit her, Finito."

Susan's story gave a likely ending: that he hit her and killed her. Then he threw her body in one mine shaft, her bag in another shaft, and then dropped explosives into each shaft to collapse the dirt in on top of her and her things, to bury them where they would never be found.

His diary did not say that. After the "Finito," she simply vanished.

What was chilling was the lack of remorse Mark seemed to feel about what he had done. The next entry was several funny stories about two bush characters he met at Cloncurry pub, seemingly written a couple days later. He seemed to have discarded her from his life and casually moved on without second thoughts- a minor annoyance put aside.

The next entry, another day later, was lots of gruesome crocodile pictures and the caption, "I dreamed of crocodiles last night. They fill my soul and I feed on their hunger. It is a kind of twisted joy."

Anne wondered, *Was that a remorseful scream coming through a dream or was it only a lost soul going to ever worse places*?

Part 7 - Cathy

Chapter 37 - High Class Hooker

Cathy and her sister, also called Cathy, were inseparable when they were little. Actually, when she was little, everyone called her FiFi, as Fiona was her real name. It was only later, after the real Cathy had gone away-, well died- that she had taken Cathy's name to keep the memory alive. She hoped, back then, that by taking her sister's name, after she was gone, she would be able to keep some of the joy they had shared together. But, after that, her life was empty. Then, the other stuff had started, and it had gone from bad to worse, until she just had to escape.

Cathy left home when she was sixteen, the earliest she was allowed to go and find work on her own. It was not that she had any falling out with her parents; she remained close and would ring them regularly even though she would tell them almost nothing about her private life. Rather, she had a huge sense of guilt over what had happened to her sister and did not want to inflict more pain on her family. Although she could not bear to talk about her own life, things that she had done and what had been done to her, she decided that she wanted to spare her parents as much anxiety as she could over her own safety.

Cathy would ring them at least once a week and chat to her Mum and Dad. She recounted things about her work, happy stories, nothing dark. At least once every three months, she would come home for a weekend and pretend they were all a family again and she was still their little girl. It was like playacting and not too hard to do, although by the end of each visit she would find herself exhausted inside at the effort to sustain the pretence. Still, it was worth it. They went on with their lives, blissfully unaware of the real person she was for the rest of the time. As they were country folk at heart and almost never came to any city, she felt little concern they would find her darker secrets out.

When Cathy left home, she first went to Edinburgh and got a job as an administrative assistant to the boss of a manufacturing company. The wages were poor and it was hard to earn enough money to live on. It was also too close to home, only an hour's drive from the village her family lived in. While they did not come to town much, she feared she'd find them walking down the street when she least wanted to see them.

Cathy soon worked out that, for someone like herself, sex was the best exchange medium. She gave in to the boss's groping hands and pawing in his office, but on the basis that it advantaged her in both pay and other benefits. As both his public assistant and his private mistress, she doubled her salary and got a generous expense allowance on top.

After six months, she moved to Glasgow where her boss arranged a job for her with a friend of his, another MD in a business that he worked closely with. She had paid for that job reference in kind: giving him a last, all-night, loan of her body, and indulging all his wild fantasies.

It had been a similar deal with her new work in Glasgow. Her type of administrative assistant did as much work on the couch in his office, with the door locked, as she did on the phone or as a typist.

By the time she was in Glasgow, she had worked out that, if this was part of the deal for many bosses, she might as well make it pay for her in other ways. She got a night time job as a higher-class working girl, more discreet than those who worked the streets: no drugs and protection from catching something unwanted, baby included.

Cathy still kept her day job going. For one, it was easier to maintain the pretence with parents and friends back home that way. Of course, there was no way she could afford such a nice flat and all her nice clothes on an ordinary admin assistant's wages.

Then, she moved on to London. There was a bigger pool for daytime jobs and it was also better for other work. Here, lots of rich Arabs fancied trying a milk-skinned girl from the north with a touch of Scottish brogue. She had a knack of keeping her daytime bosses happy. She was good at organising other people to do work, using the boss's authority to persuade and cajole, sometime threaten and occasionally putting her own personal charms to work as well. Over five years, she had a succession of day jobs- always a step up from the job before. By now, she could easily support herself in these grandly titled Executive Manager roles. The night work was cream. More importantly, it filled an empty hole inside her: that part broken when her sister had died.

She knew, deep down, all men were bastards; all were determined to get one thing no matter what it cost the woman. She gave them that thing, but on her own terms and at her own price.

Apart from the men who paid her day job wages, Cathy had no friends. Neither the other night girls, nor the men she serviced, knew anything about her except a first name. No work colleagues or clients had her real address or private contact details. For those who needed to locate her, she gave a mobile phone number: one for day work and one for nights. Except for required business social functions, she never went out with her work colleagues. For night work, she met clients in discreet places where total privacy and security came as part of the package.

Cathy had one life at her family home as the dutiful and loving daughter who contacted and visited her parents regularly. When she came home, she said hello to the others in the village, as if they were long lost friends.

Then, she had another life in the city where she wore different clothes, had a comfortable apartment, well-paid work, both day and night, and a healthy bank balance. Her life drifted on by like that for seven years until she was twenty-three.

One day she woke up faintly bored. It was OK, her life was broadly satisfactory. But there was nothing in it she cared about, other than her parents, and she could never let them see inside her. She did not want a boyfriend or a long-term lover; she had met no one she trusted enough that way to let them see inside her world. It was better to let those who wanted or desired her to pay to rent her body for a short time and then be gone. But she wanted something more important in her life than that.

Sometimes she thought that, maybe, she should get a pet: a fluffy dog or a cat that gave her company when she was on her own. But she knew that that would involve a new form of dependency, some creature whose life depended on her coming home each night and providing food, water and exercise. Perhaps, a walk in the park. She did not want that level of commitment. She could always pay someone else to do this part, but she did not want that either as it would involve letting someone else into her private life by sharing apartment keys or whatever.

When Cathy did not work, she read. A few novels, but mainly true stories about other places. Some were books of explorers, some travel books of trips to other places, of their peoples of yesterday and today. Slowly, an image formed in her mind of going to live somewhere else, a place where no one knew her. She had more than a hundred thousand pounds from her night work in a Swiss bank account and her day job had its own bank account with several thousand pounds of spare cash.

One day, she came home from another ordinary day. She worked for the boss of a big city finance firm. Today, he was feeling frisky and decided he wanted to play with her more away from work, but she'd avoided that.

Cathy had met his wife at the office last week. Unlike some of the other wives who were vacuous airheads, only out to build their own image, she had genuinely liked this lady. As expected, her boss told Cathy how his wife did not appreciate him, how he was thinking of leaving her, how he really wanted something more than a casual romp in the office with Cathy, something ongoing and meaningful, a shared life.

Cathy had heard these lines too many times before. She knew they were another form of the eternal excuses these men used to justify their weak morals. Normally, she did not care. Provided the pay and other benefits were right, she would let these platitudes flow over her.

But, somehow, this man's clear lies irritated her. Tonight, he'd asked to take her out for dinner. Cathy had begged off, claiming a prior engagement. She did not want to spend an evening in bed with him- the days on the couch in the office were enough.

Tonight, was a rare night when she had no other engagements booked and she did not want any. She had been thinking about quitting her day job completely for a while now, she did not need the money. She had kept it going to maintain a veneer of respectability for the sake of her parents, still the dutiful daughter, not the high-class hooker.

Her day job also gave her something to do. She otherwise found her days to be mostly empty and purposeless. Over the years, she had come to hate weekends when she was mostly alone, with only her own company, during the day.

Cathy was sick of the inevitable bartering she did with her bosses around her availability for sexual favours. She decided she would rather just get paid for what she did at night. It was much simpler. No one lied. The men did not try to con her with promises of a future she did not want, they just paid for and got sex. She could not say she really enjoyed it- but at least it was a simple, straightforward transaction with no strings attached and no lies spoken.

But it meant living an ongoing lie, a lie which started when Cathy was eleven years-old and her uncle had raped her. That was bad. But when she discovered her had done it to her older sister, too, and, as a result, her own sister committed suicide- something broke apart inside her.

She hated her uncle; she never let him come near her again when she was alone. She would be polite to him in company, but only because she could not bear for her parents to know about his double betrayal.

After that first time, she had walled the memory off. But she had let it happen with other boys at school after that, hoping to find something in the act that was better than what had happened that first time. Even though pleasurable, it did not fill the emptiness inside her.

Cathy left school as soon as she was able. Soon after that, she began to use her body to make money, to buy her independence from everyone and everything. Yet, now, she seemed eternally trapped in living a double life and could not see any future ahead that she wanted.

Cathy was not suicidal. She had seen and lived through the way this action had torn a hole in her and her parents' lives. She could not bear to be that selfish and wasteful of her own life. But she could not think of any different thing she wanted to do. That is, until recently.

It was not as if a new life idea had opened before her. Rather, she knew she did not want to live here or like this, anymore. The idea of escape, travelling off to another place or places in an anonymous way, with a new unknown identity, became appealing. She began to make plans for a new life where nobody knew anything about her. Perhaps, it would allow real friends or deep relationships. Perhaps even, after a few years, a new and better relationship with her parents. An adult to adult one, not this one, forever trapped as the younger sister of a long-lost child and as a person who tried to live for both of them.

Tonight, Cathy was restless at her apartment, searching for something new. She decided there was no better time to make the move than now. She would do it in a respectable manner, she would give her current boss a month of notice so he could organise a replacement; she would do the same for her night time work. She would go on the internet now and look up flights and travel options to different places.

She wanted to go to the opposite side of the world. As far away from this place and this life as possible, maybe Australia or New Zealand, a place where they spoke English. She had enough money in her regular bank account to cover her flights and her living costs for at least a few months, without having to touch the other, much larger, bank account. She would travel as a backpacker, on the cheap. It fitted better with the image she wanted for her future: not as a high class hooker travelling the world and staying at posh hotels but, rather, a simple girl from the back of Scotland who had worked in various jobs across the UK and had now decided to see the world to make a new life for herself somewhere else.

After a week of researching various other countries, she settled on Australia as the place she wanted to move to.

Chapter 38 - A New Life in the Antipodes

Just over a month later, Cathy found herself in Melbourne.

Despite all the income from her former work, the furthest she had ever travelled before was to Paris, to which she had twice made day trips on the Eurostar from London. Her apartment in London had been her refuge from the world outside. She had chosen to stay there at all times, except when she was visiting her family in Scotland. The only exception had been these two trips to collect items of jewellery.

This arose because she was given an item from a master goldsmith in Paris by an appreciative lover. The maker's name was inscribed on the box. She had liked the style so much that she rang this man and ordered further pieces on each of her next two birthdays. Each time, she had gone and collected them in person.

These trips also allowed her to have discreet meetings with her Swiss- based financial advisor who was pleased to meet her there as part of the service of managing the funds she regularly deposited.

Despite numerous requests to accompany her clients on trips to the continent and beyond, she had consistently said "No" to their invitations. They could visit her, or she would go out and about with them in London, but that was the limit of her accommodation to them.

So, until this trip, she had never even been on an aeroplane, let alone gone over an ocean like the one which she could see below her.

Cathy decided to fly from Heathrow via the Middle East for no particular reason, other than it was the most direct route. She chose Melbourne as her destination. It was a similar-sized city to Sydney- but with a lower international profile. She had a vague dread of meeting a wealthy client in an airport, where her avoidance options were limited.

She enjoyed the flight, being left alone in a crowd, with no unsought attention. She ignored the couple beside her. Instead, she gazed out over the endless expanse of water, as countless miles of oceans passed beneath her. She was revelling in the sense that, at trip's end, she really would be on the other side of the world, a place where she thought her freedom was assured.

In Melbourne, she stayed for two weeks in a comfortable, self-contained apartment in the city. She liked this city. It had a comfortable old-world feel, not dissimilar to London. However, on her fifth day, she glimpsed a former client walking down the other side of the Bourke Street Mall. That decided her, it was too well patronised by the jet-set for her taste. She had her hair cut short with a red rinse, to reduce the chance of her being recognised by this man or others she had known from her former life.

That night, Cathy caught the train to Adelaide, deciding it was a far less visited city by the "Glitterati". This time, rather than staying in a swanky apartment, she became one of the backpacker-crowd, staying in a crowded hostel in downtown Adelaide.

She found it liberating to be surrounded by a mass of travellers from all corners of the world. So many pasts and futures intermingled. She was just plain Cathy, now a reddish brunette with a short bob hairstyle which was almost boyish looking, though her curvaceous body belied any idea she was asexual.

A few hopeful men from the hostel tried it on. She was so practised at deflecting unwanted attention that she barely noticed.

She had no clear idea where she would go or what she'd do now.

Two weeks passed as she drifted in and out of this place. She spent them walking around the city streets, shopping, catching the beach tram to Glenelg, having drinks and exchanging tales with other backpackers.

After a week, she sent a postcard to her parents. She felt she should let them know where she was, to spare them worry. She gave the address here to allow them to write, saying she expected to stay another month before she moved on and, when she did, she would soon give them her new address.

Cathy had never indicated she was not planning to return home. There would be time enough to let them know this when she had worked out a clear plan for her future.

She liked Adelaide. It was a comfortable city, not too big, with nice Victorian-era houses, similar to those found in many parts of London. It made her feel safe and at home. She thought that, perhaps, in a month or two, she would look for a place of her own here. A two-bedroom cottage in one of the suburbs near the city was something she could afford with her savings. Then, she would find a job where she used her brain and organisational skills to support herself. It would definitely not be a job that included supplying favours in return for advancement.

She enjoyed listening to the tales of travel told by other backpackers, but found little desire to go off exploring the cities and other famous places around the coasts of Australia. The one place she wanted to visit was the inland. It seemed to be a vast area, thousands of miles across, loosely termed "The Outback".

Her plan was not well-formed. Cathy remembered, from long ago, reading a book by a man named Neville Shute called, "A Town Like Alice." From this memory came a vague desire to see this place. She knew it was in the middle of Australia. The train line north from Adelaide to Darwin ran through it. It would be easy to travel that way. It was something to do before she found her own place, a job and settled into life in Adelaide.

Chapter 39 - Vanished

One day Cathy and three others, two girls and a bloke around her age, were sitting in a bar around the corner from the backpacker hostel. It was a typical afternoon, the type where one person said to anyone else in the lobby, "I am going for a drink, any other takers?" She and another girl, Julie, that she knew slightly, joined the proposing couple.

After half an hour, a man a few years older, looking to be in his early thirties, walked into the bar and greeted Julie. It was not a highly familiar greeting, just the sort that passing acquaintances make. He bought a drink and came over, asking Julie if he could join them.

As he sat down, he looked at Cathy with a searching intensity. She wondered why and moved her eyes away. He seemed to realise and apologised, explaining, "Sorry to stare. It is just you have a look that reminds me of someone else I used to know. For a half-second, I felt as if I was looking at her. But it is gone now, I'm sorry if it made you uncomfortable."

She shrugged and smiled, "I am sure it is just one of those deja vu moments we all sometimes get. I'm certain it was not me you knew."

He nodded, "No, similar but different."

At this point, the other couple got up and left, excusing themselves with other things to do. So now it was just three. First name introductions were made: Julie, Cathy and Mark.

They fell into the easy conversation of strangers. Cathy liked Julie, she was easy-going. They had chatted briefly three of four times and shared a couple drinks before today. Julie was Canadian and had worked in Sydney before coming here. She was heading for Perth next week to meet her boyfriend. She had met Mark, in passing over a cup of coffee, at the hostel the day before. After half an hour, Julie left saying she, too, had things to do.

Now, it was just Cathy and Mark left. They each bought another drink. Mark offered to buy this one for Cathy, but she declined, saying she was averse to buying rounds as then one had to keep score.

He nodded, not any way put out, as if he understood this need for personal independence. He asked Cathy where she was from. She used her standard story of a girl from Scotland who'd taken a city job in London and now wanted to see the wider world. She asked him about himself in return.

He said, "I am from everywhere and nowhere. My home is out there somewhere," indicating to the north with a broad sweep of his hand.

She was intrigued, "Out there is a lot of places. Is there nowhere in particular that you call home?"

Mark did not reply, immediately, but a flash of something passed over his face that she thought was pain. He covered it with a grin. "Well, you are right; out there is a lot of places. In the course of an average year, I live and work in many of them, scattered across inland Australia, what some folks call, "The Outback". Really it is the next place past where most other people live.

"At times I work on cattle stations, other times mines, sometimes I fix houses for my black friends, sometimes I go overseas to work for a bit.

I think of that big place out there as my home. I cannot point to just one place and say that is where I really belong. Tomorrow, I am heading up towards Alice Springs, a short drive of around 1500 kilometres. Sometimes, I stay there for a bit. But, this time, I am heading on through and going further north to do some work on a cattle station."

Cathy found herself being unexpectedly frank with this man, not giving any details of why but saying that she had found she really liked Adelaide and had started to think about settling here. She also told him of her long-standing interest to visit Alice Springs and the Outback, and how it was funny that he knew and was going to that place.

Mark said, "Well, if you want to head there tomorrow, make a one-way trip to Alice, come back by yourself, I am happy to offer you a ride."

Cathy shook her head, saying, "Thanks, but no thanks. I think I may go there, but not quite yet. When I do, I will take the train. I like travelling that way and I like the independence of making my own arrangements, not asking for help from others or fitting in around them."

Mark nodded again, "I am impressed, one of the very few completely independent people of the world. Don't you like the company of others?"

Cathy shrugged, "I wish I could say I do. My experience is most people want to give me something, whether I want it or not. Then, in return, they want something back- often a part of me. I don't want to be that something. I find it easier to live a life without obligations."

The talk drifted into safer topics, another hour of talking about the world at large and things and places of interest.

Cathy had an unformed sense that this man understood what she meant about being one's own person. It seemed to fit him as well as her. But there was also something more, as if they both had parts broken inside from their past, that trust was their missing commodity, neither trusted the world to give them good things, nor expected them of others.

As more than a week had passed since Cathy sent the letter to her parents, she checked at the hostel reception for any return letter as she came back into the lobby.

Sure enough, there was an envelope in the familiar hand of her mother, dated only three days before with an express sticker on the outside. She went and sat in a chair in the lounge to read it.

The first page was just the general chit chat of Scottish village life. The second page began with, "Your uncle called last weekend and asked how you were going on your travels. I told him you liked Adelaide and would be there for a bit. Amazingly, he is also on a trip to Australia himself, flying out the day after this letter, two days in Sydney before flying on to Adelaide. He asked for your address so he could call to see you and say hello. I gave it to him. I will post this by express mail so, hopefully, you will have got it before he arrives and be expecting him."

Cathy did her sums. The letter postmark date was three days ago. Her uncle could even arrive in Adelaide this afternoon, probably tomorrow or the day after was most likely. But it could be today!

Of all the people in the world that she never wanted to meet again, he was number one. She hated the way this nightmare had followed her here. It would be hard to avoid him if he came to this place. She just could not bear to see him. She must go somewhere else. She could not reveal this to her parents or he would know and may follow her again. She must vanish.

She was sitting lost in her own world, oblivious to the one around her. She became aware of a person sitting in the next seat.

She looked up. It was Mark.

He said, "Sorry to intrude, when I came inside I saw you sitting reading a letter with a shocked look on your face, like someone died. Is there anything I can do to help?"

She looked at him, surprised by her own directness, saying, "You said you were leaving tomorrow, going to Alice Springs. You offered me a lift.

"Could you leave tonight, that is right now? If you do, I will come with you, if that's OK?"

Mark shrugged, "Sure; today, tomorrow, it is all the same to me. My business in Adelaide is done; my car is in a car park around the corner. I can pack my things and be ready to go in five minutes if that suits you."

Cathy went upstairs and was packed in a minute. On returning to the lobby, she saw there was no one at reception. She scribbled a quick note telling of her early departure. "Something has come up and I need to leave unexpectedly. Don't worry about the extra days I have paid for- I don't need the money back."

As she finished writing, Mark came alongside. She folded the note, left it on the counter and they walked out to his car. There were two other people she recognised waiting in the lobby bar, so she waved to them and called out, "Goodbye, I'm leaving now."

That night, they stayed in side-by-side rooms in a little motel in a town called Burra, an old copper mining town.

In the late evening, they walked around parts of this historic town, chatting and enjoying the dusk stillness. They did not intrude any further on the other, both taking room service and going to bed early. Mark said he would call her to wake up at six am, as he wanted to get away early.

Chapter 40 - Hunting in the High Hills

Cathy was in a deep sleep when the knock came to her door.

"Six o'clock, time to go."

She dressed quickly and brought her bag outside. It was still dark, just a faint glow in the east, and the air was cold. She shivered, glad of her thick jumper though her legs were cold in the shorts.

Mark had the car engine idling and already there was faint heat in the cabin. She climbed in and curled her legs under her on the seat.

Mark looked at her curiously, "Bit cold, huh. Don't worry, in another minute it will be roasting and you will be able to stretch out like a cat in the sun. I always try to get going first thing; it's a habit of station life. In a couple hours, we can pull up for some breakfast and really enjoy it.

Seeing this is your first time to the bush, I thought I should show you a few sights along the way. We are heading up through the Flinders Ranges. There are spectacular mountains and view of scenic gorges which I thought you might like to see. Then, you will know where to come and visit next time you are up this way from Adelaide."

Cathy smiled at him. There was something warming in his manner. It came through as an obvious love for these places and a real pleasure in showing others. She said, "Well, aren't I the lucky one? Getting my own tour guide as well as my own Outback Tour. I can't imagine why I refused your kind offer the first time you made it."

He gave her a wicked smile back, "It is my pleasure, Ma'am. I always aim to please."

Cathy found herself laughing, really laughing. It felt so good, just to laugh and be happy, to become a carefree person, again. She could not remember the last time in her life when she had laughed with totally unexpected joy. She settled down to enjoy the journey, determined to make it a trip to remember and glad of this unexpected turn in her life.

As they drove along, the sky to the northeast slowly brightened, going through the full range of dawn colours. It had rained lightly during the night, just odd puddles on the road. But the remnants of cloud sat off to the east. The light captured them, high up at the edge of the world. It lit them with the softest mauve light. Then, as the light brightened, the hue changed to a rich pastel pink, flecked with orange and red edges.

Cathy watched spellbound. It took her back to her earliest childhood, faded memories of sunrises and sunsets of the Scottish Highlands, though here the colours and light were different. A tear trickled down her cheek, remembering a lost childhood and innocence gone; it was so long ago. She brushed it aside with her hand, determined to leave the past behind.

The sunrise had moved to a new level of surreal colour; a riot of mauves, pinks, reds, oranges and finally gold as the first light shafts streaked up from the still hidden sun disk. Soon, this distant extended kaleidoscope covered half the sky, layer on layer of cloud infused colour.

As suddenly as it came, it went. In another minute it had faded, now just the orange and gold remained as the light streamers grew ever brighter. Then, it was just gold as the sun disk touched the horizon.

Cathy turned to Mark and said, "I have seen many beautiful sunrises and sunsets as a child in Scotland. But this surpasses all that have come before. Did you turn it on just for me?"

Mark said, "I wish! Even for me, a hardened bushie who gets to see a new dawn most every day, that was one to remember. I think you deserve credit, if you had not prompted our early departure last night, I expect I would still be eating my breakfast in Adelaide. I will keep you as my good-luck charm if you keep bringing such special sights."

They breakfasted at Peterborough, a pastoral town an hour north of Burra. As the shops were now open, Mark stocked up on provisions for the trip. He suggested Cathy buy a pair of hard-wearing jeans, RM Williams he recommended, some shirts, a jacket and sturdy walking boots. He told her he was planning to take her walking the hills over the next two days.

She took his advice, modelling her new gear, which made them both laugh. She felt a simple sense of real joy, an almost forgotten emotion.

That night, they planned to stop at Wilpaena Pound Resort, arriving at lunch time. In the afternoon, they walked around the magic circle of mountains, their colour changing endlessly as the afternoon light moved around, the sun rays lighting one distant peak after another.

It was approaching dusk before they were back. They had walked for many hours with occasional rest stops to admire the view. They had adjoining motel rooms again and, tonight, they shared a meal and glass of wine in the adjoining restaurant, dancing firelight shadows from a roaring log fire were their welcome companion.

Cathy started yawning, unaccustomed to the early morning and all the walking; it must have been ten miles that they walked this afternoon. Her legs were aching from the unexpected exercise and her body glowed with a euphoric feeling from exertion and fresh air.

She said to Mark, "What is tomorrow's plan?"

He replied, "Have you ever been hunting? Tomorrow, I want to hunt goats in the ranges fifty miles north of here. I can usually bag three or four in the course of a day, which fills up the ice box on the back of my truck. Goat meat is a welcome change of diet for people who live up north of the dog fence. Up there are lots of dingoes but no goats. I have a Greek friend up there who likes nothing better than a meal made from a big old billy goat.

I promised him one on my next trip. To get it I will be leaving really early and it will be hard to get out of bed. The reward is being on the high mountains of the northern Flinders Ranges for a dawn which promises to be every bit the equal of what we saw this morning, with the difference that it will only be the two of us looking out from the top of the world.

However, it's OK if you want a sleep in. I am happy to go on my own and come back here to meet you again in the afternoon."

Cathy said, "Well, if you are prepared to put up with me, I am game. I sometimes went out with my father hunting pheasants when I was little, although he never let me shoot. I doubt I will be of any value as a hunter, but I would like to walk along with you and see this place at dawn, if I am not in your way. Please, tell me if I am, and I will stay here."

Mark looked at her appraisingly, "Well, you are a good walker, you proved that today, and you don't complain. If you promise not to talk at the times while we are stalking goats, I would enjoy your company."

Cathy nodded, "Deal, I have been silent most of my life. I only talked when I was little. I seemed to forget how to talk after my sister died. So, despite my chatter today, it is my normal state to be silent."

Mark put his hand on hers; an affectionate rather than intimate gesture. "I liked your talk. I am often silent and alone with my thoughts too, so the change is welcome. Please keep talking, it is sweet music. It is only during the hunt part you need to stop. "

Cathy turned her hand over and curled her fingers around his. "Thank you, I like talking to you, too. I think we have both lived most of our lives inside ourselves. It is good to have a friend to talk to."

A huge yawn came over her. She said, "I must go off to bed now or I won't be able to get up when you call me in the morning."

It seemed even darker than yesterday when Mark knocked on her door, saying, "It is time for the hunters to be out on the hills."

She looked at the bedside clock; it was only 4:30 in the morning. Blearily, she pulled on the clothes for the day, her RM Williams jeans to protect against the wiry grass and prickly bushes, a long-sleeved country shirt in a bright check that Mark had chosen for her, a waterproof safari jacket that she had chosen for herself, thinking it fitted the bush image, and the sturdy walking boots she had broken in yesterday, with thick socks inside, to protect her feet from any rubbing. Last of all was her Aussie style Akubra hat which Mark told her was an essential part of the get up of any self-respecting Aussie outback girl.

She smiled as she looked in the mirror, hardly glamorous but it was definitely a new appearance from what she had known.

Mark was waiting outside the door, fully dressed and also looking sleepy. He looked her over, nodded appreciatively, "I like it, someone who does not let fashion get in front of practicality. I see you have dressed the part."

Without further ado, he led her to the car and they drove away.

It was almost an hour until the first glimmers of light came into the eastern sky. Now, the landscape was a surround of high and higher ridges as they followed a narrow dirt road climbing up a valley.

As they turned onto it from the main road, Mark told Cathy it was about a half-hour drive to where they would leave their vehicle and the road was steep and a bit scary in places so she should just keep calm and enjoy the view. He had come up here several times before and the road was not as bad as it looked. He promised her that, at the end of the climb, it would be worthwhile.

The light was much brighter by the time they came to the top, a small clearing in a basin in the hills, with just enough space for three or four cars to park and turn round. The last five minutes had been really steep and, despite Mark's assurance, she felt anxiety as the vehicle slowly ground its way up a loose rocky track, wheels slipping and sliding as they gained and lost purchase. Sometimes, the car's lean to the side was so steep that it pushed her hard against the door or into Mark's solid arms which gripped the wheel.

She was pleased when the climb stopped. She stepped out into crisp autumn air and surveyed an almost perfect ring of further rising hills, olive scrub and pale white grass adorning pink-orange hillsides which glowed in the pre-dawn light.

Mark unpacked the gear from the tray of his vehicle, handing Cathy a backpack with a water bottle, snacks, a first aid kit and survival gear. It was relatively light. He put a bigger and heavier pack on his own back, then picked up a rifle with a shining scope and asked her if she wanted to try using it.

She took and examined it carefully. It felt solid but was less heavy than she'd imagined. "Yes, I will try it out, if you show me what to do. What type of gun is it?"

"It's a Browning 223, one of my favourite guns for hunting mid-sized game, like goats and pigs."

She saw it had a webbing strap for carrying and slid this over her shoulder to test how it felt as she stood there.

Mark took it back and showed her how to open and shut the breach, how to check to ensure it was not loaded, and how to best carry it in a way that left her hands free for walking and climbing. He picked up another gun, bigger and heavier looking, though not huge. He said it was a 243, similar but with more stopping power for the big old billy goats.

They headed off following a literal goat track. It skirted their clearing and wound its way up the shoulder of a hill, heading directly towards the lightening sky. Mark pointing out signs of recent goat activity, hoof marks in patches of soft dirt and fresh dung, still steaming in the cool air.

They climbed steadily. Cathy could see her breath steaming in the air as she breathed deeply to power her climb. Her legs were aching now, a legacy of yesterday's unaccustomed use, now followed on by this morning's fresh challenge.

Mark looked back at her, eyebrows raised in inquiry as to how she was coping. She gave him her best grin and a 'thumbs up', signalling she was doing fine. They kept on, climbing ever upward, stepping up over boulders, grabbing and pushing the brush aside, dodging the prickly bushes. At last, the effort eased as they came to where the steep hill shoulder eased into a gentle slope climbing to a ridge above. The path widened and they walked side by side. Mark put a finger to his lips and Cathy nodded.

Fifty yards back from the crest, he took off his pack and rifle, quietly placing them on the ground, indicating to her to do the same. From his pack, he took a set of binoculars. Now, he led her in a low crouch to the ridge crest, going the last few yards on hands and knees, stopping just as their view cleared the ridge. They were now lying, facedown, stretched out side by side, looking out for miles.

Before them lay a huge bowl shaped from grassy hillsides. Dotted across it were at least a hundred white, brown and black dots, some multicoloured. Most were several hundred metres away and, as she watched, they gradually resolved themselves into discrete goats: mothers with their kids alongside, big billy goats with horns standing sentinel, mid-sized animals with spiky little horns. Interspersed between them were other animals which she now recognised as kangaroos, perhaps wallabies, all sharing this grassland in the early morning light.

It was like an African panorama from a wildlife documentary.

A small creek came down from a gap between two hills and pools of water along its course glistened below in the soft light.

She looked up. The whole eastern sky was alight; not so many colours in the clouds as yesterday, but faint high streamers of high cloud glowing a brilliant red and below soft pinks, oranges and gold of hills and sky joining and sliding into one another. It was a place where all the colours seemed to merge into layer after layer, making it hard to separate earth and sky. They lay side by side watching spellbound until the sun finally crested the horizon, bathing their whole world in golden light. It was breathtakingly and awe-inspiring.

They felt as if they were two lesser gods watching the sun god recreate the world anew. The word 'beautiful' seemed inadequate, closer to puny, as a way of describing this sight.

Cathy felt an immense gratitude to this man for bringing her here to show her this. Her whole trip across the world was worth it for this moment alone, a place where earth and sky met in a perfect fusion of light and colour.

She reached over and put her hand on his shoulder. He looked up and met her eyes, inquiring.

She whispered, "Thank you for bringing me. This is a sight that will live forever in my mind. No photo or words could ever do it justice. I am glad I shared it with you. It is a memory to hold forever."

He nodded, silent but seemed to be moved by her words.

As the gold light faded into day, reality returned. He brought her back from the ridge and explained their tactics. He would take her around the side of the hill which they were now on, to the place where the creek cut through. They would follow the creek bed down into the middle of the fields.

There they would choose an ambush point, using one of the rocky knolls that marked its passage.

He gave her a quick lesson on using her rifle, showing her how to use her pack to support it. How, while lying prone, to sight it and hold it steady, how to ease the trigger back while breathing steadily.

She said she was not sure she could shoot when the moment came, but she would bring the rifle along and see how she went.

They headed off and worked their way around the hill shoulder, staying below the crest. Mark said they did not need to be quiet for this part, as the hill would block the sound and sight of their passage and their downwind location would block their scent. But, once they came to the creek, they would have to be totally quiet and be really careful. These goats were regularly hunted, at the weekends, by hunters from Adelaide and, as a result, were very wary.

For now, they walked and talked, saying nothing significant but making little notes on the life around: the distinctive call of an eagle high in the sky, bright colours of feeding parrots flashing past, the smell of damp earth and an occasional place infused with the semi-sweet fragrance of a flowering shrub.

The walking was easy, a gentle downhill passage with only occasional boulders to navigate. They came to where the creek ran in little cascades down a steep rocky hillside before spreading into pools below. It was steep coming down over the rocks and boulders. They went slowly, carefully, placing each foot on a solid place before advancing, gently pushing aside any branches to allow passage.

Cathy's mind was totally in the moment, all else ignored as she gave full attention to making silent steps. They reached the bottom and kept following the creek bed. The ground had looked flat from above but, down here, the creek ran below head high banks, with dense foliage hiding the foreground. It seemed like a lost place. They came to a rocky knoll where water trickled down. The view opened and Mark led Cathy forward, both going on their hands and knees. The goats were now much closer; the nearest group was about 200 yards away.

Mark pointed to another rocky knoll further down, two thirds of the way to the nearest goats. "Our target is to get to there, unseen," he said.

After this second knoll, it was only open ground with the creek breaking into bigger pools. Several kangaroos were drinking at the closest pool. It looked like a group of goats were heading there to supplant the kangaroos at the watering point.

Mark led the way now, climbing up to the outside of the creek bed but staying within the shelter of the fringing trees. Once past the open rocks, he led them back into the creek's full shelter. Now, glimpses of goats were visible, grazing below. There was a light wind blowing into their faces.

Mark watched the goats intensely as he placed each step, several times pausing in mid-stride as a sentry goat raised its head, sniffed the air and looked around intently.

It seemed to take forever to cover this part, held in a state of suspended animation. Cathy felt her heart beating strongly in her chest and ringing in her ears, it sounded so loud she thought the rest of the world must hear it, too.

At last, they were in position. The goats continued to graze undisturbed. She settled herself with her pack on the ground in front. Mark took her gun and loaded five bullets into the magazine, then inserted one more into the breach, closed it and slid the safety catch on. The only noises from his actions were faint, almost inaudible, clicks.

He signed, indicating that when she was ready to shoot, she should slide the safety catch off. Now, it was up to her.

He loaded his own rifle, positioning himself two metres to her side on a higher ridge. He indicated a group of six goats walking towards the water. He pointed to the leader, a big billy goat with well-formed horns. "Mine," he mouthed and signed.

Cathy nodded. After billy goat gruff came three females with young at foot then, at the back, two almost grown goats, spiky little horns on their heads. Mark indicated that she should select between these two to choose her target.

She acknowledged and calmed herself. The goats kept coming until the billy had his forelegs in the water, having a last look around before he lowered his head to drink. All the other goats reached the water's edge and started to walk in to drink, except the female with the largest kid. This goat seemed to be standing sentry, nervously looking around and raising its nose to scent the air, while the others drank.

Mark indicated Cathy should shoot when she was ready. He slid off the safety catch of his rifle. She did the same and brought her rifle into line, with her vision looking through the scope. She selected the rear-most of her two goat targets and placed the cross hairs on its mid chest behind the point of shoulder, as she'd been instructed.

Now or never, she thought, giving all her concentration to holding steady while she squeezed the trigger. The huge blast reverberated from in front of her. A split second later, the second blast came from her side.

When her senses returned, she looked to where the goats were. The front billy was resting on its chest, nose in the water, having fallen where it stood. Her target had not moved; although perhaps its head had come up slightly.

The other goats had jumped in alarm, as if to flee, looking around for the source of the sound. As they searched for danger, a second crack sounded from her side. The second juvenile goat slumped to the ground.

Cathy kept watching as a long, slow second passed. Now, her own target had crumpled at the knees to an ungainly sitting position, on its chest with its head resting on the ground. The remaining goats rushed away towards the distant hillside.

Mark came across, removed the bullets from her rifle and handed it to her, breach open. His own was already similarly disarmed. He led the way across the open ground to the pool below.

Cathy looked in amazement at her goat as she approached. It seemed quite beautiful, brown skin with mottled white patches. It looked startled in death, eyes wide, as if caught by surprise as it sat there.

Mark pointed to the entry hole where her bullet had struck, two inches higher and three inches behind where she had aimed.

"That was a good shot. It took out the major blood vessels at the back of the heart, with death in seconds from massive blood loss."

He paused and continued "I don't think it felt anything," seeming to sense her concern that it had not suffered. "The bullet goes so fast it would have been through it before it knew. With that damage, there would be no blood to its brain and no awareness from then on."

She felt relief that it had been done without suffering but, most of all, she felt great exultation- the successful hunter had made her first kill. This satisfaction of a primal instinct washed over her.

She watched as Mark quickly eviscerated the bodies and removed their heads and feet. Then he found two poles, each about two metres long. He asked Cathy if she felt she could help him carry them back. He explained they would need to do it in stages: first to the top of the hill, where they would have a big rest, before carrying them down the other side to the car. This first bit to the top of the hill would be hardest, lifting the weight. They would try to do it in one go but he could always come back a second time, if needed.

Mark estimated the dressed weight of the three goats combined was 80 to 90 kilos. He said he thought they could manage it if he arranged the weight so that he took about two thirds and she took about a third. He would go at the back as they went up the hill, using his strength to push them both forward as they climbed.

Cathy was unsure if she was strong enough but she said she'd do her very best.

Soon, the goats were tied to the two poles, the smaller two to one side and the big one on the other side, to give balance. The weight was towards the back. Mark got Cathy into position to stand at the front. He lifted the poles on her shoulders, picked up his heavy ends and rested them on his shoulders.

"OK, off we go, nice and steady, watching where you step. Don't be scared to drop them if you lose your balance or they get too heavy."

It was hard work but manageable. As the angle of the hill increased, she could feel the weight easing as more load transferred to the back, but now she had to lift both herself and the poles. She could feel Mark's steady steps continually pushing her forward. She kept stepping ahead, a foot at a time, her legs straining to lift with every step.

After five minutes, Mark called a halt saying they were past halfway to the top. They sat side by side on a rock until they got their breath back. Considering he had been lifting most of the weight, Mark seemed in good shape, breathing hard, but otherwise showing little sign of strain. After his breathing returned to normal, he did a couple stretches before they pushed on. The next stage was much steeper and harder. Soon, her legs were screaming and she could hear Mark grunting with the effort of each step as he walked behind her. They did just over half before Mark called another rest. The crest of the hill was in sight, but the steepest part lay in front. He separated the poles, and they came up the last leg carrying one pole at a time. Finally, all three goats were at the top.

They both sprawled out on the ground sucking in air until their heart pounding and breathing slowed and their legs regained strength.

After a few more minutes, Mark stood up and began searching the ground. Soon he found a particular rock and picked it up.

Cathy asked what it was.

He showed her that this rock had a fossil in its centre, a perfectly formed snail outline. He told her it had been made hundreds of millions of years ago when this land lay at the bottom of a shallow sea. Since then, it had been thrust up far into the sky.

It was a time so distant that it lay beyond her comprehension. She held the rock herself and traced the outline with her finger, feeling as if this was a time machine drawing her back into an incredibly ancient past before even dinosaurs walked. She hunted around amongst the other rocks, now looking at each fractured face carefully. Sure enough, within a minute, she found another fossil, similar but different, another ancient creature of the sea, this one oval-shaped, with stripes running across the middle. Mark called it a trilobite. Almost reverently, she put it down again. She looked at the land below her feet with new understanding of its antiquity and history and, in a small way, began to share the passion for it that so obviously permeated Mark.

Mark hunted around some more and found fragments of aboriginal flint chippings, showing these to her. He told her they were made by the aboriginals in the process of making a stone tool like a knife or spear head, which they would have used for hunting.

Now, she had a second picture in her mind. She imagined these dark people of millennia past, sitting here on this hilltop, surveying the view as they prepared their tools and planned their hunts. She wondered if they had also used the creek as an ambush point. She asked Mark.

"Almost certainly," he said. "They are such skilful hunters. I have seen a black man from this country stalk a kangaroo so close that he reached out and caught its tail without the need for a spear or stone.

"They would have used the creek and the water pools as we did today, but they could also catch animals by stalking them across ground so open that to us there seems nowhere to hide."

They each took a drink and snack bar from their packs before heading down the other side. The view was still marvellous, but the magic of early morning light was gone, along with the animals, now seen only as distant dots of far hillsides.

The walk back to the car seemed easy after the climb. They had a trail to follow and Mark was now at the front taking most of the weight while she walked easily behind, supporting her end and enjoying the view. The drive back was uneventful, and they had a restful afternoon at the camp. Cathy went for a walk by herself along the creek, while Mark stayed in his room.

They ate an early dinner in the bar and retired early, both tired. Over dinner, Mark had said he wanted to be away early again the next morning, to drive on to Coober Pedy, where they had a dinner date. He told her of a phone call he had made there this afternoon to tell of his hunting success, saying he would bring a promised goat. He said the man asked if he could be there by early afternoon, they were planning a big family celebration that night and the billy goat would be a perfect centrepiece for a traditional Greek feast. So, despite previous plans for another day of sightseeing, they needed to go early and directly to this place. He promised the dinner would make it worthwhile.

They rose and left at five. This morning, the sunset was behind them unseen. They drove southwest for two hours stopping for a quick breakfast at Port Augusta. After that, it was many long and featureless hours of bitumen driving, heading north along the main road to Alice Springs, the Stuart Highway. They arrived, as they had planned, in the early afternoon.

Coober Pedy was a strange and dusty town, a hot-potch of buildings which took all shapes and styles. Its central feature was an endless sprawl of shops selling opals.

They pulled up outside a big gaudy house, obviously owned by a prosperous inhabitant. It rose high above its neighbours and boasted one of the few flower gardens in sight out the front. Mark tooted the horn. A burly man, thick set with dark hair turning to grey, came out.

Mark called out "Nikko, I have your goat, as promised. I hope we are in good time for the feast tonight."

"Marco," the man exclaimed, "You have come most fast. I told my Athena you would come soon; but she said not till later, too far to drive so quick from the goat mountains; mountains like in our Greece."

They were shown inside and given large tumblers of a sweet, green iced drink which tasted faintly of limes, lemons and green herbs. It was refreshing after the heat of the day. They were only part finished when there followed retsina, ouzo and a selection of bread and dips.

Athena served them; she was a small woman with a mass of jet-black hair. She looked years younger than her husband, with a ready smile, saying, "Marco, who is your friend? You must introduce us, it is most impolite not to do so. I have fixed your regular room for tonight, the big room with the balcony you like at the top of the house. I will show Catherine around while you men talk."

As Cathy followed her up the stairs, Athena explained that tonight was an unofficial engagement party for their daughter Cassandra- Cassie, as most people called her. She and her fiancée, Stefan, had gone off to Adelaide yesterday, shopping for a ring. They were due back in town later this afternoon. When they returned, there would be a celebration.

It turned out that Nikko was a prosperous opal and gem trader who owned a busy shop in the middle of town. He bought from miners and sold both wholesale to other jewellers and to the town's many visitors.

Over the years, they had prospered in this place. Now, their daughter was marrying into another local Greek family, also in the opal business.

Athena's stories rattled out, "You would think that with so many stones in Nikko's business there would be one to suit my daughter, one that could be made into a ring. But no, she told Stefan she wants a diamond, a big, fat diamond, paid for in hard dollars by her future husband, not some cut price stone taken from Nikko or Stefan's business.

"So they went to Adelaide, to visit the most expensive jewellery shops. Last night, they rang to say they have bought the perfect ring and are bringing it back to show us all and celebrate."

So, on the strength of this and a phone call from Marco yesterday, telling us he had a huge goat to roast, Athena explained they had decided to have an impromptu engagement feast tonight.

There would of course be a more formal engagement party on the due date, but she and all her friends had all got to work today making many foods: sweet pastries, lamb dishes, salad's, roasted lemon chickens, "much food and most delicious."

It was to be a surprise for the returning guests. But, the most special part, was the whole roast goat. It would be cooked on the spit for many hours, according to Nikko's secret recipe, ready for a night of feasting.

As she talked, Athena walked Cathy from room to room, showing her the main features. Despite what appeared to Cathy as a gaudy exterior, the interior of the house was a classic piece of the Mediterranean brought to this faraway place, done with exquisite taste.

They came to the third level, just an attic room with a big balcony. They ascended by narrow stairs. It was a lovely open room, looking out above the other houses of the town. In its centre was a huge bed and around the perimeter were various pieces of furniture: chairs, a dresser and a marble washbasin. Folding doors led to a marble terrace with terracotta pots and wrought iron chairs.

"This is Mark's special room. He has stayed here many times when he visits. He and my husband have done much business over many years which has made them both lots of money. When Mark comes, this is always for him- even if we have other guests, we always give this to him. Mark is like a son to Nikko, though now, Stefan will be that son. I think you will find the bed comfortable and have a good night together, yes."

Cathy realised that Athena had assumed that she and Mark were a couple; the bed was for them both to share. Perhaps Mark had come here before with other women.

She felt a flash of embarrassment; she did not think this was Mark's plan. She realised it would be impolite to say otherwise, it would cause embarrassment to her host and seem ungracious. She turned and smiled at the lady saying, "Thank you so much, it looks very comfortable."

As they came downstairs, the goat was being carried to the courtyard at the back. A fire of coals was glowing, and it was lifted onto a spit where it was basted with oil and herbs and then set in place to slowly turn away for hours.

It was a wonderful night, great company, so many stories that had her laughing until her sides ached. Nikko was a natural story teller and Athena could also hold her own. Between the stories came plates of steaming food, with aromas to die for: roast goat slices, chickens with lemon and garlic, moussaka, souvlaki, spicy lamb meatballs on skewers, then sweet delicacies, little deep fried sweet dumplings, yoghurt with honey and walnuts, delicious honey and almond pastries. It was all washed down with endless glasses of retsina and ouzo.

As the night progressed, it turned into music and dancing. Everyone joined in, forming lines and groups that ebbed and flowed. One of the dances reminded her of the Zorba music, others Cathy did not know and they had unpronounceable names- but she joined in with abandon, as did Mark, sometimes dancing briefly together, mostly with other partners.

At last, the night subsided into quiet reflexion as the guests departed. Now, she was yawning and tired. Athena turned to Mark, "Lady Catherine is tired. I have shown her where her room is and brought her things up. Now, you must bring her up to it, Mark."

Mark had the good grace to look sheep-faced as her rose to escort her. She was feeling light-headed from all the wine. At times, he put out his hand to steady her as they climbed. She liked the solid feeling of his arm against her shoulders as he did. She decided that there were far worse things than having this man's body next to hers in bed, whatever followed. It was not her plan, but it felt right.

At the top landing, as Mark opened the door, Cathy felt quite tipsy and her body swayed. His arm went firmly around her shoulders and she leaned into him saying, "That feels good, your arm around me like that."

He brought her over to the bed. She lay back, her head spinning. She felt him take her shoes off. She thought the undressing would continue, not minding. Instead, she felt him pull back the covers, lift her under then tuck her in, snug and warm.

She had a half-formed intent to invite him to come alongside her. But her mind was drifting and the words would not form. She had a vague awareness of him taking a pillow from the other side and a blanket from the cupboard as she fell into a deep sleep.

She woke with a dry mouth and needing to go to the toilet. She remembered it was down on the next level and stumbled down the stairs. She found a glass and drank water to clear her head.

She was not used to having more than one or two drinks on any occasion, even when entertaining guests. She had mastered the art of appearing to drink but stopping after the first couple. It had been much better in her previous life to keep a clear head.

But, last night, she was captivated by the fun and her glass was endlessly full. She kept drinking it down, sip by sip. Now, she felt faint embarrassment and hoped she had not been silly in her exuberance.

She walked back upstairs feeling cold and almost sober, though she knew that was a mirage. It would get worse before it got better. She was in for a hangover of the sort she had not had for many years.

She felt like being minded, the way her mother still did for her when she was at home, tucked into bed with a warm bottle.

Cathy tried to go quietly, but her balance was still not fully there. She tripped on her bag lying on the floor as she walked back to the bed, stumbling and reaching out for support.

Suddenly, Mark was alongside her, steadying her and guiding her to the bed. She did not know where he had come from; he was so silent and moved so easily, like a cat.

He sat her on the edge of the bed and went to pull away. She held onto his hand and pulled him back, "Come, lie next to me. I think I am still drunk and will have a hangover in the morning. It would be nice to have you next to me, minding me, like the way when I was a little girl I used to cuddle in next to my mother and father."

She climbed under the covers and moved across to the centre, indicating a space for Mark to lie next to her. She realised she was still wearing her clothes from the night before, as was he. He was lying on his back, as if self- conscious. She took his hand and pulled him towards her so he was lying on his side facing her. She moved her shoulder in against his chest saying. "I hope you don't mind. I just want to be held."

As she spoke, she turned her back into his chest and felt his body push along her length, hard and strong, yet enfolding. She took his hand and pulled it over her, holding the flat of his palm against her belly in the mid-place. He pushed his hand gently against her belly and lightly stroked it as she snuggled tight against him. Her eyes were closing again. She felt comfortable and sleepy and drifted away, as if floating on a white cloud.

The sky was light, but it was still early when she woke again. Mark was sleeping beside her, breathing softly and regularly. His hand was still resting on her belly. It felt so good. She pushed it more firmly against her and he stirred. She turned to face him, enfolded in his arms.

His face looked seriously intent as she moved her face almost up to it, kissing him lightly on the nose. "I know I will feel sick later, but for now, lying here like this, I feel unbelievably comfy. Thank you for minding me in the night. My experience with men had not been so good over the years. It is wonderful to find one I can trust."

Mark's arms tightened around her. She felt his aroused maleness, it was a normal part of waking for most men, and a big part of her wanted to relieve it.

He said, "I am glad you feel can trust me, I am first and foremost your friend. Though, when I feel you lying here, your body touching mine, I am not so sure I trust myself that much. I will try to pretend there is no gorgeous woman lying here."

She kissed his nose again. "Oh, that," she said looking down at his waist. I don't mind about that- you are definitely a man. What I mean is that I trust you because you have not tried to make me do anything I don't want to do, that is something very precious.

"I think I want that part of you," she said, looking directly into his eyes and then taking his hand and placing it on her breast, undoing the buttons with her other hand and sliding it under her top where he could feel her nipple. He stroked it gently and she could feel both her arousal and his growing.

But then, her mind reasserted itself, saying, "Before we both decide if we really want that to happen, I need to tell you about me. It is something you deserve to know and it is my moment of truth- a part of my life untold to anyone before. It is not a pretty story, but I want you to know who I am and why."

She turned away from him as she spoke, deciding she needed the anonymity of not seeing his face as she revealed her past to him. She felt his arms go back around her, this time holding her whole body against his, maintaining an intimate physical link that gave her an amazing sense of security. It felt so good just to be held in this embrace.

She started her story at the beginning, when she was a little girl, describing her memory in the third person, almost as if it had happened to somebody else- it seemed less painful that way.

Chapter 41 - Story of a Little Girl

Anne had read through the next part of the diary several times. She had thought, as time went by, she would get inured to the awfulness of the story that Cathy had told Mark and yet she had not. Each time she read it she felt fresh outrage rise at what had been done against an innocent child- in fact, two innocent children.

She had never fully understood the word hate before. Now, it inhabited her in a totally visceral way as this story emerged. If someone did this to her child, she would kill them like a person stepping on a cockroach. And she could feel this emotion well-up inside Mark, too, in a way that was far scarier; to him killing was a thing of little moment that he was practiced at. She had a sense that if Mark had ever met the perpetrator of this horror, his action would have been swift and fatal.

Now that she needed to tell this girl's story, Anne struggled to find a way to put into words what she read. It was too private, painful and intimate to add it directly from the diary into her book, the way she had done with many other parts of the story. It was a secret that Cathy had been determined not to share with others. So, it was impossible to tell this in a book read by others. Still, she owed it to this person not to let the story be buried and slide away. In writing it out, almost word for word, it was clear Mark decided it must be recorded. Anne felt the need to be faithful to this, too.

In the end, Anne realised she needed two versions: a simple, public version that told of this girl having a difficult childhood, with the devastating loss of her sister, who was two years older than her, when she was ten. The consequences of this catastrophe flowed through into her teenage and adult life, so that she became a person who kept almost entirely to herself, living a mostly hidden life- except for visiting her parents regularly.

Then, Anne wrote out the private version, almost verbatim from Mark's diary. It was a thing that should go to the UK police for further investigation, though in a highly-sensitive manner she thought. She understood that the NT police had made some preliminary inquiries with their UK counterparts, but they had not provided them with this transcript as yet, leaving it to Anne to pursue her own inquiries first.

In the meeting Anne had in England with Cathy's parents, she had given no clue to this story. Their only observation was that they not seen Cathy's Uncle since before he travelled to Australia, saying he hoped to catch with his niece. As he was in the military, often on secret special deployments into remote parts of the world for extended periods, they had not found it remarkable that a couple years had passed without hearing from him. Anne found it strange, though. She understood the NT police had made discreet inquiries with UK police as to this man's whereabouts and they, in turn, had inquired with the UK army without getting a clear answer back.

This was not in a situation where charges were likely. Without Cathy to tell it or Mark to give first-hand testimony, what he said was done to the child in the story in his diary, was only hearsay.

Anne wrote out this story, word by word and line by line in a separate file titled 'Cathy's Story'- *an innocuous title for a house of horrors*, was the way she thought of it. She saved it on a separate memory stick which David encrypted, to stop others from unintentionally seeing it. Each night, she read the part she had written to David, as a way of letting this piece of poison leave her mind. She wrote it as a third person narrative told by Mark:

Cathy told me how she had an uncle who was in his early twenties, and who seemed incredibly handsome to her and her sister when she they were little girls. He was always around at her place, seeing her and her sister, and particularly paying attention to her sister who was two years older. She would often sit in his lap as would her sister. It had always seemed harmless fun.

One day, when she heading off to visit friends, she saw her uncle walking with her sister, going alongside the lake, towards the forest.

That afternoon her uncle was not there. Her mother said he had left to go away overseas tonight, this was his last visit for a few months. She stayed talking to her Mum for a while, eating fresh cookies she had baked. There was no sign of her sister, she wondered if she had gone out.

Her Mum said Cathy told her she had a headache and had gone up to her room, after her Uncle had left. She went up and tried to open the door, but it was closed and locked. She could hear her sister in the bedroom crying and she would not let her come in. She said she had a still had a headache and wanted to be left alone.

Next day her sister was nowhere to be found, they searched the house and surrounding fields but did not find her. They called the police and the police organised a search, but nothing was found.

People thought she must have run away, she sometimes got cross and moody, and a few times she had gone off to the next town, saying she was sick of being at home and was going away.

But that was only normal older sister stuff, she would always say "Fifi, I am going off on my own for a day. Don't tell anyone, I just need time out but will be back in a day."

And she had always come home the way she promised. The others thought this must be what she had done, and she would turn up the next day or the day after at most.

But she did not believe it because her sister had not said goodbye to her this time. She felt really worried, particularly as she had locked herself in her room the day before, crying.

They found her on the third day, or at least a fisherman did. She was floating face down in the middle of the lake, way out from the edge. She was only wearing a nightie with nothing underneath.

They would not let her look, they said the fish had been nibbling at her for three days, it had made a terrible mess, eating lots of bits of her face and skin and private parts.

They did a post mortem and said it was inconclusive, they thought she must have had an accident and fallen into the water from the jetty early in the morning, while still in her night clothes.

The police called it accidental drowning, although that did not seem right to her, it was unlike her sister to go down to the lake before she got dressed, she had never known her to do this before.

That was when she took her sisters name. The funeral was horrid, all those people standing there and saying nice things about her sister and her Mum and Dad standing there crying, so heartbroken. Her uncle was not there, he was over in the Middle East.

On the day of the funeral she decided she wanted to try and make her parents happy again, to become her sister and, by living the part of her sister, make them forget about that awful thing that happened.

The next day she announced that from now she would be called Cathy and she tried to act like her sister. People had gone along with it and humoured her as if this was just a strange request from a little girl that they needed to accommodate. She heard people say, a couple times, that it was her own way of working through her grief.

It was a year until she saw her uncle again. Now she was starting to grow up herself, she had little bumps on her chest now and the place where he used to touch her between her legs was changing too, little hairs growing around the edges. One day her uncle was there when she came home from school.

Her parents were both out, but her uncle was sitting in an armchair, as if waiting for her. She ran and hugged him. He told her to come and sit on his lap. She did, but now felt self-conscious that he would see the way her body was changing. She was not sure she wanted him to see or touch her in those private places anymore.

He asked where her Mum and Dad were. She said, "They have gone to a meeting in the town and then will stay there for dinner. They said they will not be back until late. They told me to fix my own dinner."

At that her Uncle gave her a great big smile. "That is great. That means I have you all to myself for hours. I can't wait to see how you have changed since I saw you last."

He looked critically at her chest. I can even see little bumps growing where there were none before. Then he took her to her bedroom, telling he wanted her to take her dress off so he could have a closer look.

She did, feeling even more self-conscious. He sat her back on his lap, wearing only her panties and he fondled the little pimples on her chest as he called them. It did feel nice and she could feel that hard lump in his trousers again. Then he picked her up and carried her over to the bed where he lay her down, pulling off her panties and saying he wanted to look at that place.

She let him and felt him put his fingers inside, much further than before. At first it felt nice but then it hurt as he pushed in further. Then he took his clothes and she saw him standing there with his huge red thing, she had seen it before but she had never seen it with all his clothes off.

He told her to stay lying on the bed and he was going to have a feel inside that place with his thing. She did not want him to do that, she knew now it was a thing that only grown-ups did, and she was still a little girl. She shook her head and tried to say no. But he held her down on the bed and put his body on top of hers. He forced legs apart and pushed and pushed there with his thing. She started to cry, saying to stop, that he was really hurting, but he would not listen, it seemed like he pretended not to hear her, even though she was crying out to stop.

He just kept pushing and pushing and it hurt more and more. Finally something gave way and it went right inside her. Then he lay on top of her pushing it in and out, over and over again, until suddenly he gave a big shudder and lay still.

After, when he got dressed, he told her she must never tell her parents about this, or they would both get into big trouble. She promised not to, she did not know what else to say.

Then she fixed him some dinner. He seemed in a hurry to go, even though she said he should stay to say hello to her parents. They ate quickly and she thought he would go after that. But, just as he was leaving, he said he had changed his mind and he could stay a bit longer.

He brought her back up to her room, saying he wanted to try it out with her one more time before he left. So, he did it again. This time it did not hurt quite so much. Soon he finished again with another big shudder.

As he dressed to go he said to her. "I thought I would have to wait another year until you were ready. But, even though you are a year younger than your sister was when I first did it to her, you were ready too and I really liked it with you, just as much as with her. Soon you will learn to like it too."

Now she glimpsed a terrible truth. She asked him, "What do you mean; you did it to my sister?"

He said, "Last time I was here, a couple days before she died, I took her for a walk in the forest, down by the lake. When we got there, I made her take her clothes off, just like with you. Then I made her lie down on a blanket I brought and I did it with her, just the same as with you.

"She was bigger and stronger, and she tried to fight me off. But I held her down until I had finished. She was cross and crying afterwards saying I should not have done that.

"I told her she would soon get used to it and enjoy it, that we would do it lots more times until she learned to like it as much as I did.

"She ran away back to the house, and I went back to the army base because I had to leave that night. I was sad when I heard she had died as I would not get the chance to do it with her anymore.

"But once I got back from overseas, I decided to come and visit you to see if you were ready to try it too. It is lucky I found you here all by yourself, so I did not have to wait to try it with you. You even have her name now. So, it is like one Cathy has gone away and I have the second Cathy in her place, just as good as the first one."

Cathy stood looking at his gloating face. She could not understand how she had ever liked him. Now she understood what had happened on that day, that what he had done was the reason why her sister had died.

She felt white hot rage towards him. Despite her small stature she screamed at him. "Get out, you murdering bastard. You raped my sister and she killed herself. You did not care that she had died. The only thing you cared about was doing the same to me as well. I will not tell my parents because I could not bear for them to know. But you will never, ever touch my again, if you do I will kill you, I promise you that."

She ran to the kitchen and got the biggest knife she could find and stood in the corner waving at him lest he try to come near her again.

He looked at her, shrugged, then got in the car and drove away. After he was gone she felt so sick and disgusted with herself, even though she pretended she was happy to see her parents when they came home, determined they should never know.

Anne got to the end of her writing of this small part after three tortuous days. It was only five pages of printed text, but she felt she had lived a lifetime in writing these words, telling and reliving a monstrosity done to a child by an evil man.

She placed herself in the mind of Cathy, in the circle of this man's comfort and imagined how it might have gone. She felt Mark's arms tighten around Cathy as she worked her way through the story, telling every intimate detail. When she had finished the most awful part, Mark wrote that, when she turned her face back to him, he said, "He deserves to die. I will make sure that one day soon he will."

The diary told Anne that Cathy pushed her finger to Mark's lips, telling him to calm down, she would never let her Uncle find or touch her again and how she had watched unspeaking until Mark's rage abated.

When Mark was calm again, she'd continued her story; how her life had drifted out of control after that, with this terrible secret that she could not tell anyone about, how this man destroyed both her childhood and her sister's life. She was sure, although she could not prove it, that her sister went off in the night and flung herself into the water of the lake to wash away the shame.

She did not know if her sister planned to kill herself or if she had drowned by accident, but the end result was the same; her uncle had effectively murdered her. And yet, Cathy knew, but there was no way she could tell her parents about it without destroying their lives as well. So, she had borne a secret no child should ever have to carry, and it had torn her own life apart.

All the time she spoke, recounting this later memory in detail, Mark kept an arm around her gently hugging her and running his fingers lightly through her hair to comfort her as one would a child.

When she finished, there were no tears in her eyes. Even though part of her anger remained, she said she felt comforted for saying it to someone at last. Then, she told him of the new letter, coming from her mother to Adelaide, telling of her Uncle's planned visit and how, because of this, she needed to escape. That was why she had asked him to bring her with him.

Mark hugged her tighter, saying, "If it will help, I will go back to Adelaide and take him for a drive. No one will ever see him again, after that and he will never bother you again. I will put him where no one will ever find him. That is what he deserves for what he did to you."

Cathy shook her head, "Please do not do that. Killing him can never undo what he did, but it would hurt others. It is enough that I have told someone. I have been trapped with this secret for far too long."

It seemed that Mark had accepted her request and let the story continue, but then again, perhaps not. Mark's diary wrote and underlined his own comment at the end of this section. It seemed a fitting close.

'He deserves to die, very slowly and very, very painfully. Perhaps to burn that part off him, slowly, while he watches, would be fitting.'

Anne felt a strange concordance with this man. She should abhor his use of violence to gain justice- and yet, she applauded his sentiment, perhaps even his intent for action. She wondered if he had spoken these words aloud to Cathy and made her afraid that he would really do this thing. However it seemed more likely that he had written this later- perhaps after she was gone. At that time, maybe, he had said no more and let her story continue.

After this, as she lay beside him, she told him of her life as a prostitute: selling her body to men for money was the only way she knew to regain a measure of control until, finally, she needed to end that, too. So, now, she had come to Australia, intending to start a new life as a completely different person.

When Cathy finished, she put his hand between her legs, holding it there and saying, "I have never done this with a person I really liked. But, I think I am ready to try it- with you."

Mark shook his head, "No, I would be lying if I said I do not want that with you. But, for now, all that matters is that I am your friend. I would not be your true friend if I took advantage of you in this place. You have bared your soul and told me your most awful secret.

"Tonight, I must tell you something of me that is as dark and see if you can still like me, the way I like you. I will tell you the story of Belle and how I killed her with my own hand, and how, in doing so, I killed the thing I most loved."

Chapter 42 - Fragments of Nothing

That was it, really, the end of the story of Cathy.

Mark's diary told of their next night very briefly; them lying together in a swag under the stars, him telling her the story of Belle, how he had shot her, and of the awful grief and remorse which followed. Cathy had comforted him with her body, the way that only a woman could, lovers at last, taking his pain inside herself and giving a little healing in return.

The diary did not record him telling her about the other deaths he had caused. That suggested he had not told her of these, perhaps he thought this was a truth too bad for even her to hear.

The story ended with the words:

"I lay with her under a starry desert sky and bared my soul, I spoke of Belle and how I loved her, yet how I killed her, and how that killing of what I loved was now killing my soul. There was something in Cathy that was like my Belle, a look, as if she saw into my soul and judged me not.

"Cathy comforted me as only a woman can, this woman whose soul was torn by her own anguish. She took my body inside her own. I emptied my seed within her and it felt as if some part of the badness in my soul was emptied too. She loved me with her body.

"As I held her, I was comforted. In some small measure I hope I gave her comfort too, though a part of me fears I betrayed our friendship by taking what too many men had taken before.

"But, after it was done, she said this night it was different, she had given herself to me with love, something she had never done before. I hope our shared pleasure has given her a little healing. But a part of me knows fear for her; fear that I have added another layer to her pain, giving her my pain to share."

After those lines telling of them as lovers, giving and returning love, Cathy was gone. The only other time her name appeared was a brief mention in a poem. It was placed after a page on which he had drawn a picture of an eagle in the sky and a dingo standing alone and proud on a ridge top- mouth open and howling at the night sky.

Anne wondered if it was symbolic of the eagle flying away and him, left alone yet again, howling into the desolation.

The final entry with her name was poetic and cryptic:

Cathy vanished, I know not where
I searched for her and found only air
Perhaps she has gone to a place in the sky
A place to which only the eagles can fly
I hope I have not harmed her
In my dreams I have fear
That something terrible has happened to her.
But where she is now I have not any clue
In heaven or hell, only God knows what is true
I wish her well in this life or the next
I most wish to hold her and again feel her breath
But still with her leaving I have her wise words
'I have started again, Mark, so also must you
One day you will find her, your own new queen
You will travel with her to a place never seen
Would that queen was me, perhaps in time it can be
But first I must heal myself, mend my own broken soul
For a beginning of this I thank you, my friend of all worlds'

Then, on the same page under the poem, was a single line that may have referred to her uncle. 'One day he will pay, I will make it so'

So, Anne had a detailed picture in part: three days of their trip in the diary, an intimate and detailed account of what Cathy had told him of her own rape and life as a prostitute. This story was so explicit that it seemed as if, after she was gone, Mark recorded every word as she had spoken it, so others could know of the awfulness done to this child.

After Cathy told of her life, the story jumped straight to the intimate account of the night when they became lovers. It must have been a subsequent night, probably the next night, but that was only a guess.

There was no description of them leaving Coober Pedy on the morning after the party, though others confirmed that they had: their holding hands at breakfast, hugging their hosts and promising to come again, then, a last sight of them driving away towards Alice Springs.

There was no clear record of them being in any other place. That final night was not a story about a physical place where they became lovers, nor about the act itself. It was a story about an emotional connection, a second part of their joint healing as she took his body within her own and gave comfort to his soul's pain. And, in a strange way, it also seemed to be a closure to the story of Belle, as if Mark saw something in this woman that was of the other, a look and a kind friendship. It seemed to Anne that, when he was with Cathy, a truth was told and accepted and that gave him a way forward.

But Cathy, so alive and vibrant, just vanished. All Anne held in her hands to mark this passing was these fragments of nothing.

Was she alive or dead? The story gave no clue. Perhaps Mark had really not known. After the tenderness of their few days together, it was impossible to believe he set out to kill her. Yet, she was also gone, and tragedy seemed to stalk all the companions of this man.

It could be so, that she was dead, but Anne was determined not to abandon this one to the same lost fate as the others, as a truly lost girl. She lived in hope that Cathy had just vanished somewhere to escape the story she could never bring herself to tell her family. Perhaps, she was fearful of what Mark would do to her Uncle, if he ever met him.

This part of Mark's dairy told a deeply personal story of this girl, a story she had told to only one man in the confidence of a night together. Anne understood she did not have Cathy's permission to it share with others, not even Cathy's own family, it would betray her clear intent after all she had done to keep her awful secret.

Chapter 42 - And Along Came Susan

Anne felt she had travelled as far along the path as Marks words would take her in the search for Cathy. She was a highly significant person in Mark's life, as evidenced by the pages he had written about her. But she appeared for but a short time, bright though her impression was, seen like a shooting star lighting the night sky. And, once gone, no shadow of her presence remained.

But Mark's diary story still had fifty pages to run, concluding with Susan, who occupied most of the last thirty pages, her part only finishing on the last night.

Anne had two tasks yet to do to complete telling the story in this 'Diary of the Lost Girls'- the title her mind had assigned Mark's book.

The first was to come to know Susan through Mark's eyes, in the hope that this understanding might give some further insights into what followed. Some of Susan's reactions and actions were surely driven by the Mark she had discovered in the month period in which she had known him. Perhaps this book would even give clues to where Susan went in the end.

Anne did not believe this, but felt she still must search it, just in case. More, she felt she had to try to understand the contradictions at the heart of this story. Why, for all but one day, had he treated her as a most loved person, but, for on that final day, he treated her as an animal, trussed as if wild and dangerous. Mark had made Susan believe that he deliberately killed these others and would do the same to her, that he would callously murder her and give her body to the crocodiles. He let her spend a day and night in abject terror, believing this. Her fear was so real that she had killed him, seeing this as her only escape. But, after this was done, Susan still stayed fiercely loyal to him and his memory, seeking for Mark's name to remain unsullied.

Anne thought it was, in part, to protect her unborn children, but she was sure there was more than that. Whatever happened on that last day and night was an enigma within an enigma: the enigma of Mark, the why he did what he did, and, within it, the enigma of Susan- both before and after she killed him.

In Susan's telling of the story, captured on the tape, this part was most scant. She told in detail of the phone texts, she told of Mark tying her up, carrying her locked in the cooler box, of becoming his lover again on the last night, a thing in which she was a willing participant. She told how he returned her to captivity with the apparent intent of her death, after he told her his life story.

She told of finding the knife, using her seductive powers to lower Mark's defences, seizing the opportunity to end it by ending him: using the knife and the branch as her weapons. She told of dragging his body to the billabong, not sure if he was really dead, and of watching the feeding frenzy as three crocodiles tore his body, limb from limb, until only blood and tiny scraps of flesh remained in the water.

Then, she told how she systematically hid all evidence of them being in this place, so all that remained was the box of buried passports and a few metal objects consigned to various watery graves.

Last, she told of how she had driven to Darwin, cleaned and left the car, and flown home, maintaining a fiction that all this had never been.

The chronology of this story was complete and verified. But something was missing, that ongoing story of 'Why?'

Why had Mark treated Susan one way and then another?

Why had she also done the same? What drove these reversals?

Was it just two crazy, irrational people or was there a layer of this story still hidden, a Russian Doll within a Russian Doll.

Anne did not know if this book would give her the clues she sought, but her job was unfinished until she tried to discover these answers.

She read and reread these last fifty pages, over and over, seeking a deeper understanding that refused to come.

Still, gradually, two things became clear: that there was no evidence of any girls after Cathy and before Susan: whereas, before, brief presences of many were dotted through the narrative, most came and went quickly for temporary visits, a night or two, at most a week. He described these freely and intimately but with little emotion, "she was a good lay" was the sort of way he spoke.

Cathy seemed a shadow of his love and friendship with Belle. This seemed to give him a measure of forgiveness for his past. And it seemed she left him with a promise, the new Queen would come.

After Cathy was gone, nearly a year passed until Susan came. In the next twenty pages of notes there was no female presence: the story seemed to be mostly records of work and trips abroad, odd mentions of Vic and Buck, but, mostly, he was in the Middle East. It seemed he was there doing something significant, perhaps a major work project there-although, it seemed more of a search for an unnamed thing or person. At its end, this part suggested he had found what he sought. Returning from that last trip, he wrote, "It is done. Search over. I am glad."

The day after this was written, Susan appeared, glimpsed through trees on a beach in Cairns. She appeared 'Goddess like', and almost immediately it was clear he had found his new queen, successor of Elin, to whom he once promised an inheritance of a desert kingdom. This time, an inheritance was given, written in a will, although Susan never saw it and its fate was unknown.

Last time, the Queen died. This time, it was his turn instead.

She killed the king and yet remained loyal, strange indeed!

Anne saw a pattern like an ancient prophecy, predicted and fulfilled. What she did not understand was why one or both must choose to die.

It seemed like the Abraham story, with a life sacrifice at its heart. But it was not a story which belonged in Old Testament times when God and man walked side by side.

Part 8 - The Emptiness

Chapter 43 - Endless Emptiness

The year had passed and a new year had begun.

Anne had returned from her travels in October, having gone to America after her holiday in the outback with David. She spent the final months of the year cataloguing all her information and turning it into a draft book called "Lost Girls". By Christmas, she had a good draft with her editors for review. She felt in great need of a rest after a gruelling year.

She had lived an emotional roller coaster as she found out story after story- small parts happy, but, in totality, a trail of appalling tragedy.

She felt profoundly sorry for all the girls and their wasted lives, Susan especially. But for Susan's chance meeting with Mark, a thing that had thrown her off the rails, her future had seemed so bright.

But, most of all, Anne felt profound sympathy for the man at the centre, the man whose own life had been a series of ever-increasing horrors. In the end, he was perpetrator as much as a victim. Part of her felt it was fitting that there was closure with his death.

Having walked so many miles in his shoes, she could not find it in her to blame him, despite his final, remorseless murders. She only wished it could have been otherwise, particularly before he had met Susan.

She thought that Vic's Mum had got closest to the truth; Mark had lost a mother and her love. It seemed that what had followed, as he had gone through so many relationships, was an increasingly desperate and demented search for another love, a new queen.

Many times, he could have found her but fate intervened. The final outcome was an act in a classic Shakespearian tragedy where the death of the villain was preordained; but to get there, he destroyed all he touched. With hindsight, it seemed to have become inevitable, like a death wish in waiting.

Anne wished there was a way to wind back the clock and make it otherwise: if only Elin had lived, his first fairy queen, if only Belle lived, she seemed the nearest in this story to simple love, if only Josie, but for jealousy perhaps she would have had Mark's measure, if only Amanda had not tried to wrest control of his soul. The final two deaths were darker, but it did not appear that Mark formed a premeditated plan to harm them, rather it was that they were broken inside, too, and each had failed to understand he was even more broken than them and just how dangerous that made him.

Cathy was the strangest; in a way, she was the most broken of all. Yet, for the first time, there appeared to be a person with a power to heal and be healed, perhaps it was her need that brought goodness from him. But, before that had run any natural course, she, too, was gone.

Still, the Mark that came after her seemed a less damaged person, the poem of the new queen seemed to be something he had taken to heart, seeking a new beginning.

Then, along came Susan. The way Mark described her, she had fulfilled the new queen prophecy- first described by him as a Greek goddess. And she had the look, that ineffable look shared with Belle and Cathy, the dark hair and searching eyes but something more, a mix of mischief and joie de vie, perhaps love of life was the best way to say it. It seemed to reach into Mark's soul and connect with him. Was it a look, glimpsed as a child, of his long lost mother?

Anne had first seen a photo of Mark's mother, taken on her wedding day, but this was a posed photo without life. While her hair and face were similar, she could not judge if she, too, had that look-but, perhaps. She knew Sandy had other family photos from Mark's past, but she had not viewed them. Perhaps, they would show something if she did.

When Susan had come along, she, too, had a look which was common to Belle and Cathy which caught Mark's attention and made him arrange to meet her. It did seem he was seeking to start afresh, determined not damage this one. He begged her not to seek his past. Yet, it could not be. She needed to know about the man and the truth was uncovered. Under pressure, Mark reverted to type: in-part professing love, but tying her up like a dangerous animal, in the end unable to reconcile his two parts.

Then, a final place of clarity. He realised he could not kill what he loved this time, yet he could not stand by and let his history come out. He saw that to impart to Susan knowledge of who he was would inevitably sow the seeds of future destruction, that the knowledge would tear her apart, little by little.

So, he had chosen. Anne had no doubt that, if Susan had not acted first, he would have swum out to join the crocodiles: the outcome would have been the same, but without Susan having his blood on her hands.

But then, as Anne thought further, even that alternate place seemed to be no solution. For Susan to watch her doomed lover being torn apart would most likely have damaged her equally to what her own act had done. Susan was in a trap of circumstances, too; she saw no way out either. At last, Anne felt she was in a place to understand the hopeless desperation that consumed her friend's soul, emptiness feeding on yet more emptiness, without escape.

She was now at the end of her own search, seeking a solution, but there was none. She understood that, sometimes, life dealt shit cards giving no solution. And this story had a whole royal flush of them.

By the end of the year, Anne was totally numb from living this human storm, day after day, week after week. It was a relief to be alone with only David and his family, to be in a place where no one talked further about this last year. As she sat in the sun watching David's family at work and play, she felt normalcy gradually return to her life.

Chapter 44 - The Inquest

Anne returned from a New Year's holiday at David's family home to Darwin in late January for a formal inquest into the disappearance and possible death of five girls: Elin, Isabelle, Amanda, Cathy and Susan.

Susan's disappearance had no direct connection to the others, in Mark being the person likely to be responsible for their deaths. Yet, Susan, was still inextricably part of the whole story, her life having run a very parallel course.

After a preliminary argument and counter-argument, the coroner agreed that Susan also should be a subject of consideration of this inquest- if only to more clearly establish her role in the other disappearances. This would lay to rest some of the malicious rumours circulating that she was part of some grand plot, rather than just another victim, even if her role was after the event.

Neither her parents nor Anne had any objection to Susan being a person under consideration, their only interest was to find anything further that may lead to her or allow an understanding of what had happened to her.

The judge also named an unknown further person of interest who may also have become deceased while in the company of Vincent Mark Bassingham. This person was of unknown identity and, for the purpose of the proceedings was only known as "J," as this was the only clear evidence of identity within the diary. No one had come forward to give a possible identity of this unknown person so, in evidence, "J" she remained. Still in the media and in peoples' conversation, she soon became known as Josie. And at least it gave her a human face, perhaps it was her real first name.

The judge ruled that "J" was not a formal subject of the inquiry, but rather, a person about whom the court was seeking to establish facts which may lead to an identity and a subsequent investigation.

On a steamy, wet season day in Darwin, the inquest got underway, the lawyers, police and witnesses moving quickly from air-conditioned cars to courtroom coolness, while a media scrum sweated out in the sun, hoping for sensational shots of the main characters coming and going.

The coroner called all to order. There were two main lines of evidence for the inquiry. The first was the police investigation led by Alan for the NT Police. The second was the evidence of the diary, provided jointly by Anne, Alan and a psychologist who sought to establish some key facts about its author including his mental state, history and personality type. The diary's accuracy was also evaluated extensively, on the basis of its internal consistency and all the other known history of Mr. Vincent Mark Bassingham.

The police evidence was led off with Alan taking the stand, supported by many others, working through what the police had discovered. Alan described how the investigation initially discovered the metal box with the passports and then how the police had established the identity of the four girls whose passports were found there. He showed, in photographs, the former hiding place of the metal box in the vehicle of Vincent Bassingham, also known by his various aliases. Then Alan described the evidence leading to a connection between him and these missing persons.

Various police officers then gave evidence as to how they had investigated the identity of each of the four girls and how, at the time when the passports were found, all the girls were considered missing persons but without any specific evidence as to their fate. The police described how they contacted the parents and others who knew each girl and obtained statements about their knowledge of the circumstances preceding each disappearance.

All the parents and many of the friends were in court to corroborate this testimony. It established the last known places of residence and intended travel plans of each girl, although it was clear that such knowledge in each case was very limited and fragmentary.

The coroner was heard to remark that these girls seemed to typify many backpackers who came to Australia, with only a vague knowledge of where they were going and what they would do.

The police then outlined their other lines of inquiry to find last known locations of each girl. This placed Elin's last known location at Birdsville in the company of Vincent Bassingham, otherwise known as Mark Brooks, on the basis of evidence of the landlord of the Birdsville Hotel. Isabelle's last known location was at Derby, where it was confirmed she stayed the night in a room in her own name, but in the company of Vincent Bassingham, yet again with an alias of Mark Brooks. It established that Amanda's last known location was at the Emerald Hotel, where she had shared a room with Vincent Bassingham, now with the alias of Mark Brown. For Cathy, it established the last known location as the private residence of Nikko and Athena Christos, where she also shared a room with Vincent Bassingham, who they knew as Mark Bennet.

Thus, all parties agreed that Vincent Bassingham, in various aliases, was the last person known to be in the company of each of these girls and that all had appeared to travel willingly with him at that point.

The evidence then moved to Anne who described first the transcript given by Susan, as captured on tape. Short excerpts of the tape were played to confirm the veracity of some parts and a full transcript was provided to the coroner. Anne led them through a summarised version of this tape describing its key events from Susan first meeting Mark on the Barrier Reef to travelling with him from Alice Springs to the Top End of the Northern Territory.

Anne told of the succession of discoveries Susan made, beginning with the multiple number plates, then of the metal box with the passports and the multiple identities of Vincent Bassingham, the various Mark Bs, then of the text she sent and its reply. Finally, she told of the events from Mark's discovery about the texts, Susan's captivity and coming to the billabong of the crocodiles, then of the final night and the next day. As she worked her way through this story, she could see journalists running in and out of the court room, capturing ever more details, many horrific, as this story was finally revealed and, then, rushing off to tell their various media outlets.

It surprised her that this story, which she carried in such detail inside her head, was as largely unknown to the outside world. Of course, while the police had released some parts, it had never been told as a coherent, whole narrative until this day of her testimony.

Anne then described the verbal story, as passed on to Susan by Mark, that he admitted to killing some of these girls, particularly one whose story matched that of Amanda.

Her next evidence was to be about the information within the diary. However, before she was called to give this, the psychologist, who had also investigated the contents of the diary, to appraise the mental state of its author, was called.

He said he had formed the view that the diary was mostly a credible and accurate document, which predominantly showed its author was a rational and lucid person, although it increasingly showed evidence of anti-social and psychotic behaviours in its later parts.

He also explained that it included parts of creative writing and poetry which were, in some instances, apparently fictitious. He said in many cases it was difficult to distinguish between the parts giving true information and the fictional parts. His overall assessment was that the diary of one, Vincent Mark Bassingham, who called himself Mark B., should be generally treated as providing an accurate description of the facts it recorded.

The police were also questioned about their investigations into the diary's veracity and confirmed that, in places where information allowed, they had been able to verify many specific facts.

Anne was then recalled to continue telling of her discoveries of the fate of these girls from the diary records, later corroborated by other sources- particularly the various girls' parents.

She told the judge that, subject to his permission, she would use the name Mark to describe this man as that was his identity within the diary and was also the name he was known by to all the girls. She explained how she had read the full diary document through several times and had begun by cross- referencing the parts which told of Susan with the descriptions Susan had given of the same events. This had helped her to familiarise herself with Mark's writing style and gave her a sense of the veracity of his descriptions. It also helped her differentiate between factual and creative components.

Overall, she had found close corroboration between Susan's story and the diary records- although she noted that Susan's story was more comprehensive and complete for the parts she knew.

She then began giving the substance of the diary records made of Elin, which described the time period after they left Birdsville and travelled into a remote part of south-western Queensland where they had spent about a week removing opals from an abandoned mine shaft until its collapse led to Elin's death. She told how Mark described this event, in apparent anguish. He told of his attempted rescue and how he buried her alongside a nearby billabong, marking the grave site with rocks which he placed on the ground above, to outline the boat he buried her in, following the custom of her Viking ancestors.

The police corroborated the account of the diary and confirmed there were innumerable abandoned mine shafts in this part of Queensland, which had an estimated area of about 100,000 square kilometres. They said, to date, it had proved impossible to locate the site of the mine or the grave- although searches were continuing, mainly using satellite images.

Anne then told of her visit to Sweden and described how this burial site matched the form of burial of Elin's own mother, providing a further and independent source of corroboration for the diary account.

From there, the coroner moved to examining the circumstances of Isabelle's disappearance. Anne took them through the key points of the diary account, in this case, the joint handwriting of both Isabelle and Mark with Isabelle's French annotations, now translated and confirmed as being in her handwriting by her parents and other experts. She then spoke of how Mark wrote of her fall from the cliff into the water below, surrounded by five large crocodiles, and how he said he had shot her in the head with his rifle in the final seconds to alleviate her suffering.

There was audible gasp of surprise from the press gallery at this revelation and Isabelle's parents covered their faces in pain as it was recounted. The judge admitted these facts were deeply distressing to all parties and called a recess. After the recess, the police advised they had searched for the location of Isabelle's demise without success but, as there were hundreds of kilometres of coast in this area, it was another needle in a haystack.

Next came the story of the unknown "J." Anne gave her account based on reconstruction of the events within the diary. The police confirmed that Mark owned a flat in Katherine which fitted the description of the time spent there. They also confirmed the visit of Mark and a girl at around this time to Rosewood Station, although the girl's name was not remembered. They had also located a track and billabong matching the diary description of the final site where they were together. They had been unable to locate any evidence of their occupation of the former camp site. In relation to the identity of 'J', they had been unable to find any leads and the area where it was claimed she was buried was so vast as to be impossible to even begin a search. They confirmed the account of the barman in the Top Springs Hotel of an altercation taking place between Mr Bassingham and another patron which led to this man being severely beaten, needing prolonged hospital treatment for a ruptured liver. The man, himself, was located but refused to provide further evidence.

Now, came the story of Amanda and, again, Anne led them through the diary account, corroborated by evidence from her parents. The professor, who voluntarily attended the inquest of his own accord, provided details of their past relationship. Parts of the Amanda story were corroborated by Susan's tape transcript, which was played alongside. Of the mine shaft holding her body, the police again indicated the potential area was so vast they did not know where to begin to search- in a similar way to the burial sight of Elin. They speculated that both could be in the same region.

At last, they came to Cathy. Her presence in Adelaide was confirmed by her parents from her letter and by the backpacker hostel. Her presence in Wilpaena Pound and Coober Pedy was confirmed by witnesses who agreed with the diary account. But then, there was nothing further, other than an enigmatic poem to explain her vanishing or her absence.

The coroner sought Anne's opinion about her likely fate. Anne asked to speak to the coroner and counsel in private, with only Alan present. Anne took them through the abuse allegations about her uncle from the diary, as described by Mark.

Anne asked that these not be disclosed as she thought it remained most likely that Cathy had vanished to escape from her uncle and, if she was alive, she clearly did not want these allegations publicly aired as they would cause her parents further distress. Alan advised that the NT police had already passed these allegations on to Scotland Yard for their own investigation. He considered public disclosure at this stage would be prejudicial to this investigation.

The coroner agreed to withhold this evidence from public release and Anne was glad. It was a small service she could do to this girl, she was as much a victim as the others, even if still alive.

So that was that. The story of the diary and the best information they knew about the fate of five girls.

The coroner then turned to the disappearance of Susan, establishing the sequence of events beginning with her release from jail, then of the days she spent with Vic at Alan's flat and the final day at the hospital, with her departure captured on a hospital lobby camera just after eight o'clock in the evening. Alan led the first part of the evidence, concluding with a final likely sighting of her taking a lift south at Berrimah.

Vic and Alan then explained the role which the media articles appeared to have played in her disappearance that night, then Alan and Charlie told of the discovery of the sandals she had been wearing, confirmed by her DNA and fingerprints, found near the billabong.

The fruitless search since, the public appeal for information and the various unlikely sightings which had been made since were also described. This was a story in which Anne had little role, mainly told by Vic and Alan who were both visibly distressed in the telling.

After two weeks of evidence and innumerable witnesses, the coroner retired to consider the facts and write his findings. A month later, the court resumed for the coroner's verdict. He called the court to order and began to read. Anne scribbled his spoken findings down on a legal notepad, not trusting her mind to keep track without this written record.

I find that Elin Nordquist met her death by misadventure resulting from the collapse of an abandoned mine shaft in an unknown location in South Western Queensland. I find Vincent Bassingham had no direct role in her death but may have had an indirect role though encouraging Ms Nordquist to assist him in the excavation of a dangerous mine shaft.

I find that Isabelle Rollande met her death by being shot in the head by Mr Vincent Basssingham. While there are extenuating circumstances such a death constitutes murder under the Northern Territory and Western Australian Criminal Codes. However, as Mr Bassingham is also deceased no further action for this event can be taken

I find that Amanda Parker met her death by a blow delivered by Mr Bassingham. However, as there is testimony that Ms Parker was attacking him with a knife there is no basis for any finding beyond self-defence for Mr Bassingham's role in her death.

I find that there is insufficient evidence to rule on the likely fate of either Fiona Rodgers or Susan McDonald although I express my view that serious concerns are justified about the fate of both girls. I encourage the police to continue investigating both disappearances.

In addition, I find a likely case of murder exists by Mr Bassingham against the unknown person, J. However, in the absence of evidence of her identity, I am unable to make any further finding. As Mr Bassingham is now deceased, a murder charge is unable to be sustained. I encourage the police to continue to search for the identity of this person as, should this be established, it is likely that closure could be brought to the case of this missing, even "lost" girl.

I commend the NT Police and Ms Anne Smithfield for the extraordinary work they have done in investigating and bringing closure to many parts of this tragic investigation.

I convey my profound sympathy to the parents and the many friends of these missing girls, whose fate may never be fully known.

Chapter 45 - Telling the Story

Two weeks after the coroner made his findings, Anne was contacted by a leading commercial TV channel. It wished to do a 'Lost Girls Mini Series' run over three nights, telling the story of her investigation.

It was to be a story in three parts: the first the tale of Mark, beginning with his troubled childhood up until the events of the first two 'lost girls', for whom he clearly had great affection. It was a story of a man seeking to rise above adversity, yet endlessly caught up in tragedy.

The second part was a story with a dark heart, the man who had become a wilful murderer, killing with no apparent remorse, as if in the possession of a dark or evil spirit.

The third part was Susan and Cathy's stories, where still some hope remained- but the hope was only slim. Each of these told a story where elements of friendship, hope and love re-emerged, despite all the destructive forces still at work.

This part would end up as a testimony of hope for continued life of these final two brave girls and with it a second appeal for more funds to keep searching for these and other lost girls from across the country.

It was to be followed by a memorial ceremony where plaques were placed for these missing girls and for others that the public at large were still searching for, in an appropriate place.

Anne rang all the girls' parents. All agreed to the story being told, despite the further distress of reliving the pain in public. It was an important story and, if it helped find others, that was reason enough.

The TV channel promised that the stories would be sympathetic to all girls and that each girl's parents would have a right to veto the release of any private information that they found distasteful before it went to air. The TV station did not need this permission about information that was already in the public domain, but it agreed that it was in everyone's interest that the story be tasteful and sympathetic.

Anne found herself as principal narrator of this bizarre and awful series of events. At times, she found it so distressing that the cameras had to stop as she recomposed herself. But, she stuck at it over six weeks of filming, two weeks per episode and, finally, it was done. She had put her heart and soul into the search. Now, she put her heart and soul into telling the story, hoping through it to reach someone, anyone, who knew a fact that was real, new and which would help bring closure.

After the story was made, it went into two weeks of editing and Anne was consumed by the pre-publicity. She became an instantly recognisable film star with her flaming red hair and photogenic husband. Together, they captured the public heart of Anne's new country.

Already, the story had been syndicated to the UK, France, Sweden and Canada. Negotiations were advanced for the USA though Amanda's story was the hardest to tell in a way that evoked public sympathy. But here, the Professor was her firm ally, having agreed to give unlimited access to his experience with this girl who, despite the bad things she had done, also had redeeming features which he described with clear affection. Somehow it worked, giving Amanda a kinder side while keeping faithful to the facts.

At last, it was done. Anne came home and collapsed into bed. David pampered her for the final three days until the first show went to air.

For three nights, they sat at home watching and reliving, with tears in their eyes. She was surprised that, even though she knew it all, it still moved her beyond words. She prayed something good would come of it.

Chapter 46 -Nowhere Search

The documentary screened on primetime Monday night, at the end of May, for an hour with the two follow-up episodes running on successive nights. It was called 'Nowhere Search.' It was the highest rated show of the year. At the same time, they reran the "Lost Ones Appeal" and, until after midnight on the third night, the phones rang off the hooks. By the end of the last night, over two and a half million dollars was pledged. Over the next week, with postal, internet and phone donations, they comfortably passed three million dollars.

The day after the TV documentary finished, the book "Lost Girls – Nowhere Search" was launched. It had five main parts, one for each of the girls, then, at the end, a small part titled Josie. Each part told a story of a girl's life up until the time she disappeared.

After that, where they could, they had used Mark's diary to fill in blanks. It was story of four dead girls and of another two girls, with their fate's unknow. It was generally agreed that Elin, Amanda, Isabelle and Josie were all deceased.

In the week after the program screened, hundreds of calls came in which needed to be investigated. The police and missing persons' organisations worked their way through them all, successfully re-uniting three families with long- lost children, so that was something good.

But, of the fate of these four presumed-dead girls and of the two still listed as missing, nothing new came.

Anne felt, at her core, that Susan and Cathy were probably both dead- yet she refused to let her mind go there. Something beyond explanation was at work here. It sustained an unending hope in her for one of them to walk through the door. But she was utterly exhausted with the looking.

In the end, she realised she'd done all she could. Her own search was concluded and she must get on with her own life. She knew that, if Susan was here, she would have told her to do exactly that, she would not want yet another life damaged through her actions.

She and David set a date and agreed that they would go ahead and get married as soon as possible once the final memorial day had passed.

With that, she thought she could move on and finally close the book on her "Nowhere Search".

Chapter 47- A Glimmer

Anne somehow found herself unable to just let it go as the days and weeks passed, to acknowledge the search was really over. It felt like a final disloyalty to Susan to admit defeat. The story kept going round and round in her mind always searching for what else to do; whatever new lead there was to pursue.

Her life had been consumed by the search. Was it only a year since she had started? She remembered, clearly, the fateful day when Susan had begun telling her story, that futile attempt to cast off her past and return to her childhood 'Emily' identity. It lasted less than a week until the day when the evil spirit, which seemed to have taken residence in her soul, overwhelmed her.

At least that was the way it felt, after all this time, as she looked back. She was still no wiser as to whether Susan was alive or dead. No glimmer of a new identity or of an existence after that night had emerged, but she refused to let her mind concede there was no hope.

She had to admit it looked bad, the sandals she had lent to her friend and the crocodile totem found next to the billabong must mean Susan had come back to this place of the crocodiles before vanishing.

While nothing further had been found, it was hard to believe that, after coming there, she had gone elsewhere rather than into the water.

Since that day, when Alan had rung to tell her of the discovery, she could not bear to allow herself to follow those thoughts to where they led- a second body torn apart and consumed. But, dreaming of other possibilities, was futile. Her mind spun in an endless loop of "maybes."

Both she and David carried a burden of joint and personal remorse for going out to dinner that night, rather than calling to see Susan and ensure she had some support.

It was at least as bad for Vic, who she could see had become instantly and totally captivated by this vanished girl. Vic blamed himself, even more, for agreeing to have his operation so soon, rather than staying with her and delaying it until after the babies were born. But, if it had happened the way everyone thought, then there were no babies anymore either: not one, but three lives lost. It was too awful to contemplate what it all meant.

Yet Anne, despite knowing she had done all she could, was not able to put it from her mind: it was always there, an unresolved grief.

The good thing was it had not poisoned her relationship with David; that was stronger than ever- although, they had mutually agreed to push the wedding back and defer marriage plans until next Christmas to allow Anne to pursue all the leads that she could uncover unhindered. Once they got married, they planned no delay in beginning their own family and, with that, her free time would vanish. She knew she must bring this search to something approaching a conclusion before then.

Now, it was June of the year after: fifteen months from when Susan had vanished and a year since the fundraiser which had launched the public campaign, not just for Susan but for all the many other people who had vanished in Australia without a trace.

Others were using funds to search for other missing people; she had concentrated her search only on Susan, the other girls whose passports were found and the girl, J, who Mark had spoken of in his diary.

Last month, when the TV channel screened the documentary which accompanied her book, the response was huge. The millions of dollars of additional donations from that night were now funding the building of memorials and the following of leads for other missing people.

Next month would be the final event in which she would take a part, a memorial service in Darwin. They would place the six plaques with the girls' names at the end of East Point where the harbour met the sea, a place which looked out to the west where the sun set over an ocean called the Timor Sea. Anne's mind associated the setting sun with the passing to new life and eternal hope. This felt fitting.

Today, as all those thoughts of the search ran round and round in her mind, she was sitting in the sunny living room of the flat she shared in

Glebe with David. It was actually his place, but now her travels around the world were finished, so she had moved in with him, set up her computer and all the other mod cons for her writing.

It had a glorious view out onto Sydney harbour, with ANZAC bridge dominating the skyline. In the early morning and evening, she would watch the dragon boat crews practice their racing skills. Other times she would glimpse large ships further out, sometimes the luxury cruising boats with millionaire owners who moored them immediately across the bay from her.

She loved this view, especially on winter sunny mornings when the sun streamed in. Often she sat her in her track pants and slippers, having a leisurely breakfast, after David had gone off to his office in Camperdown to work. She thought of him and his tousled blond hair with affection, as she had last glimpsed him leaving this morning.

The phone rang, startling her out of her reverie. It was someone from the TV channel, one of the administrative people who had been dealing with the donations for the appeal. She could not recall this lady's face, but her name sounded familiar.

The phone voice asked if it was Anne? When Anne confirmed it was, the voice said, "I have this slightly unusual letter addressed to our appeal and with your name and then; 'Private and Confidential' written at the top. I have not opened it, it seemed like I should check with you first.

"Perhaps it's another parent asking for help, and they did not want to disclose what has happened more widely, but are asking you to read their request privately before you do anything further. I wondered, should I send it on to you? Or, alternatively, if you are coming past our office in the next day or two, you could pick it up?"

Anne felt intrigued and curious. There had been lots of requests for help early on, mainly after the first appeal. These, they had worked on with the police in deciding what to do, helping where they could. But, generally, these came to the well-advertised help line and address, not via the appeal which was used as a place of public donations.

Anne felt she needed to read the contents of this envelope first, just by herself, to honour the sender's wishes. As David's flat was at the bottom of Glebe looking out to Blackwattle Bay, it was only a fifteen-minute walk to Pyrmont, the location of the TV channel office, from where the call came.

Anne had not been out today; it would be good to stretch her legs. She replied, "It is only a short walk from here to your office. So, if it is OK, I will pop around in about half an hour to collect it."

"Sure," the person on the other end of the phone replied.

She had a quick shower and changed out of her tracksuit into a smart business suit, then walked out in the crisp winter morning air. It was a glorious Sydney day, the sun low to the northeast and shining in her face, warming her as she walked. She loved this walk around the bottom of the harbour, passing people of all shapes and ages, the fit brigade, cyclists in fluoro gear on the way to a late work start, people walking dogs, elderly people taking in the morning sun and fresh air. She passed the coffee shop on the point and resisted the temptation for coffee and cake; she could feel weight was creeping on with the last month of 'at home' inactivity combined with good eating and drinking. Perhaps, she would indulge on the walk home.

Soon, she was at the TV office reception. They all knew her from last month's program and greeted her like a long-lost friend. The admin person came out to the front desk and passed Anne the letter. Anne thanked her then looked at it, curiously.

It was a small plain envelope with a single postage stamp postmarked 'Adelaide' in one corner. At the top was her name – then Private and Confidential underlined, followed by the appeal address from the TV program. It had been meticulously transcribed in neat handwriting using capitals. There was no return address and no other distinguishing features on the outside.

Anne thanked them and put the letter in her jacket pocket, wanting to respect the sender's wishes to open it in private. She waved her goodbyes and walked back into the street.

It was only a few minutes' walk back to the cafe where the coffee and cake had tempted. She decided to return there before opening and reading this letter. She found an outside table in a sheltered nook. Once her coffee and a lemon tart were served, she savoured a lingering sip and bite before retrieving the envelope.

She did not know why, but she sensed this was a thing of importance. She opened it with a nail file from her bag, carefully lifting the flap with a minimum of tearing. Inside was a single sheet of paper, folded once. There was writing on the inside of the folded sheet. She took the sheet, opened it, and spread it on the table in front of her.

In the same writing she read:

Dear Anne,
You do not know me though you have told part of my story.
I saw it on TV a few days ago. I found it very hard to watch, the hardest part was when my parents appealed to know where I am.

I did not deliberately set out to hurt them. I ask you to let them know I am alive to ease their pain. Perhaps one day I will be able to bring myself to contact them directly. In the meantime, I ask you do not disclose this information to others. I do not want police or media searching for me even though I do not think they will find me.

There is one other thing I want to say. It is that the Mark I knew was a good person. He was kind and never sought to hurt me.

I wish I could say more but I cannot.
Thank you.
Cathy

Beside the name Cathy was a funny little squiggle that did not mean anything to Anne.

Anne felt like a bomb had exploded in her hand. It could be a hoax but it did not feel like it. She wondered if it was true, that when all the other searching failed, the TV program had reached one soul who now wanted to lay her ghost to rest.

She did not know what to do. They had all promised to share any information that came their way, that is between the group of close-knit friends and family that had led the search.

But this girl had expressly asked that the only communication be directly with her own parents and, even then, she could not release to them what she thought was the key, the story of the child. She decided to talk to David and together they would decide what to do.

She picked up her mobile phone and dialled his number.

He answered on the first ring.

She said, “Could you come home for a bit? There is something really important I must show you.”

As she walked to the front of the block of flats, his car was turning into the driveway. She sat in the passenger’s seat as he stopped alongside her.

Wordlessly, she passed him the envelope.

He read it, his face furrowing. “Wow,” was all he said for a minute.

Then, he said, “This is the best news in a year. Let’s go inside and ring her parents together. I know it is the middle of the night over there. but if it was me, I would want to know without losing a minute.”

They found their number in Anne’s contact list. There was the inevitable delay as the links connected through the different exchanges. Then, they could hear it ringing. It rang and rang. At last, a groggy Scottish male voice came down the line.

David asked, “Is this Mr. Alastair Rodgers?”

There was an affirmative grunt.

David introduced himself and Anne. They had both met Mr. Rodgers several times before.

"Oh, aye," came the reply; then, "What news?"

David handed the phone to Anne. As she picked it up, she heard a female voice, a bit distant, come down the line. "Who is it Alastair?"

"Those people from Australia, the ones looking for Cathy, ye know who did that TV program."

"Oh my God, Alastair, what are they saying?"

Before he could reply, Anne spoke down the line, "Mr and Mrs Rodgers, we think we have got a letter from Cathy, it says it is from her."

There was a sense of stunned silence coming down the line, a sense of people too overcome by emotion to find words. Anne could feel tears in her eyes. She started to speak again, finding her voice was choked, too.

She passed the letter to David saying, "Could you read it to them?"

David took the letter and the phone and said, to the continued silence, "Are you there Mr. and Mrs. Rodgers? Could I read the letter out to you? It is only a few lines long and we are not sure if it is real, but we knew you would want to know about it straight away. "

Two voices came down the phone line, almost together; a female, "Please do," and a male, "Och Aye, Please Yes, for God's sake."

David read as slowly and clearly as he could. A couple times, his voice had a slight tremor.

Then, he said, "At the end, just near where she signs her name Cathy, she had put a funny little squiggle, half like a face but not quite.

They heard, down the line, the female voice, "God be praised, it really is our girl." The male voice was silent, but they could hear what sounded like a man sobbing.

After a minute, it calmed and he came on the line again. He said, "With the squiggle you describe we are almost sure it really is our girl. It was a thing she and her sister had for communicating together when they were little girls. It is like she put it there to tell us it is really her. We are both a bit overwhelmed with emotion right now, but would it be possible to send us a copy as quickly as you can? I have an email in my home office so perhaps you could scan it and send it through?"

It was done in a minute while they stayed on the phone. Another minute later, the voice came back again, "Yes, we have the letter now. It is her handwriting and her signature. That squiggle is something that could have only come from her; so, praise be to God, our prayers are answered. We know our girl is still alive."

There was not much more to say. The Rodgers' said they would ring back next day once they had time to digest the news and decide what to do. They were already booked to come to Australia for the memorial ceremony in Darwin next month. Perhaps, they could bring that forward and come for a couple extra weeks to try and find their Cathy.

It was agreed they would talk again the next morning, Scottish time.

Chapter 48 - Laying the Ghosts to Rest

On a cool breezy day in late June, over fifty people gathered at a headland called East Arm. It looked out over Darwin Harbour on one side and on the other looked out across a vast flat ocean called the Timor Sea to a distant land below the horizon called Indonesia. Occasional sail boats moved slowly across the far sea sky horizon.

A rock, a big square slab of natural sandstone, taller than any of the people assembled, had been erected. It was set into the ground amongst other natural, earth-coloured rocks of the headland. It faced four ways with each flat side bearing a name at the top.

There was Elin's side, facing directly to the northern ocean and across the world to a Nordic sea, a place from where a warrior queen may choose to sail in search of distant lands.

There was Isabelle's side, which faced towards a less distant Kimberly coast where some fragments of a former life still lay hidden.

There was Josie's side, which pointed south towards what was believed to be a distant desert grave, a grave once covered in dead flowers which held the last remains of an unknown girl.

And, pointing back across the city of Darwin and out to the east, was Amanda's side, the city girl who had come to the bush, the girl from the land far across the Pacific Ocean, the girl who came to an unfamiliar land where she did not belong and was now lost somewhere to the far east or southeast of this place. If Amanda's spirit could choose, Anne knew she would have chosen it to reside in a city of buildings- not an empty desert.

Each rock face was inscribed at the top with words carved into the stone, a short story of the life and loss of a girl, simple things like date and place of birth, hometown, favourite things. The final part was a telling of what brought them to this land and of where and when they died, as best known.

Below these inscriptions were other brass plaques telling the stories of other missing 'lost' girls and some missing men, too. Half a dozen adorned each face but there were many more to follow.

For Cathy and Susan, there were no inscribed rock faces- that would be an abandonment of hope. All who had known these two girls were determined to still find hope. Even so, they were still lost to those who loved them most.

A simple bronze plaque told, for both of them, the story of what had brought them to here. Susan's faced east, on Amanda's side, pointing to the place of the river of crocodiles where she had left her lover and may have returned. Cathy's faced south, to somewhere between Coober Pedy and Alice Springs where she was last seen. On her plaque was written the poem from Mark's diary. It seemed a fitting way to remember her.

Anne walked around the stone and came to a stop facing out to the sea, searching for the warrior queen of a distant horizon. Somewhere over the glittering sea of waves, sparkling in the breeze, she imagined she could now glimpse her: Mark's first loved Elin, forever travelling away to unknown lands. Anne could picture her clearly, the girl with the golden hair, the Elfin Queen, sailing a proud ship further and further out to sea. She really wished Mark was still standing beside his Elin, sailing off to a better place. Then, this world of loss and heartache, for so many, would have never been.

But, if she could have one wish and only one wish, it would be to see her friend Susan again, home safe, no longer another lost girl.

Vic walked up beside her and took her hand. "We will find her; I know, deep down, we will find her when the time is right."

About the Author

Graham Wilson lives in Sydney Australia. He written and published twelve novels and a memoir.

They comprise two series:

1. The Old Balmain House Series – three novels
2. The Crocodile Dreaming Series – five novels and two book prequel

He has also written stand-alone novels, *The Glitter* and *Mysteries*, and a family memoir, *Kaleidoscope.*

The *Old Balmain House Series* starts with the novel, *Old Balmain House*. Its setting is an old weatherboard cottage, in Sydney, where the author lived for seven years. Here, a photo was discovered of a small girl who lived and died about 100 years ago. The book imagines the story of her life and family, based in the real Balmain, an early inner Sydney suburb, with its locations and historical events providing part of the story background. The second novel in this series, *Lizzie*, builds on the Balmain house setting. It is the story of a working-class teenage girl who lives in this same house in the 1950s and 1960s. It tells of how, when pregnant, she is determined not to surrender her baby for adoption, and of her struggle to survive in this unforgiving society. The third novel in this series, *Amelie*, follows the next generation of the family in *Lizzie*. Lizzie's daughter is faced with the awful choice of whether to seek the help of one of her mother's rapists' in trying to save the life of her own daughter who is inflicted with an incurable disease.

The Crocodile Dreaming Series is based in Outback Australia. It starts with the novel, *Visitor,* which tells the story of an English backpacker, Susan, who visits the Northern Territory and becomes captivated and in great danger from a man who loves crocodiles. The second book in the series, *Victim*, follows the consequences of the first book, based around the

discovery of this man's remains and his diary and Susan being placed on trial for murder. The third book, *Void*, is about Susan's struggle to retain her sanity in jail while her family and friends desperately try to find out what really happened on that fateful day before it is too late. In this book, *Vanished,* Susan disappears too. It tells the story of the search for her and four other lost women, whose passports were found in the possession of the man she killed. The final book in the series, *Invisible,* is the story of a woman who appears in a remote aboriginal community in North Queensland, without any memory except for a name. It tells how she rebuilds her life from an empty shell and how, fragments of the past return. With them come dark shadows that threaten to overwhelm her.
The two books in the Prequel are collectively titled Vengeance, with the first part, *Vertigo*, the story of the life of a boy, become man, Mark, and of the series of tragedies that surround him and repeatedly throw his life out of balance. In the second part, Vortex, the story becomes increasingly dark as he seeks retribution from those who have harmed both him and those he loved. Over time, he increasingly becomes a monster and is ultimately destroyed, as the vengeance he seeks destroys himself.

The novel, *The Glitter* is a tale of corporate greed and corruption in Sydney, and the novel, The novel, *The Mysteries* is a historical fiction story set in early Sydney about a very old house with a hidden basement and a rediscovered story of the people who once lived here and how that flows through to today. It also tells of the search for a mother and child who disappeared without trace 30 years ago and how this mystery is resolved.

The memoir, *Kaleidoscope*, is about the author's life in the Northern Territory: his childhood in an aboriginal community in Arnhem Land, in Australia's Northern Territory, the people, danger and beauty of this place, and of its transformation over the last half century with the coming of aboriginal rights and the discovery or uranium. It also tells of his surviving an attack by a large crocodile and of his work over two decades in the outback of the NT.

He is also in the early stages of planning a memoir about his family's connections with Ireland called *Memories Only Remain* and is compiling information for books about the early NT cattle industry, its people and its stories and about the history and stories of people who worked for the NSW National Parks and Wildlife stories.

Graham writes for the creative pleasure it brings him. He is particularly gratified each time an unknown person chooses to download and read something he has written and write a review - good or bad, as this gives him an insight into what readers enjoy and helps him make ongoing improvements to his writing.

In his other life Graham is a veterinarian who works in wildlife conservation and with rural landholders. He lived a large part of his life in the Northern Territory and his books reflect this experience.

More information about Graham and his books and writing is available from the following sites:

Graham Wilson – Australian Author on Facebook
Graham Wilson's Profile on Goodreads
Graham's website: www.grahamwilsonbooks.com

If you want to contact Graham directly please use the email:
grahamwilsonbooks@gmail.com

www.ingramcontent.com/pod-product-compliance
Lightning Source LLC
Chambersburg PA
CBHW021234060726

47590CB00005B/1762
9780645588736